Conte[nts]

Foreword

"

Having been involved with university admissions processes for over ten years, I can sympathise with the anxieties and hopes of prospective candidates. The competition for a place at Oxford or Cambridge has never been fiercer.

Many school leavers feel that the odds are stacked against them and that only those who have privileged access can ever be successful. Extra tests and the prospect of an interview can make potentially successful candidates give up before they begin. They feel that there is some secret formula or hidden key that is denied to them. This is entirely untrue: anybody with the right qualifications has an equal chance of success, and what may seem from the outside to be a system slanted in favour of those who can buy success, is in fact a system designed to select the best candidates regardless of their background. If you want to apply and have the appropriate grades, you have as good a chance as anyone else.

In the admissions tests and at interview you are treated as an individual and not a statistic, and it is a level playing field for all candidates. The universities do not have any hidden agenda or favoured type of candidate. All they want are the students who perform best in the application process, taking into account their work in the admissions tests and at interview. And by 'best', they don't mean the person with the most crammed knowledge – they are looking for all-round intellectual ability linked with academic curiosity and commitment. Nobody can obtain these things over the counter: they are intrinsic to any individual who is prepared to stretch themselves to the limit and aim for the highest. Background is irrelevant.

The competition for places continues to grow, as more candidates attain high grades at A level. Exam boards are bowing to pressure to differentiate between A grades by awarding A★s as marks of distinction, and a typical Cambridge offer now includes at least one A★. The universities are also attaching more importance to the tests they set for candidates at interview, as they do their best to sift through a highly talented pool of candidates in as fair and efficient a way as possible. All this makes the interview even more important in the selection process.

A difficult situation inevitably arises: at interview the universities want to gauge those things which the A level and UCAS form cannot properly reveal – things like potential and motivation. These are things which cannot be prepared for – innate qualities that haven't been taught and which can't be bought by those with greater access to facilities or specialist teaching. Candidates can expect to be given some unseen material to be discussed at their interview, usually given to them just before the interview itself. The tests will tend to concentrate on how you apply your mind rather than your ability to recall facts, and how you can think under pressure. All candidates (and parents), however, will of course ask themselves 'how can I prepare for these extra hurdles?'

It is clear that at one level the answer is: 'You can't, nor should you be able to.' That is, you cannot change your personality, nor suddenly improve your academic and intellectual potential overnight. What you can do is consult those whose experience can help you to show yourself as you are now to your best possible advantage. This is what the education consultancy Oxbridge Applications and the authors of this book are aiming to do. Nobody is offering that secret formula because none exists. What is on offer is a wide range of expertise to help you both play to your strengths and avoid the pitfalls into which so many students fall, preventing the interviewer from getting a true impression of their abilities.

It is important to realise that the interview is intended to discover what is unique about you; not how you fit into some pre-conceived mould. Your UCAS form will have shown how much you know about the basics of the subject you have chosen to study, so the interview is unlikely to concentrate entirely on this. More important is showing how you react to unexpected academic and intellectual challenges: the interviewer will want to judge how much you are likely to develop over three or four years. You need to be able to show that you are a committed and engaged candidate; if you aren't, you shouldn't be entering the competition!

This is not a conveyor belt – the admissions process is about individuality rather than conformity – and there is no brain-washing or attempting to beat the system: as explained, that would be as unethical as it is impossible. What is possible is for you to raise your game by sensible discussion and advice. It has been a pleasure to see so many candidates from a variety of backgrounds improve their chances through this common-sense approach, and the success rate suggests that it has been a valuable experience for many. But remember: anyone can offer advice, but only you can turn advice into success.

”

Barry Webb
Former admissions tutor and
member of the Oxbridge Applications' Advisory Board, August 2010

Introduction: So you want to go Oxbridge?

All students deserve the best possible advice when applying to Britain's best universities and since 1999, we have been continuously fascinated by how they can fulfill their potential, make the most of themselves in the challenging and demanding Oxbridge selection process and learn from graduates who have been there and done it.

What do successful applicants do? How do their minds work? How do they prepare? What books do they read? What regrets do they have? How do they handle demanding questions in interviews? These questions are at the heart of this book and we thought the best way to answer these was to ask thousands of students from diverse backgrounds who have successfully applied to Oxford and Cambridge. The result is this book – *So you want to go to Oxbridge? Tell me about a banana...*, written by Oxbridge graduates, for Oxbridge applicants, just like you. We've spoken to those from public and private schools, from grammar and state, to those based abroad, to those who prepared for months, to those who grew up with a weighty expectation to follow in their parent's Oxbridge footsteps, to those who were the first generation to apply to university, let alone to Oxbridge. What they all have in common is that, regardless of their background and their experiences, they all went through the application process and succeeded.

Can you be trained or coached for cracking the Oxford and Cambridge admissions process? No. Can you go through past interview questions and prepare scripted responses? No. Can you copy what those who have done it successfully did and expect the same results? No. So does this mean there is nothing you can do to prepare yourself?...No.

Like all challenges in life - learning to drive, a big sports match or mastering a musical instrument, there is always a mixture of ability and sheer determination, preparation and focus that leads to success. Yes, the geniuses will get their place, but what about the rest of us? It is this that we want to help you to convey here - you at your best in the selection process, which is all any rational and reasonable admissions tutor can wish to see. For them to miss students of ability – just because they are not confident, lack the right insights into what tutors are looking for or simply cannot communicate their intelligence is tragic.

The idea that you should just be yourself in interview is a truly lovely thought. It is difficult to know what this means if you have no idea what admissions tutors are looking for, haven't grown up in an environment that facilitates academic style conversations around a dinner table or breakfast brunch (even just a simple case of listening to Radio 4), and have a tendency to say 'erm,' 'basically' or 'like' all the time. While being good on paper, you may have no idea how to translate those core academic abilities (thinking things through, being logical, analytical and objective) into success in an interview scenario. In this case, 'being yourself' may not reflect your academic potential. You may not actually know how to be yourself in the context of an academic, one-to-one interview.

Having worked with over 45,000 applicants we think that, if you do apply, all anyone can ask is that - come the January after you have submitted your application forms, sat an admissions test and hopefully been invited to interview, you have done everything you possibly could do to excel. And one way or another, whether you end up at Oxford/Cambridge or another good university, your mind can rest easy that you gave it your best shot.

So what do successful applicants do and what themes can we draw out? Well, firstly they really want to study their chosen course at their chosen university. They understand what the course entails and why it's a good fit for them. They then apply every realistic ounce of effort and energy to achieve that goal - this is something that they really want. They delve a little further into their subject area, not because they 'have' to, but because they have a genuine love for their subject – they 'want' to do it and in so doing, have something interesting to say in their personal statement and at interview and show tutors they are capable of independent learning.

They take time over their application to prepare for the various hurdles that present themselves - from the UCAS form to an admissions test, from written work to selecting the right college. Why do they do this? - because they are convinced that studying that course at that university is right for them.

Finally, they focus on the interview; a key aspect of the Oxbridge admissions process. They accept that whilst some people can 'wing' an interview, this is a relatively new experience for them. The idea of being in new surroundings, with unfamiliar people, talking about challenging academic material is understandably for many, a nerve-inducing prospect.

Whilst they know they cannot be coached, they accept that, like any examination, they can prepare for this experience. They can think about what tutors are looking for, get used to tackling hard questions and structuring arguments using real detail. They take feedback in the run up to the application process about how they can improve and have the humility necessary to understand how they might come across to a stranger – be that too shy or sadly - too often the case - a little arrogant! Successful applicants tend to understand that the person sitting across from them is making a decision about whether they want to teach that person for three years and potentially more. It's a big decision for a tutor to make, deciding to spend hours of their lives discussing their academic subject with a particular student. Successful applicants will give that tutor all the information they need in order to know they are making the right decision, by making sure the tutor understands the truth – that they really do want to study that course at that university.

Of course, there are no guarantees – and even if you do all the above, that offer may still remain elusive. With nearly five of the best qualified students going for each place available, the need for motivation, enthusiasm, talent, commitment and a real interest in the subject outside of the curriculum is as high as ever. For many, the Oxbridge application process may be the first time they do not succeed academically and for some this is a difficult pill to swallow.

We have written this book to give advice and information from thousands of students who have been through the process. We've heard the regrets, 'I wish I had not been so nervous,' 'I wish I'd read those books on my personal statement,' 'I wish I had brushed up on my school work' and as much as possible, we want to help you to make your application a positive experience.

So you want to go to Oxbridge? Tell me about a banana… has been written by those who want to give you great, juicy advice to help your application reflect its true potential. If you've already picked up this book and read this far, you've already demonstrated staying power! Keep it going and we wish you the very best of luck.

Rachel Spedding & Jane Welsh
& the publishing team at Oxbridge Applications

1. Choosing a course

Advice on choosing the course that most inspires you.
We explore undergraduate courses at Oxford and Cambridge
(with opinions from graduates who have read those courses).

Without a doubt, choosing a course to study at university can be a tricky decision. At university you have the opportunity to study many courses you may never have heard of before or encountered academically. Although many university studies focus on one discipline such as English, some join two together such as History and Politics, and others apply academic skills already developed at school to different subject disciplines, such as Engineering with its use of Maths and Physics. Similarly, if you enjoy History, Classical Civilisation or Human Geography, you may enjoy learning about the development of society and culture in the course Archaeology & Anthropology at Oxford or Cambridge. If Physics, Chemistry and Maths are the subjects for you, would you consider studying their application to our planet and matter with a degree in Earth Sciences at Oxford?

University gives you the unrivalled luxury of being able to discuss your subject with leading minds. The rigidity of the academic guidelines will depend upon the course that you choose, but on the whole, university gives you the opportunity to discover your own path and explore new academic interests through independent study, lectures, seminars and the Cambridge supervision and Oxford tutorial systems. It is no wonder then, that in your personal statement and interview you need to show genuine interest in your chosen course and that you are open to new ideas and ways of approaching it.

Choosing a university course is an important personal decision. You owe it to yourself to take the time to think carefully about your choice. After all, we are talking about the next three years of your life! Being totally absorbed by the idea of an offer from Oxbridge, and not spending enough time thinking about what you want to study, or just applying for subjects that you think are 'easy bets' is not something we would recommend.

Receiving an offer you have worked so hard for is just the beginning of your Oxbridge journey. When you arrive, you must conquer the increased pace of learning, new ideas and the deadlines that come with three (or maybe more) years of university study. You may need to cope with (coffee-fuelled) dissertation-drafting, and the well-renowned strains of the final exams ('finals'). Both the application process and your actual time at university should be less stressful and more enjoyable if you love your subject, so do choose wisely. Plus, likely odds are that if you're enjoying something, you'll be better at it!

A key mistake many people make when choosing a course is to assume that because they are good at certain subjects at school, they will be good at them and enjoy them at university as well. Although this can be true, and the two often go hand-in-hand, it is important to consider how different university courses will be from A levels (or equivalent) and the only way to do this is to spend time doing your research.

Another mistake is to misunderstand the differences between courses offered at both Oxford and Cambridge. While there are obvious similarities between the two universities, there are key differences between the courses at each institution. Cambridge's curriculum is deliberately structured so as to allow undergraduates to gain a broad understanding and knowledge of their subject before specialising in a certain area. Courses are split into Parts I and II – with the chance to change disciplines after the completion of Part I. At Oxford, undergraduates engage with their subject in more depth from the outset. One such comparison can be drawn between Natural Sciences (Physical) at Cambridge, and its nearest equivalent, Physics at Oxford. Oxford Physicists get an earlier induction into the specifics of their chosen subject. In contrast, Cambridge Physical Natural Scientists gain a wide view of the available options in their first year before settling on one subject. Both courses have their own advantages and it is down to you as an individual to decide how you would prefer to spend your three, or possibly four, years of study.

To help you decide which course you might like to plump for, we've put together some simple questions for you to ask yourself.

What am I enjoying about my current studies?

Enjoyment is the first rung on the ladder towards demonstrating real motivation and potential for your chosen subject. Besides, if you want to secure a place, your interviewer (usually a university tutor) will need to know that you would enjoy interacting with the subject in tutorials and supervisions. 'I chose PPE at Oxford,' says James, who founded Oxbridge Applications, 'because I was fascinated by how societies work and PPE allowed an analysis from three different angles: how power is distributed, how resources are allocated and whether something is morally right.' Similarly Tom, a recent graduate from Oxford, had a long-standing passion for Physics, which served him well, both at interview and over the three year course. 'Physics applies maths, logic and experience to help understand the universe and all its machinations. Why wouldn't you want to study that?! Beyond its intrinsic value though, studying Physics is also a great way to train your mind to formulate creative solutions to quantitative puzzles. Almost everything that can be measured can also be modelled using insights from Physics.'

Is there an area beyond my A levels (or equivalent) that I find interesting?

Perhaps you've found yourself discovering the powers of Eastern philosophy or have started to develop a taste for Viking poetry and Pictish stones? If this is the case, one of Oxford or Cambridge's more 'unknown' courses could be the right one for you. Genuine interest and excitement for a particular specialism will stand you in good stead – the interviewers are looking for keen amateurs.

It is worth noting, however, that just because on average these courses are less over-subscribed, this does not mean you should apply speculatively because you think you stand a greater chance of being offered a place. ASNaC (Anglo-Saxon, Norse and Celtic) at Cambridge might have had a relatively high application-to-offer ratio in 2009 (52/25), meaning applicants had a 48% chance of being offered a place, but students who apply for such courses will usually be really keen on the subject in question and able to demonstrate this. Don't be lulled into a false sense of security and choose a subject you consider an 'easy bet'. If you do feel a course is right for you, then make that application because you want to study the subject for three or four years.

As much as the university is looking for 'keen amateurs', they will expect you to have a clear understanding of what the course entails. For example, a number of students might like the sound of Philosophy at Cambridge, but in the admissions test you sit at interview and then in your first year, you will have to grapple with logic (which requires a mathematical approach). If you do not have a core understanding of what logic is or how to approach it, you will find the application process and, if you are successful, your first year, quite tough. Make sure you know what you are getting yourself into. It's a really good idea to read the full course prospectus so that you can see what you will potentially be studying each year in detail.

What do I excel at?

The enjoyment factor is not the only thing to consider – you need to be extremely able too. You may love football, but if you can't play it well, you're never going to get into the England team (not that it is necessarily a benchmark of quality these days!) As two of the top universities in the world, Oxford and Cambridge are looking for the best and brightest. All-round academic achievement is extremely important, and you need to have the grades on paper (at GCSE and A level or equivalent) to match your desire to study the subject. If you have studied the course before, you need a track record of academic success. If not, you need to show an aptitude through achievement in similar science or arts subjects.

What academic area do I feel really confident talking about?

This is a key factor to consider before the interview itself, and also because at Oxford or Cambridge, you will need to talk intelligently about your subject for three or four years!

What do I want to do after university?

While you should try not to worry too much about picking a course that leads directly to a career (the majority of students do not know what they want to do when they finish university, let alone start), it is always good to be aware of the future. If you already know you want to be a heart surgeon or a lawyer, you should look to choose the most suitable course to give you the necessary qualifications and experience to achieve that goal. Our advice however, is that you should only apply if you feel absolutely certain of your choice. Not only do these courses tend to be among the most competitive but they also tend to test your total commitment and understanding of the profession at interview. In 2009, the applications-to-offer ratio for Medicine at Cambridge was 1,702/276. That's an average success rate of 16.2%, which is well below the university's average success rate (for all subjects): 25%.

For Law, it can be helpful to have an understanding of some of the key, fundamental legal concepts, as in most interviews applicants are asked to discuss and analyse moral and legal dilemmas. In 2009, one applicant was asked: 'if there is a law allowing the military to shoot down any plane that is about to crash into a building, is that a good law or not?' Another interviewer posed the question: 'is pushing someone's head into the water, in order to kill them, and leaving someone else's head which is already in the water, in order that they would die, the same thing?'

Many applicants feel compelled to apply for courses such as Law and Medicine, because they fear that, if they do not, they will miss out on the option of those careers forever. If you feel this pressure, you should remember that a Law conversion course only takes one year longer than the equivalent qualification for a Law student, and that Magic Circle firms take approximately a third to a half of their trainees from non-Law backgrounds. There is also a graduate fast track programme for Medicine, reducing the five year training to four years for those with the relevant science A levels.

Similarly, many applicants believe that without an E&M (Economics & Management) degree from Oxford, or an Economics degree from Cambridge, a career in the City will be beyond reach. This is absolutely not true. There are many successful graduates, from disciplines as varied as History, Engineering, Maths and Land Economy, who are now excelling as slick operators in the financial world. It is also worth noting that E&M at Oxford and Economics at Cambridge are fiercely competitive, with a success rate of 8.9% (over the past three years) and 12.75%

(1,396, applications to 178 offers) respectively. Oxford explicitly states that it expects to invite approximately 30% of applicants to interview. Interviews are tough, and applicants will be expected to have a sound grasp of economic theory, not just business – another common misconception. Applicants must also be able to confidently solve mathematical problems, as well as have an understanding of the macro-economic situation in Britain. Last year, some applicants were asked to prove Pythagoras' Theorem algebraically, explain quantitative easing, talk about GDP growth, interest rates, VAT and what they thought about bankers' bonuses.

Next steps

There's no substitute for good research. A great place to start is at the university and course open days. These days give you a fantastic opportunity to meet with tutors and current students and to ask (burning and intelligent!) questions. Current students are usually open to discussing their studies with potential applicants - after all, they enjoy what they're doing and want to see new protégés entering the discipline. A faculty tour is a brilliant insight into the workings of the department, and many will host a lecture to give you a taste of the working life of a student. After visiting the departments, you will probably have a gut feeling as to which subject you could envisage yourself studying at Oxbridge. There is also a wealth of information on Oxford and Cambridge's university websites and prospectuses, which should be your first port of call.

Many applicants find speaking to their teachers and/or Oxbridge advisor (if you have one) useful, as they know you academically, and can talk to you about what you have enjoyed about your current studies as well as which subject areas you excel in. It can be helpful to talk to your parents (even if they have not been to Oxford, Cambridge or university). They've lived a little longer than you have and can provide helpful insights and a different perspective on you and your future.

To help inspire your journey of course discovery, in the next section of our book we've put together profiles of courses currently available at Oxford and Cambridge, written by graduates who have read those courses. They'll give you a little taster of the key elements of the course and what they loved most about their studies. We have also included whether you would need to take an admissions test, submit written work, and whether there are any particular A levels preferred or required by the universities for each subject. Make sure that you keep on top of the requirements listed on the university website (as this should include the most up-to-date information) and ensure that you check out individual colleges' entrance requirements on their websites as these do vary from college to college.

As with all aspects of the application process, finding the right course takes a fair amount of effort, background research and decision-making. This is why we have included suggestions of other courses you might like to look at. If your interest is piqued by a particular subject, you may be keen on a discipline which tests similar skills and covers cross-over topics. Exploring the options available to you and working out where your academic strengths lie are very valuable exercises, which will prove beneficial throughout your Oxbridge application.

Which course will it be?

To keep you thinking, why not pick up a pencil and in the next section tick the courses that look good to you. Small steps... big decision.

□ ASNaC (Anglo-Saxon, Norse, & Celtic)

Anglo-Saxon, Norse and Celtic – more commonly referred to as 'ASNaC' – is, to all intents and purposes, unique. No other university in the UK offers the breadth of scope that ASNaC provides in its field, and certainly not at undergraduate level. For those applicants interested in studying the literature, language and history of the so-called 'dark age' of Britain, Ireland and Scandinavia in-depth, taking the ASNaC Tripos at Cambridge provides the best opportunity, in an endlessly evolving, fascinating, and enjoyable degree course.

Duration of course: 3 years

Admissions Test: Some colleges set their own admissions test at interview.

Written Work: Most colleges ask applicants to submit school/college essays.

Entrance Requirements: No specific A levels are required, but languages and humanities are preferred. Certain colleges have additional requirements.

Past Interview Question: How could you go about dating an unknown manuscript?

"

The amount of choice was amazing – essentially students can design their own degree, and dissertations allowed us to contribute towards the field of scholarship.

"

ASNaC graduate

Not the course for you? Take a look at **Classics, English** or **Modern Languages** at Cambridge or Oxford.

□ Archaeology & Anthropology

'Arch and Anth,' as this course is commonly referred to, provides a broad introduction to past and contemporary human societies, from a social, biological and material perspective. An interdisciplinary approach is taken in the first year through emphasis on a wide range of components from the Archaeology, Social Anthropology and Biological Anthropology departments. The variety of views and perspectives that students gain from these components creates an atmosphere that encourages interchange and discourse. Students are able to specialise in one of the three branches for their Part II, in the second and third years.

Duration of course: 3 years

Admissions Test: Most colleges set their own admissions test at interview.

Written Work: Many colleges ask Archaeology & Anthropology applicants to submit school/college essays.

Entrance Requirements: No specific A levels are required. Certain colleges have additional requirements.

Past Interview Question: What, in 5000 years, would people be able to understand about our society if all the evidence they had to go on were graves?

"

I am fascinated by studying cultures comparatively and I loved the way I could focus on this throughout the Arch and Anth course.

"

Arch and Anth graduate

Not the course for you? Try **Archaeology & Anthropology** at Oxford, or go in a different direction with **Classics** or **Human Sciences** at Oxford.

□ Architecture

Architecture is one of the few subjects in the university that combines the intellectual challenge of a Cambridge Tripos with the opportunity for creative design. It provides a wide-ranging education in the principles of architectural design and its theoretical background. The course is intended on the one hand to establish the basis for a body of technical, historical and theoretical knowledge and, on the other, to apply this knowledge to the study of the principal questions of building and of the built environment.

Duration of course: 3 years

Admissions Test: Some colleges set their own admissions test for interview.

Written Work: All applicants are expected to show a portfolio of recent work at interview but this isn't expected to be work of an architectural nature. Some colleges ask applicants to submit school/college essays or set their own projects/tasks for applicants.

Entrance Requirements: No specific A levels are required, but AS level Mathematics or Physics and A level Art are preferred. Certain colleges have additional requirements.

Past Interview Question: What would you say is the most important building of the 20th century?

“

I loved so many things! Most of all, the opportunity to learn from a very inspiring set of tutors.

”

Architecture graduate

Not the course for you? Take a look at the **Engineering** and **History of Art** courses at Oxford and Cambridge, or the **Materials Science** or **Fine Art** courses at Oxford.

□ Asian & Middle Eastern Studies (Oriental Studies)

Asian & Middle Eastern Studies, while developing language skills, also covers history, philosophy, literature and current affairs. This is not solely a language course: the course works towards a complete understanding of Asian culture and tradition. Although this makes for a very varied course, at times some students find it rather demanding.

After all the hard work, the sense of achievement at being able to interact with people from such a unique and fascinating culture is truly remarkable, and, after completing the course, students should find themselves in a position to be able to communicate with almost another quarter of the world population.

Duration of course: 4 years

Admissions Test: Some colleges set their own admissions test.

Written Work: Most colleges ask applicants to submit a school/college essay.

Entrance Requirements: No specific A levels are required, but an A level in a modern or ancient language and/or a humanity or a social science are highly recommended. Certain colleges have additional requirements.

Past Interview Question: How will life in the Gulf be transformed if its oil supplies run out?

“

The sense of achievement after the four years have been completed is one that can only be achieved after studying a completely new language and culture from scratch, and certainly makes the course worthwhile.

”

Asian and Middle Eastern Studies graduate

Not the course for you? Check out **Modern & Medieval Languages** at **Cambridge** or **Modern Languages** or **Oriental Studies** at Oxford.

□ Classics

Classics at Cambridge is unique for a number of important reasons. Firstly, figures have shown that around half of all those applying to read Classics at Cambridge are admitted. Secondly, in contrast to the course offered at Oxford, which is longer and is regarded as the more traditional, at Cambridge you sit exams every summer over the three years. Thirdly, in the second year of Classics at Cambridge, students get the opportunity to explore a rich and expansive volume of Latin and Greek texts, before narrowing down their focus considerably in the third year to specialise in just two topics. At university level, Classics is radically different to the experience of studying it at school, where students often complain of many tedious hours doing exercises about Caecilius or translating Xenophon's rhetoric. Instead, undergraduate students are allowed to select whichever elements of the entire sphere of the ancient world they find of interest (within reason). It is no longer a requirement for applicants to have studied a classical language at A level as it is now possible to opt for the four year degree. After an intensive first year studying just the Latin language and the Roman world, the course follows the same structure as the three year degree.

Duration of course: 3 years, or 4 years if the applicant does not have Latin and/or Greek to A level or equivalent.

Admissions Test: Some colleges set their own admissions test at interview while others may ask applicants to do some preparatory study at the interview or in the weeks before the interview.

Written Work: Almost all colleges ask applicants to submit school/college essays.

Entrance Requirements: A level Latin or Greek is essential for the 3 year course. No specific A levels for the 4 year course are required but an A level language is highly desirable. GCSE Latin and/or Greek are considered useful. Certain colleges have additional requirements.

Past Interview Question: Is Aeneas a modern hero?

"

I think the thing that I enjoyed most about my course was the third year. You were then able to study the sorts of things that interested you most.

"

Classics graduate

Not the course for you? Try **Classics** at Oxford, or go in a different direction with **Archaeology & Anthropology** courses or **ASNaC (Anglo-Saxon, Norse and Celtic)** at Cambridge.

□ Computer Science

Cambridge has a rich computing heritage – listing Alan Turing ('Founder of Computer Science') as a previous student, with the impressive claim that the world's first fully programmable computer, EDSAC, was built there, and, as the first university to provide a Computer Science course.

The course is well tailored, and the mix with other sciences makes for an interesting and flexible degree. It is an excellent option if an applicant is not entirely sure at this stage what they want to do. In addition, the great range of choice and the wide scope for project and practical work means that this is a course which is not just exam based.

There are, however, some important points to consider. Compared with similar courses at other universities, the Computer Science degree offered at Cambridge is considerably more theoretical. The mix of subjects taken in the first year, including Natural Sciences, makes for a varied degree if those extra subjects are of interest. However, those who wish to focus exclusively on computer science may find that this course is not for them.

Duration of course: 3 years, with an optional fourth year Masters.

Admissions Test: The Cambridge TSA (Thinking Skills Assessment) is required by most colleges, while others may set their own admissions test at interview or ask applicants to do some preparatory reading in the weeks before the interview.

Written Work: N/A

Entrance Requirements: A level Mathematics is essential. A level Further Mathematics and/or a physical science are considered highly desirable. Certain colleges have additional requirements.

Past Interview Question: 'The game of Chess will be played perfectly by the computers of 2011.' What is the meaning of this statement and is it likely to be true?

"

I enjoyed mastering something that is so fundamental but which few people really take the time to investigate.

"

Computer Science graduate

Not the course for you? Try **Computer Science** at Oxford, or go in a different direction with **Mathematics** or **Engineering** courses at Oxford or Cambridge.

□ Economics

Economics is considered to be one of the most prestigious courses on offer at Cambridge. Of course, that makes it one of the tougher ones to get in for, but if you're successful, you'll be in for a pretty thorough education. The course focuses on giving students a solid understanding of the core features of economics, both pure and applied. The specialised nature of the degree will enable the student to concentrate on studying the subject in considerable depth, but it will also allow significant breadth, giving them the opportunity to consider things from an interdisciplinary perspective, taking in history, sociology, mathematics, statistics and philosophy. There is no doubt that at the end of the degree, an Economics graduate will have a very marketable qualification.

Duration of course: 3 years

Admissions Test: Some colleges ask applicants to sit the Cambridge TSA (Thinking Skills Assessment). Some colleges ask applicants to complete some preparatory study at interview.

Written Work: Some colleges ask applicants to submit school/college essays.

Entrance Requirements: A level Mathematics is essential. A level Economics is preferred (A level Business Studies is also useful if the student is unable to study Economics at A level). Certain colleges have additional requirements.

Past Interview Question: Should a Walmart store be opened in the middle of Cambridge?

"

I believe that the course had a good mix between both model development and understanding, as well as more essay-based analysis.

"

Economics graduate

Not the course for you? Try **Land Economy, Geography, History** or **Mathematics** at Cambridge, or **PPE (Philosophy, Politics & Economics)** or **E&M (Economics & Management)** at Oxford.

□ Education Studies

Cambridge has offered educational training for over 130 years and the undergraduate course is one of the best in the country, with a reputation for academic excellence.

Cambridge's Tripos is unique in that it allows students to combine the academic study of education with another subject, effectively offering students a Joint Honours degree. This is a rare opportunity to develop another academic subject to degree standard whilst also focusing on the various disciplines of education, acquiring skills and knowledge within both fields. The specialist subjects on offer with Education Studies are: Biological Sciences, Classics, English and Drama, English, Geography, History, Mathematics, Modern Languages, Music, Physical Sciences (Chemistry or Physics) and Religious Studies. Most of the teaching on these subjects is the same as that offered to students on the degree course in its own right.

Duration of course: 3 years

Admissions Test: Some colleges set their own admissions test at interview.

Written Work: Some colleges ask applicants to submit school/college essays.

Entrance Requirements: An A level in the subject the student wishes to study alongside Education is essential. Certain colleges have additional requirements.

Past Interview Question: What makes a good teacher?

“

I enjoyed the supervisions more than any other aspect of the course because they enabled me to explore the issues discussed in lectures in more depth.

”

Education Studies graduate

Not the course for you? Check out the specialist subjects on their own at Oxford or Cambridge.

□ Engineering

The Engineering Department at Cambridge is arguably one of the most prestigious of its kind in the country. It is one of only a small number of top engineering departments to offer a general base to its engineering course. All students take common papers in their first two years (Parts IA and IB of the Engineering Tripos), regardless of their final disciplinary specialisation. Not everyone will find everything covered in these two years of interest to them, but the skills and knowledge gained are valuable in equipping students for multidisciplinary projects after graduation.

Entering the Engineering Tripos keeps a student's career options open. Those wishing to pursue the Chemical Engineering Tripos follow either the Engineering or Natural Sciences Tripos in their first year, before transferring in their second. Engineering students entering their third year can branch off to follow the Manufacturing Engineering Tripos, Management Studies Tripos or the standard Engineering Tripos. All Tripos, with the exception of Management Studies, are four years and lead to MEng status.

Duration of course: 4 years

Admissions Test: Most colleges ask applicants to sit the Cambridge TSA (Thinking Skills Assessment). Some colleges ask applicants to sit a short Maths Test or the STEP (Sixth Term Examination Paper), while others make an assessment on the interview alone.

Written Work: Applicants are not expected to submit written work.

Entrance Requirements: A level Mathematics & Physics are essential and a third mathematics/technology/science A level is desirable. Certain colleges have additional requirements.

Past Interview Question: Why are British aircraft carriers shorter than American ones?

“

I loved being able to specialise in subjects that I enjoyed in my third year and being able to explain the results that would be generated through theory and lab sessions.

”

Engineering graduate

Not the course for you? Try **Physical** or **Biological Natural Sciences** or **Mathematics** at Cambridge or **Engineering, Materials Science** or **Physics** at Oxford.

□ English

English at Cambridge is not the same as English at any other university. The course is rigorous, stretching and far more flexible than it may first appear. The scope of literature studied ranges from Ancient Greek classical texts to modern poetry, prose and drama. The backbone of the course is practical criticism (commenting upon unprepared texts), and although its examination is now only compulsory at the end of the degree, each term will see students honing their skills in this discipline. If applicants can demonstrate an aptitude for that kind of practical criticism, then they stand a good chance of being accepted to study English at Cambridge.

Duration of course: 3 years

Admissions Test: Most colleges set their own admissions test. A few colleges may ask applicants to do some preparatory reading in the weeks before the interview.

Written Work: Most colleges ask applicants to submit school/college essays.

Entrance Requirements: A level English Literature or English Language & Literature is essential. Certain colleges have additional requirements.

Past Interview Question: Why do we read literature?

“

I loved the people! English is such a discursive subject, so it really helped having intelligent people around who challenged your ideas and forced you to think more deeply and creatively.

”

English graduate

Not the course for you? Try **ASNaC (Anglo-Saxon, Norse and Celtic), PPS (Politics, Psychology & Sociology)** or **Philosophy** at Cambridge or **Modern Languages, History** or **Classics** at Oxford or Cambridge.

□ Geography

Geography at university is very different to Geography studies at school, and differs considerably from the preconceived ideas which most students have. Whilst typical school-level geography themes are to be found (e.g. environmental hazards, coastal management, industrial and urban planning, and analysis of forest resources) there is much in the geographical Tripos to be surprised by.

Students may encounter discussions about the role of prostitutes and sexual deviants in shaping Victorian England, be forced to consider the relationship between post-modernity and post-modernism and the role of the reflective qualities of water and soil types in remote sensing. On the whole, students are able to pick and choose the areas that interest them, with the general philosophy of the Geography Department being to provide students with a multidisciplinary set of tools with which to tackle problems. It follows that Geography graduates can hope to leave with enhanced logical and critical thinking ability, the ability to interpret texts, numeracy, practical skills, graphical and design skills, fieldwork experience and the ability to work under pressure.

Duration of course: 3 years

Admissions Test: Some colleges set their own admissions test at interview.

Written Work: Most colleges ask applicants to submit school essays.

Entrance Requirements: No specific A levels are required. Certain colleges have additional requirements.

Past Interview Question: Discuss the problem of AIDS in Africa and possible solutions.

“

The Geography course prompted me to question why humans consider our world, society and landscape in the way that we do. It was a transformative course for me as I began to look at everyday problems more analytically.

”

Geography graduate

Not the course for you? Have a look at **Land Economy, Economics** or **Natural Sciences (Physical)** at Cambridge or **Geography** or **PPE (Philosophy, Politics & Economics)** at Oxford.

□ History

History at Cambridge offers the chance to study a hugely diverse range of topics from British economic and social history, to Ancient Greece, the History of the USA or even the History of Political Thought – and that's just in the first year! Beyond that, students can go almost anywhere they like and specialisation and independent research is positively encouraged. The breadth and flexibility of the History course at Cambridge means that historians can find themselves sharing classes with students in Politics, Psychology & Sociology, Anglo Saxon Norse & Celtic, Modern & Medieval Languages and Classics, as well as focusing on more philosophical questions in courses such as Historical Argument and Practice. Thanks to the Cambridge Tripos System, historians at Cambridge are in an excellent position to transfer to another course, favourites being History of Art and Law. The teaching of History at Cambridge is rated excellent and the department is well supplied by the Seeley Library, one of the largest student libraries dedicated to history in the world. All this means that Cambridge is one of the best institutions in the world for history and the department's alumni are provided with the skills to succeed in diverse and fascinating careers.

Duration of course: 3 years

Admissions Test: Some colleges set admissions tests which are sat at the time of interview.

Written Work: Most colleges ask for a school/college essay.

Entrance Requirements: A level History is highly desirable. Certain colleges have additional requirements.

Past Interview Question: Who writes history?

“

I loved the subject matter, excellent teaching and freedom to pursue my own interests.

”

History graduate

Not the course for you? Check out **ASNaC (Anglo-Saxon, Norse & Celtic)** at Cambridge or the **Archaeology** and **Anthropology, Classics,** or **History of Art** courses at either Cambridge or Oxford. **History** is also offered at Oxford, either as a Single Honours or as **Ancient & Modern History.**

□ History of Art

History of Art is for those interested in studying works of art and understanding them in their historical and social contexts. It is distinguished from art criticism, which is concerned with establishing a relative artistic value upon individual works, or sanctioning an entire style or movement and art theory or 'philosophy of art', which is concerned with the fundamental nature of art.

History of Art at Cambridge is a small course with only a handful of fellows. This makes for an intimate department in which there is a good mix between students and staff of different colleges. For this reason, it is considered a course with attention paid to the individual student, and a corresponding flexibility for students to make it what they will. Students are able to draw on the wealth of resources in Cambridge: for example the excellent Fitzwilliam Museum, illuminated manuscripts, stained glass windows, architecture and sculptures by distinguished artists such as Henry Moore.

Duration of course: 3 years

Admissions Test: Some colleges set their own admissions test which is sat during the interview period.

Written Work: Most colleges require the submission of a school or college essay.

Entrance Requirements: No particular subjects at A level (or equivalent) are required for the History of Art course but subjects should be primarily academic. Subjects like History, English, Modern Languages, History of Art, Religious Studies and Classics are ideal, and Mathematics and experimental sciences are acceptable if accompanied by one or two arts A levels.

Past Interview Question: How does art reflect its society?

“

I really enjoyed the supervisions and seminars - Cambridge History of Art students are highly privileged in the amount of contact time that they receive.

”

History of Art graduate

Not the course for you? **History of Art** is also offered at Oxford. You might also wish to consider **Fine Art** at Oxford, or **History** on its own at either Oxford or Cambridge.

□ Land Economy

The Land Economy course is based on an interesting mix of Law, Economics and Environment and is concerned with how these subjects relate, and how they can be utilised to solve real world issues. The course itself is virtually unique to Cambridge, although its popularity has resulted in an increased awareness of the subject and other universities have plans to open similar departments.

An important skill undergraduates will develop over the duration of the course is the ability to respond with confidence to multifaceted problems. Land Economists are therefore highly valued in the job market for their broad-reaching approach to problems, which originates from having a background that is set in not just one discipline, but several.

Duration of course: 3 years

Admissions Test: Some colleges ask applicants to sit the Cambridge TSA (Thinking Skills Assessment). Other colleges set their own admissions test at interview.

Written Work: Some colleges ask Land Economy applicants to submit school/college essays.

Entrance Requirements: No specific A levels are required but a combination of arts and science subjects is recommended. Economics, Mathematics and Geography are considered useful. Certain colleges have additional requirements.

Past Interview Question: Why is the USA a country when Europe isn't?

"

The dissertation proved to be the high point of the course – the freedom to choose a title and topic in any field of Land Economy and carry out research and form conclusions.

"

Land Economy graduate

Not the course for you? Try **Geography** or **Economics** at Cambridge or **Geography, History** & **Economics** or **PPE (Philosophy, Politics & Economics)** at Oxford.

☐ Law

Law has been studied at Cambridge for over 700 hundred years so it should come as no surprise that the Faculty of Law enjoys an exceptional reputation both in the UK and around the world. For this reason there is no escaping the fact that the Cambridge Law degree is incredibly challenging, but also highly rewarding.

Law students are challenged to think in a deeply analytical way, approach problems from a logical position, and defend their thoughts, including written work, against criticism. Students are taught by leading figures in their field who will test their judgment and encourage them to explore a range of legal issues from new and interesting angles.

Most students who undertake a Law degree haven't studied the subject before. Instead, what is far more important is to have an interest in the subject. A good tip for anyone considering reading Law is to do some work experience in the legal sector before the interview. This not only gives applicants something to talk about in the interview but it also shows that they have a genuine interest in the subject. Whilst an undergraduate degree in Law may lead to a distinguished legal career, it is important to realise that the core skills acquired on this course are desirable in a variety of fields, ranging from academia to international business.

Duration of course: 3 years

Admissions Test: Most colleges ask applicants to sit the Cambridge Law Test.

Written Work: Some colleges ask applicants to submit school/college essays.

Entrance Requirements: No specific A levels are required. Certain colleges have additional requirements.

Past Interview Question: In a society of angels, do you need laws?

"

I particularly enjoyed the family law aspect of the course as I enjoyed the focus on the individual and the family.

"

Law graduate

Not the course for you? **Law** is also available at Oxford, with the option to take **Law with Law Studies in Europe** too. It is also worth noting that Oxford and Cambridge split examinations differently owing to the Tripos system adopted at Cambridge.

□ Linguistics

Language is what makes us human, and we have an innate ability to acquire language perfectly as children, even with impoverished input. Any linguist knows that thousands of distinct languages are spoken all around the world yet they differ so markedly from each other. How do they differ? Do certain languages offer unique expressive features that others don't? Do you agree with the Chomskyian theory of a 'universal grammar'? Linguistics – a new course, freshly divorced from Modern Languages and offered from October 2010 – aims to explore answers to these questions.

Duration of course: 3 years

Admissions Test: Some colleges set their own admissions test at interview.

Written Work: Some colleges ask applicants to submit school/college essays.

Entrance Requirements: No specific A levels are required. Some formal study of language can be useful. Certain colleges have additional requirements.

Past Interview Question: Discuss the ambiguities in this sentence: 'I bumped into a woman carrying flowers.'

"The study of different accents and dialects was the most interesting part of the course."

Modern & Medieval Languages graduate (2009)

Not the course for you? You might be interested in **English, Modern & Medieval Languages** or **Philosophy** at Cambridge or **English, Modern Languages** or even **Experimental Psychology** at Oxford.

□ Mathematics

The Cambridge Mathematical Tripos is widely regarded as one of the most demanding and rewarding Mathematics courses in the country, and possibly the world. Certainly the pace is much faster than that of many similar courses. The benefit of this advanced rate is that it allows time for a greater degree of specialisation towards the end of the course.

The emphasis in university Mathematics is on rigour and proof – particularly in Pure Mathematics, the vast bulk of time is spent proving results, and the experience of a Pure Mathematics course is often that of building a tower; each result proved rests on the results proved earlier in the course. This is less true for an Applied course, but there is still an element of proof – many results which physicists or engineers would assume or state are proved, and virtually every result is at least given justification.

Duration of course: 3 years

Admissions Test: Some colleges set their own test at interview. Most colleges require applicants to take the Maths STEP (Sixth Term Examination Paper).

Written Work: N/A

Entrance Requirements: A level Mathematics and AS level Further Mathematics are essential. A level Further Mathematics and Physics are highly desirable. Certain colleges have additional requirements.

Past Interview Question: How many 0s are there at the end of 30 factorial?

“

It was nice to push myself and find out the extent of my abilities as a mathematician.

”

Mathematics graduate

Not the course for you? You might also like to consider **Computer Science** or **Engineering** at Oxford or Cambridge, or **Mathematics** with one of its many sub-options at Oxford.

☐ Medicine

The Cambridge course is separated into a traditional style of two distinct parts, pre-clinical and clinical. The pre-clinical course is made up of two years of the Medical Sciences Tripos and a third year in what is usually a related subject. Recently the university has introduced a module called 'preparing for patients' which aims to give students their first taste of clinical practice, including visits to a GP's surgery to interview patients, and a visit to a patient's home. The third year enables students to study a topic in depth, and gain a BA in the process.

One of the first things students are told is that the pre-clinical course will provide an excellent foundation in the sciences on which medicine is built and which are essential to its practice. It is believed that this solid grounding, much of which can at times seem irrelevant, is in fact essential and will stand students in good stead to be the doctors of the future.

Duration of course: 3 years

Admissions Test: All colleges ask applicants to sit the BMAT (the BioMedical Admissions Test). This usually happens in early November (in 2010, the date is 3rd November).

Written Work: Some colleges ask applicants to submit school/college essays.

Entrance Requirements: Grade C or above in Double Award Science and Mathematics at GCSE are essential. Three of the following AS levels and at least one of the following A levels are essential: Biology/Human Biology, Chemistry (highly desirable), Physics or Mathematics. Certain colleges have additional requirements.

Past Interview Question: If you had £200million to spend in Africa, how would you spend it?

“

The first three years were essentially an academic biological sciences degree. I feel this put me in a very strong position, with a good grasp of pre-clinical concepts and helped me to learn new clinical concepts more easily.

”

Medicine graduate

Not the course for you? Check out **Natural Sciences** at Cambridge, or **Medicine** at Oxford. Alternatively, **Biomedical Sciences** at Oxford may be of interest.

□ Modern & Medieval Languages

Studying languages at Cambridge is interesting, stimulating and enjoyable. It is a four year course including a third year spent abroad. Whilst language study underlies the course, a wide range of disciplines are covered, including literature, history, culture and linguistics. As a result, a languages degree consists of much more than simply attaining fluency; students develop a number of different skills that are much sought after in the present day. Indeed, a good knowledge of languages is currently very well viewed by employers, with the employability rate of Cambridge language graduates amongst the highest out of all subjects. Furthermore, given the breadth of disciplines, there is always scope for students to focus on aspects of particular interest; the flexibility of the Tripos system ensures that the course is rarely monotonous.

Duration of course: 4 years

Admissions Test: Most colleges ask applicants to sit a language test during their interview period.

Written Work: Most colleges ask applicants to submit a school/college essay.

Entrance Requirements: An A level in at least one of the modern languages the applicant wishes to study is essential. Certain colleges have additional requirements.

Past Interview Question: What is the role of a translator?

“I really felt that my ideas were pushed to a whole different plane during an hour's supervision, it was an exhilarating and inspiring feeling.”

Modern & Medieval Languages graduate

Not the course for you? You might be interested in **English, Linguistics** or **History** at Cambridge. There are also **Modern Languages** courses available at Oxford, either on their own or in combinations with **History, English, Classics** and **Philosophy.**

□ Music

The undergraduate Music degree offered by Cambridge is highly academic, and considered one of the most challenging music degrees in the world. It commands international respect amongst academic musicians because of the advanced level of training in harmony, counterpoint, fugue and analysis. These theoretical components are offered alongside a wide range of specialist history and analysis options. Performance was traditionally kept to a minimum, but this has changed very recently, with a recital examination now an option for second and third year students. There is also plenty of opportunity for performance through the excellent college music societies and the larger university societies.

The Faculty is well equipped with an excellent supply of books and scores in the Pendlebury Library. There is an electro-acoustic lab, an ethnomusicology lab, five lecture rooms and several practice rooms, each equipped with a grand or upright piano. Most of the prestigious university concerts are held in the West Road Concert Hall situated at the Faculty.

Duration of course: 3 years

Admissions Test: Most colleges set their own admissions test to be completed at interview. Some colleges may also set a harmony test or a keyboard test at interview.

Written Work: Most colleges require the submission of a school/college essay. Some colleges may ask for a sample of applicant's music compositions.

Entrance Requirements: A level Music is essential. Certain colleges have additional requirements.

Past Interview Question: If music were a shape, what shape would it be?

“

The tutors and students I met while at Cambridge, in addition to what I learnt on the course, have enhanced and contributed to my successes as a professional musician.

”

Music graduate

Not the course for you? **Music** is also offered at Oxford, which puts less emphasis on practical skills.

□ Natural Sciences (Biological)

The Natural Science Tripos at Cambridge embraces all of the science disciplines from Physics to Psychology. Natural Sciences (Biological) covers everything vaguely concerned with living things: Zoology, Plant Sciences, Molecular Biology, Physiology and Pharmacology, as well as less obvious subjects like Geology or Psychology. Students of the Natural Sciences course (also known as NatSci) follow a broad curriculum in the first and second year before specialisation in the third and optional fourth year. The breadth of the course reflects the increasingly multidisciplinary nature of modern scientific research. Above all, the Natural Sciences course teaches analytical and problem-solving skills, as well as the ability to form strong and coherent arguments based on facts.

Duration of course: 3 with an optional fourth year.

Admissions Test: The Cambridge TSA (Thinking Skills Assessment) is required by some colleges and is sat at interview. Other colleges may set their own admissions test at interview.

Written Work: A few colleges require submission of a school/college essay.

Entrance Requirements: At least two science/mathematics A levels are essential and a third science/mathematics subject to at least AS level is highly desirable. Certain colleges have additional requirements.

Past Interview Question: Why don't animals have wheels?

“

The quality of the lecturers was probably the best bit as you got to be taught by people whose books you had read and who were very well known and respected in their fields.

”

Natural Sciences (Biological) graduate

Not the course for you? You might be interested in **Biomedical Sciences, Experimental Psychology, Biological Sciences** or **Biochemistry** at Oxford.

□ Natural Sciences (Physical)

The first year of Natural Sciences is structured to allow maximum breadth of subject choice, with the opportunity for students to specialise as they progress. If the physical sciences interest you most then you might want to choose from Physics, Chemistry, Earth Sciences and Materials Science. Options taken will influence the courses open to students in subsequent years of the degree, but other than this there are very few restrictions placed on module choice. Almost half of Natural Sciences graduates continue with further study and research, and those who do not enter various careers including consultancy, banking and media.

Duration of course: 3 years, with an optional fourth year.

Admissions Test: The Cambridge TSA (Thinking Skills Assessment) is required by some colleges and is sat at interview. Other colleges may set their own admissions test at interview.

Written Work: A few colleges require submission of a school/college essay.

Entrance Requirements: At least two science/mathematics A levels are essential and a third science/mathematics subject to at least AS level is highly desirable. Certain colleges have additional requirements.

Past Interview Question: Why does a whip make a sound when you crack it?

“

I enjoyed the variety. I loved being able to discuss science across the board with friends, from chatting about semiconductors with engineers to discussing primate behaviour with anthropologists.

”

Natural Sciences (Physical) graduate

Not the course for you? Try **Physics, Chemistry, Materials Science** or **Earth Sciences** at Oxford, or **Mathematics, Computer Science** or **Engineering** at either university.

□ Philosophy

Philosophy is the examination of mankind's most fundamental questions. What is the nature of reality? Is morality objective? What is a soul? Are there any natural rights? Philosophy is the practice of training the mind to examine how we answer questions like this and scrutinise those answers that we arrive at.

In the early 20th century, Cambridge was the centre for philosophy. Bertrand Russell, G E Moore and Ludwig Wittgenstein transformed the study of philosophy with the analytic style which is now prominent in much of the world. The main emphasis of the current course continues in this tradition with what is broadly known as the 'Anglo-American analytic tradition', i.e. mainly the current and past concerns of American and British philosophers. Particular stress is given to various incarnations of reductionism, with the logical underpinnings of language being a standard method of investigation in most of the different areas of study. Particular favourites of the Philosophy Faculty are: the conversion of the language describing mental states into language concerning the outward signs of these states, i.e. behaviour or the tendency to be disposed to certain forms of behaviour; the reduction of talk about experience and knowledge into talk about sense data; the investigation into the logical status of components of speech and thought; and the relation between thought and language.

Duration of course: 3 years

Admissions Test: All colleges set their own admissions test which is sat during the interview period.

Written Work: Some colleges require the submission of a school or college essay.

Entrance Requirements: No specific A levels are required, although a mixture of arts and sciences is useful. Certain colleges have additional requirements.

Past Interview Question: If you're not in California, how do you know it exists?

"

I found supervisions particularly enjoyable, at least with those supervisors who encouraged a relaxed pedagogical atmosphere in which one could exercise one's intellect.

"

Philosophy graduate

Not the course for you? You might also like to consider **Classics, Law** or **PPS (Politics, Psychology & Sociology)** at Cambridge. At Oxford you could consider **Philosophy & Theology, Modern Languages** & **Philosophy** or **PPE (Philosophy, Politics & Economics).**

□ PPS (Politics, Psychology & Sociology)

PPS (Politics, Psychology and Sociology) at Cambridge was a new course in 2009, when it replaced the old Social and Political Sciences degree. It offers a unique opportunity to study the complex and fascinating human world we live in by covering the three core disciplines of Politics, Psychology and Sociology, alongside, if you wish, others such as Social Anthropology. No other university offers this combination of subjects and you will also benefit from being taught by renowned academics and lecturers who are experts in their field at a world-class university.

Duration of course: 3 years

Admissions Test: Some colleges will ask applicants to sit the Cambridge TSA (Thinking Skills Assessment). Other colleges may set their own test at interview.

Written Work: Most colleges ask applicants to submit school/college essays.

Entrance Requirements: No specific A levels are required. Certain colleges have additional requirements.

Past Interview Question: How do we solve terrorism?

“ I enjoyed discussions during supervisions which were based on the content of my essays. I was able to deconstruct, oppose and defend arguments. ”

SPS graduate

Not the course for you? You might be interested in **Economics, History, Law, Land Economy, Archaeology & Anthropology** or **Geography** at Cambridge. At Oxford, **PPE (Philosophy, Politics & Economics), Archaeology & Anthropology** or **Experimental Psychology** might interest you.

□ Theology & Religious Studies

This course is perfect for applicants with an inquiring mind who wish to use their university experience to explore some of the most profound questions surrounding human existence. As well as covering a broad range of religions, including Christianity, Hinduism, Buddhism, and Islam, this degree offers the opportunity to consider deeply how religious convictions have been expressed, drawing on cultural, historical and philosophical sources. The first year offers a broad introduction to theological and religious studies, and the subsequent two years are designed to allow students a high degree of flexibility so that they may specialise in areas of interest.

Whilst it is not a requirement for prospective candidates to have knowledge of Greek, Hebrew, Sanskrit, or Arabic, one of these four scriptural languages must be studied in the first year. It is therefore recommended that those who intend to read Theology and Religious Studies should begin to study one of the languages before commencing their course. Beginners will also be able to take classes at the start of their degree.

Duration of course: 3 years

Admissions Test: Some colleges set an admissions test at interview.

Written Work: Most colleges ask applicants to submit school/college essays.

Entrance Requirements: No specific A levels are required, although an AS or A level in one or more of English, Religious Studies, History and Modern Languages is highly desirable. Certain colleges have additional requirements.

Past Interview Question: Are we in a position to judge God?

“

I enjoyed the opportunity to pursue my own interests during coursework and the emphasis on Theology as an interdisciplinary and dynamic subject within the modern world.

”

Theology & Religious Studies graduate

Not the course for you? You might be interested in **Philosophy, History, PPS (Politics, Psychology & Sociology), English** or **Classics. Theology** is also available at Oxford, with **Philosophy** or **Oriental Studies.**

☐ Veterinary Medicine

Veterinary Medicine is a six year course, compared to five years at all the other veterinary schools in the UK. These six years are divided into the pre-clinical course, which takes up the first three years, and the clinical course, which makes up the final three years. The pre-clinical course is taught with the medics and the natural scientists, although now there is an increasing drive to teach the veterinary students separately. The minor courses in the first two years are taught exclusively to the vets. The advantage this gives is that during the first three years Cambridge vets receive an extremely rigorous scientific background and understanding. The third year also provides a year to pursue any subject a student may be interested in, an opportunity unique to the Cambridge vet school. The first three pre-clinical years are based in the centre of town, where all the teaching is carried out. On completion of the pre-clinical years, students graduate with a Cambridge BA. This is then followed by the clinical years, which are taught entirely at the Queens Veterinary Hospital, Madingley Road, Cambridge. After the clinical years you graduate again with a VetMB and become a member of the Royal College of Veterinary Surgeons.

Duration of course: 6 years

Admissions Test: All colleges ask applicants to sit the BMAT (the BioMedical Admissions Test). This usually happens in early November (in 2010, the date is 3rd November). Some colleges require applicants to do preparatory study at the interview.

Written Work: N/A

Entrance Requirements: A level Chemistry is highly desirable. Grades C or above in Double Award Science and Mathematics are essential. Three of the following AS levels: Biology/Human Biology, Chemistry (highly recommended), Physics, Mathematics are essential and at least one of those subjects must be carried on to A level. Certain colleges have additional requirements.

Past Interview Question: If I put a chicken in a strong electro-magnetic field what would happen?

The practical areas of the course are probably the most fun, from gossiping about last night during practicals in the first year, to doing your first consultation with an actor in front of your friends, to the first time you perform surgery with your friends watching.

”

Veterinary Medicine graduate

Not the course for you? You might also like to consider **Biological Natural Sciences** at Cambridge, **Biological** or **Biomedical Sciences** at Oxford, or **Medicine** at either Oxford or Cambridge.

□ Archaeology & Anthropology

Commonly referred to as 'Arch and Anth,' the course provides a broad introduction to past and present human societies. This is through a social (Social Anthropology), biological (Biological Anthropology) and material perspective (Archaeology). The scope of Archaeology & Anthropology is vast, covering almost every aspect of human behaviour, giving the Archaeology & Anthropology student a fresh perspective on the sense of self and place in the world.

While initially it may appear obscure and irrelevant, it is a subject that is genuinely significant and it allows students to study a diverse range of topics and issues. How do societies structure their families, their economies, their political systems? What contextual factors affect human growth and nutrition? The interplay of these questions and the insight that can be gained from such a variety of views lie at the heart of the course.

Duration of the course: 3 years

Admissions Test: N/A

Written Work: Two recently marked school/college essays, preferably on different subjects, usually required in early November (in 2010, 10th November). In addition, applicants are required to include a statement of up to 300 words setting out their understanding of the relations between archaeology, social and cultural anthropology, and biological anthropology.

Entrance Requirements: No specific A levels are required, although a combination of arts and sciences is useful.

Past interview question: Why do humans have cultures?

"I enjoyed learning about cannibalism in South America, and the uses of pain across different cultures. The fieldwork was also extremely rewarding."

Arch and Anth graduate

Not the course for you? Check out **PPE (Philosophy, Politics & Economics), History, History (Ancient & Modern)** or **Human Sciences.** You might also consider **Archaeology & Anthropology** at Cambridge.

□ Biochemistry (Molecular and Cellular)

Biochemistry is a young, fast-changing and consequently fascinating discipline. The core of the course is the study of living things at a molecular level. Modern techniques such as NMR spectroscopy and molecular genetics have led to a renaissance in the bio-molecular sciences. Subjects relating to Biochemistry are constantly in the news and, with regular breakthroughs and discoveries, ideas are continually changing and open to different interpretations.

The Oxford Biochemistry degree is in essence quite similar to aspects of the Chemistry degree, although it does involve a considerable amount of essay writing. Biochemistry also has significant practical requirements, which give an excellent grounding for the large percentage of Biochemistry graduates who do eventually enter into research.

Duration of the course: 4 years

Admissions Test: N/A

Written Work: N/A

Entrance Requirements: A level Chemistry with another science or with Mathematics is essential. Biology and Mathematics at AS level are useful.

Past interview question: If you were a virus, how would you communicate your opinions to me?

“

Most of all I enjoyed the fact that Biochemistry is such a modern subject with so many advances made all the time.

”

Biochemistry graduate

Not the course for you? Check out **Biological Sciences, Biomedical Sciences, Chemistry** or **Human Sciences.** You might also consider **Natural Sciences (Biological or Physical)** at Cambridge.

□ Biological Sciences

With ever-changing facts and statistics to work with, Biological Sciences is an incredibly dynamic and interesting subject to study. Debate is actively encouraged on the course. This immensely diverse subject covers all areas of biology, from ecology to genetics. An important distinction to make from other science degrees taught at Oxford, including Biology, is that Biological Sciences is an essay-based subject.

The first year of the Oxford course aims to give a solid foundation in the most important areas of Biology: Cells & Genes, Organisms, Ecology and Quantitative Methods. In the second and third year, students begin to tailor their own programmes of study, choosing from a series of options ranging from animal behaviour to the study of disease. There is also a compulsory course in Evolution. Practical laboratory time and field work forms an integral part of the course, and students are given the opportunity to carry out an independent piece of original research in their third year.

Duration of the course: 3 years

Admissions Test: N/A

Written Work: N/A

Entrance Requirements: A level Biology is essential, another science or Mathematics is preferred.

Past interview question: Why don't zebras get ulcers?

"

The social aspect of the course was brilliant. We spent a lot of time together in labs and on field trips, so you got to know everybody really well.

"

Biological Sciences graduate

Not the course for you? **Biochemistry** may suit an applicant more interested in cells and genes than ecology or whole organism biology. **Biomedical Sciences** may interest those fascinated by the human body, alternatively the **Natural Sciences (Biological)** course at Cambridge is a much broader approach to the sciences.

□ Biomedical Sciences

Biomedical research is a cutting-edge discipline. Discoveries are being made all the time that change our understanding of how the human body works. Oxford has a proud tradition of standing at the forefront of new discoveries. Consequently, students on the course will be taught by many of the world's leading experts.

Biomedical Sciences is a new course which will be accepting its first students in 2011. It most closely resembles the old Physiological Sciences course and also replaces part of the course previously known as Physiology, Philosophy and Psychology (PPP). This undergraduate degree will share many qualities with its predecessors. It will continue to be an essay-based subject covering a broad range of topics, from molecular biology to how the body adapts to exercise. The few students on the old Physiology course made for an intimate and sociable atmosphere. Biomedical Sciences will continue this trend and accept a limited number of students (roughly forty).

Duration of the course: 3 years

Admissions Test: All colleges ask applicants to sit the BMAT (the BioMedical Admissions Test). This usually happens in early November (in 2010, the date is 3rd November).

Written Work: N/A

Entrance Requirements: Two of the following A levels: Biology, Chemistry, Physics or Mathematics are essential.

Past interview question: How does the structure of a cell compare to that of a city?

> "(On Physiological Sciences) The teaching quality was amazing – I had tutorials from people who wrote my textbooks in the first year."
>
> **Physiological Sciences graduate**

Not the course for you? Try checking out **Medicine, Biochemistry, Biological Sciences** or **Experimental Psychology.** You may also be interested in **Natural Sciences (Biological)** at Cambridge.

□ Chemistry

The Chemistry Department at Oxford is the largest of its kind in the Western world. With state-of-the-art facilities, including the recently opened Chemistry Research Laboratory (which has a 5* rating) and with only a fraction of leavers unemployed following graduation, there is much to attract prospective students.

Considerable emphasis is placed on lectures and lab work, which are topped up with up to five tutorials a week, making it one of the most contact-intensive courses on offer. However, for those with an aversion to essay writing, the structure and discipline of a Chemistry degree is highly appealing. Drawing upon key concepts in Chemistry, Physics and Mathematics, the focus is on three areas of Chemistry: Organic, Inorganic and Physical.

What makes this Chemistry degree different to those on offer at other universities is the inclusion of a compulsory fourth year, which is entirely dedicated to original research. This provides a unique opportunity for students to develop a number of key skills including critical awareness of developments in the field, the ability to plan and organise their own work (i.e. develop their independence), the ability to analyse their results critically and the ability to use their initiative and originality.

Duration of the course: 4 years

Admissions Test: N/A

Written Work: N/A

Entrance Requirements: A level Chemistry and AS level Mathematics are essential. A level Mathematics is highly desirable.

Past interview question: What happens to the mobility of Group 1 elements going down the periodic table?

“

The structured lecture course was on the whole very useful and informative and I enjoyed the pace at which we went through each topic.

”

Chemistry graduate

Not the course for you? Check out **Biochemistry (Molecular and Cellular), Biomedical Sciences, Mathematics** or **Human Sciences**. You might also consider **Natural Sciences (Biological or Physical)** at Cambridge.

☐ CAAH (Classical Archaeology & Ancient History)

CAAH (Classical Archaeology and Ancient History) is a fairly new degree, with the first intake admitted in 2001. The course allows great flexibility for each student, and the ability to place individual emphasis on their personal interests. Options available cover periods from around 1500 BC to 1000 AD and focus not just on Greece and Rome and their interaction with the wider world, but also on Hellenistic, Egyptian, Byzantine and Celtic history and archaeology. CAAH also offers modules on the scientific elements of archaeology and conservation, epigraphy, numismatics and ancient languages.

CAAH is a fantastic choice for anyone who wants to keep their subject options open, and absorb as many related elements as possible over the three years of their degree. The course is modern and forward thinking in its ideology, striving constantly to interlink the disciplines of archaeology and history and using the two to support each other. Ultimately, the degree aims to provide a good grounding in both academic disciplines and encourages a great deal of independent thought and creativity.

Duration of the course: 3 years

Admissions Test: N/A

Written Work: Applicants are asked to submit two recent, marked essays, written as part of their school/college work usually required in early November (in 2010, 10th November).

Entrance Requirements: No specific A levels are required, but a Classical Language, Classical Civilisation, Ancient History at A level are helpful.

Past interview question: Where do you think the Elgin Marbles should be: London or Athens?

I enjoyed the tutorials the most, I was able to discuss the topics that I found interesting and anything that I didn't understand I could have explained in a manner that suited me.

”

CAAH graduate

Not the course for you? Try checking out **Archaeology & Anthropology, Classics** and its Joint Honours or **History** and its Joint Honours. Cambridge also offers similar courses.

□ Classics

The Oxford Classics course offers the chance to study all aspects of the culture, language, literature and thought of not just one, but two, great civilisations: Ancient Greece and Rome. Graduates leave Oxford with a broad understanding of the cultures and history of the Ancient Mediterranean world on which our own is still largely based, as well as a good reading knowledge of Latin and Greek.

The breadth of the Classics course at Oxford means that it last four years (Course I), rather than three years, as is the case at Cambridge. The additional year allows more module choice and flexibility and more time to explore more obscure options. Many students prefer, however, to keep their degree to the usual three years. Students with no previous experience in either Latin or Greek have the choice of taking a five year course with intensive Latin and Ancient Greek in the first year (Course II).

Students are not formally examined until the fifth term at Oxford, which some find frustrating. The flipside argument is that there is more time to improve linguistic ability before the first formal examination.

Duration of the course: 4 years

Admissions Test: Applicants for Course I sit language tests at interview in December. Applicants for Course II must take the Classics Language Aptitude Test usually in early November (in 2010, 3rd November)

Written Work: Applicants are required to submit two essays or commentaries, normally in areas relevant to Classics.

Entrance Requirements: For Course I, A level Latin or Greek is essential. No specific A levels are required for Course II.

Past interview question: Are history and myth compatible?

I loved the translation of texts, particularly Greek comedy. The literature tutors are first class and the literature tutorials were fascinating.

”

Classics graduate

Not the course for you? Take a look at **Classics & English, Classics & Modern Languages, Archaeology & Anthropology, History** and its Joint Honours, and **Philosophy** and its Joint Honours. **Classics** is also offered at Cambridge.

□ Classics & English

Despite its name, Classics & English is not really a Joint Honours degree. In a normal Joint Honours degree the undergraduate will take half their papers in each discipline. With Classics & English however, almost half of the papers taken in the second and third years are papers that link Classics & English. It is, therefore, as much a degree in comparative literature as it is a Joint Honours degree. It is available to students who have not previously studied Latin or Ancient Greek. These students take Course II, which involves a preliminary year learning either Latin or Greek, while studying some study of the classical literature.

Since the nature of the course is so particular, it may be hard for students to gain a broad knowledge of both subjects individually. However, a student will graduate in Classics & English with an especially detailed knowledge of the relationship between the two disciplines beyond that of a Single Honours student. As the course is limited to a few Classics & English students per year, the course feels pleasantly intimate.

Duration of the course: 3 or 4 years

Admissions Test: All applicants take the ELAT (English Literature Admissions Test) in early November (in 2010, 3rd November). Applicants for Course I sit language tests at interview in December. Applicants for Course II must take the Classics Language Aptitude Test usually in early November (in 2010, also 3rd November).

Written Work: Applicants are normally expected to submit two pieces of written school/college work, relevant to either Classics or English.

Entrance Requirements: A level English Literature or English Language & Literature is essential for both Course I and II. For Course I A level Latin or Ancient Greek is essential. This is not required for Course II.

Past interview question: Why do you think Shakespeare wrote plays rather than epic poetry?

“

I liked my two college tutors very much. They were helpful in terms of commenting on essays and guiding my revision, but more than that, they seemed genuinely interested in what I had to say.

”

Classics & English graduate

Not the course for you? Try checking out the Single Honours courses in the two subjects. Alternatively, at Cambridge, you might be interested in **Archaeology & Anthropology** or **Anglo-Saxon, Norse & Celtic.**

□ Classics & Modern Languages

The Classics & Modern Languages course provides the opportunity to study one modern language (French, German, Modern Greek, Italian, Portuguese, Russian, Spanish, or Czech with Slovak or Celtic), along with Latin and/or Ancient Greek. The main focus of both parts of the course, particularly in the first year, is on literature and language, while the Final Honours School offers the opportunity to study Linguistics, Ancient History and Philosophy. For the most part the two subjects are treated individually, although there are some 'cross-over' options which allow comparative study, usually undertaken in the final year either as an exam paper or thesis.

Students may take a four or five year course (the five year course has a greater emphasis on Classics, or is for those students with no previous knowledge of Latin or Ancient Greek). In all cases the penultimate year of study is spent abroad and devoted to gaining proficiency in your modern language. The two disciplines are linked through comparative papers and the use of the knowledge of two related subject areas.

Duration of the course: 4 or 5 years

Admissions Test: Course I applicants sit a test in one or both Classical languages. Course II applicants must take the Classics Language Aptitude Test usually in early November (in 2010, 3rd November).

Written Work: Applicants are required to submit some school/college work relevant to the course. For Classics, candidates should normally submit two essays or commentaries.

Entrance Requirements: For Celtic, Czech, Italian, Modern Greek or Portuguese no specific language A levels are required. For French, German, Russian or Spanish the relevant A level is required. For Course I, A level Latin or Greek is essential. No specific A levels for Course II, although applicants should have studied the modern language they wish to read.

Past interview question: What is so strange about Cupid flying in a church in the Renaissance?

"The joy of the course was the opportunity to study a diverse range of subjects in one degree."

Classics & Modern Languages graduate

Not the course for you? Try checking out the Single Honours degrees in **Classics.** You may also be interested in **Archaeology & Anthropology** or **Classics & Oriental Studies,** or you could try the **Classics** and **Modern Languages** courses at Cambridge.

□ Classics & Oriental Studies

This course allows you to combine the study of an oriental language and culture with Latin and/or Ancient Greek and the study of the ancient world. This is a unique combination and a very fruitful degree. The Ashmolean Museum at Oxford houses collections of ancient artefacts including coins, vases and manuscripts. The new Sackler Library brings together books on the classical world and ancient Egypt and near East, with a particular emphasis on history and art.

For Oriental Studies you can select your main language from Akkadian, Arabic, Egyptian, Hebrew, Persian, Sanskrit, Japanese and Chinese, depending on your chosen college.

Duration of the course: 4 or 3 years (for Oriental Studies with Classics and no year abroad)

Admissions Test: For applicants for Classics with Oriental Studies, applicants with no prior knowledge of Greek or Latin take the Language Aptitude Test for Classics usually in early November (in 2010, 3rd November).

For applicants for Oriental Studies with Classics, applicants are required to take the LAT (Linguistic Aptitude Test) for Oriental Studies at interview.

Written Work: Two recently marked school/college essays, preferably on different subjects, usually required in early November (in 2010, 10th November).

Entrance Requirements: A level Latin and/or Greek is highly recommended.

Past interview question: If Bach is conducted by a Japanese person, is it Western or Eastern music?

“

Studying Classics with Oriental Studies allows you to organise your own timetable, and fit in everything else Oxford has to offer!

”

Classics & Oriental Studies graduate

Not the course for you? Try checking out the Single Honours degrees in **Classics** or **Oriental Studies,** or **Classics** and its other Joint Honours. **Archaeology & Anthropology** or **Classics** at Cambridge may also be of interest.

□ Computer Science

Oxford offers two courses in Computer Science, a three year BA degree and a four year Masters degree. There is no distinction between them on application and so students do not need to decide whether to take three or four years of study until the start of their third year.

The course at Oxford concentrates on bridging theory and practice, including a wide variety of hardware and software technologies and their applications. It has to be said that a great part of the course is theoretical, and some students find it too abstract, having expected a course which has more to do with writing programs than reasoning about programs. However, it turns out that this theoretical approach is very useful, putting the student in a position of understanding the underlying principles of programming, an invaluable basis from which to solve a great variety of programming problems.

The courses in Computer Science will develop students' analytic and practical skills to a very high level, making them employable in almost every field, or preparing them well for further study in the subject.

Duration of the course: 3 or 4 years

Admissions Test: Applicants are required to sit the MAT (Mathematics Aptitude Test) usually required in early November (in 2010, 3rd November).

Written Work: N/A

Entrance Requirements: A level Mathematic is required. A level Further Mathematics or a science is highly recommended.

Past interview question: How would you ensure security between two people on the internet?

> I really enjoyed the theoretical side of concurrency.
>
> **Computer Science graduate**

Not the course for you? **Mathematics, Physics** and **Engineering** at Oxford are also related, and there are many sub-options available to take. Perhaps check out the **Computer Science** and **Engineering** courses at Cambridge as well.

□ Earth Sciences (Geology)

The Earth Sciences course is a multidisciplinary approach to the study of the earth and other planets. It embraces an enormous range of topics, including the evolution of life, the nature of planetary interiors, the causes of earthquakes and volcanic eruptions, earth-surface processes and the origin and behaviour of oceans and atmosphere. The emphasis of both the teaching and research is on understanding the underlying physical principles of geological processes. Both theory and basic observation are recognised as essential elements in the Earth Sciences. While students with a strong background in all aspects of the physical sciences are encouraged to join the Department, the course also allows for students to concentrate on specific topic areas such as Palaeobiology or Geophysics.

The university offers two courses: a BA in Geology and an MEarthSc in Earth Sciences. The courses are exactly the same for the first three years. Students can then choose to continue with the four year Earth Sciences course or leave with a BA in Geology.

Duration of the course: 3 year BA (Geology) or 4 year MEarthSc (Earth Sciences)

Admissions Test: N/A

Written Work: N/A

Entrance Requirements: A level Mathematics is essential. A level Chemistry and/or Physics is highly recommended. Biology, Geology or Further Mathematics can be helpful.

Past interview question: How would you calculate the mass of the oceans?

“

I really enjoyed all the practical work and field work, and the amount of support I got in tutorials, especially in the run-up to exams.

”

Earth Sciences graduate

Not the course for you? At Oxford you might also like to consider **Geography, Human Sciences, Materials Science** or **Physics.** At Cambridge, geological sciences forms part of the **Natural Sciences (Physical)** course, a much broader approach to the Sciences in general.

□ E&M (Economics & Management)

Would you enjoy formulating and testing economic models? Are you interested in the complexities of economies? Do you light up when considering motivation behind actions? Can you simplify situations and analyse data logically? If so then the E&M course at Oxford may be an ideal choice.

Despite being relatively new by Oxford standards, E&M is still one of the most competitive for places. A big advantage of Economics & Management is that it combines academic rigour with vocational worth. This course is the only Oxford undergraduate course which allows students to study the new science of management, and is thus a perfect stepping stone into management consultancy, investment banking or other careers in business.

Duration of the course: 3 years

Admissions Test: All applicants are required to take the Oxford TSA (Thinking Skills Assessment) usually in early November (in 2010, 3rd November).

Written Work: N/A

Entrance Requirements: A level Physics and Mathematics are essential and the inclusion of a Mathematics Mechanics module is highly recommended. A level Further Mathematics is also helpful.

Past interview question: I have a rare disease the treatment for which demands a lot of resources. Should you help me live or let me die?

“I most enjoyed the variety of different modules you could take for Finals.”

E&M graduate

Not the course for you? Cambridge offers **Economics** as a distinct degree, while Oxford offers several opportunities to study Economics or Management alongside other subjects in degrees such as **PPE (Philosophy, Politics & Economics)** or **EEM (Engineering, Economics & Management).**

□ Engineering Science

The Department of Engineering at Oxford teaches a broad-based four year course that leads to the degree of Master of Engineering (MEng), accredited by all of the relevant institutions (IChemE, IMechE etc). The course emphasises the core skills the professional engineer will need, including a strong awareness of the practical skills required in the industrial sector. The course aims to instil versatility in students during the first two years, allowing for exposure to the various engineering disciplines before specialisms are chosen later in the degree.

The degree course consists of three main parts. At the end of the first year you will undertake preliminary examinations (Prelims). Once students have passed these exams, they can then progress onto Part I Finals, which are taken at the end of the third year. In the fourth year students undertake a major research project in a field of their choice, as well as completing three Finals Part II papers.

Duration of the course: 4 years

Admissions Test: N/A

Written Work: N/A

Entrance Requirements: A level Physics and Mathematics are essential and the inclusion of a mathematics mechanical module is recommended. A level Further Mathematics is also helpful.

Past interview question: How do the forces act on the Millennium Wheel?

“

I loved the way the lectures complemented the laboratory work, there were plenty of opportunities to apply what you had learned to practical scenarios.

”

Engineering Sciences graduate

Not the course for you? You might be interested in **Engineering** at Cambridge, or **Physics, Materials Science, Physics** or **Mathematics** at Oxford.

□ EEM (Engineering, Economics & Management)

EEM has a very broad syllabus, combining much of the Engineering Science course with the Economics from PPE (Philosophy, Politics & Economics) and Management from E&M (Economics & Management). The course is unique in this respect, and an equivalent is hard to find in any other major university, including Cambridge. EEM graduates are highly sought after, particularly in the banking and consultancy professions; a sound engineering base is often advantageous in understanding resource allocations within the technology sectors.

The drawbacks of EEM are to be expected when combining such a wide range of subjects. The course is hard work, and its wide breadth may be argued to leave its graduates with a very broad toolbox of skills but perhaps slightly less in-depth knowledge. Care must also be taken when choosing options and placements if students wish to gain accreditation from certain engineering institutions.

Engineering at Oxford is very broad, theoretical and extremely heavy on mathematics content, especially so for students coming from A level standard Mathematics. The advantage with breadth is that Oxford engineers are well suited to work in, and lead, multidisciplinary teams. The extra Economics and Management courses are intended to give EEMists the tools with which to understand other aspects of company operations.

Duration of the course: 4 years

Admissions Test: N/A

Written Work: N/A

Entrance Requirements: A level Physics and Mathematics are essential and the inclusion of a mathematics mechanical module is useful. A level Further Mathematics is also helpful.

Past interview question: How does a pendulum work, bearing in mind that the amplitude of the oscillations increases over time rather than decreases?

“The placement was the ultimate place to learn. It was the best aspect of the course.”

EEM graduate

Not the course for you? **Engineering** can be studied on its own, and **Economics & Management** can be studied as a Joint Honours. Alternatively you may be interested in **Physics, Materials Science,** or **MEM (Materials, Economics & Management).**

☐ English Language & Literature

English is one of the most popular degree courses at Oxford, while the Faculty is the largest English department in the country. The course gives students a chance to study writing in English from its Anglo-Saxon origins to the literature of the early 21st century. You can concentrate on English writers, or use the opportunity to look further afield to other countries. In addition, it is also possible to specialise in certain periods, or to cover the full sweep of the development of our language. Throughout the course, students develop sophisticated reading and criticism skills, and learn how to analyse form, technique and historical context.

Duration of the course: 3 years

Admissions Test: All applicants are required take the ELAT (English Literature Admissions Test) usually in early November (in 2010, 3rd November).

Written Work: Applicants are required to submit one recent example of writing by 10 November 2010. It should be a marked school/college essay and ideally, it should be an analytical discussion on topics in English Literature.

Entrance Requirements: A level English Literature or English Language & Literature is essential. A language or History can be helpful.

Past interview question: Would you rather be a novel or a poem?

“

I enjoyed the specialist papers the most; it was really good to be able to focus in on one specific author and try to read their entire output. By focusing on one author it was also possible to go beyond learning facts and gain a real sense of the author and their era.

”

English Literature & Language graduate

Not the course for you? You might be interested in one of the Joint Honours Schools with English, such as **English & Modern Languages** or **History & English.** You may also like **History, Modern Languages, Theology, Classics** or even **History of Art** on their own. You could also consider the **English** course at Cambridge.

□ English & Modern Languages

English & Modern Languages is a hybrid course, uniting half a Single Honours English degree with the opportunity to study one modern language (French, German, Modern Greek, Italian, Portuguese, Russian, Spanish, or Czech with the choice of Slovak or Celtic). The English aspect of the degree allows you to study anything from the historical origins of the language in Anglo-Saxon works through to contemporary literature produced across the world.

The modern language aspect of the degree delivers practical linguistic training and an introduction to the literature and thought of the chosen language. The range of teaching and facilities available in both Honours is enviable. Students also spend their third year abroad, allowing them to hone their language skills further and immerse themselves in the culture of their host country.

Duration of the course: 4 years

Admissions Test: All candidates are required to take the ELAT (English Literature Admissions Test) and a 30-minute test for the languages they intend to study, though not in languages they intend to study more or less from scratch. The tests are designed to test grammar rather than vocabulary.

Written Work: For the modern language aspect, applicants must submit one piece of marked classwork in the language which they plan to study, and one piece of marked writing in English (perhaps on literature, or history, or some other subject being studied at school or college). For the English aspect, applicants need to submit one recent example of writing. It should be a marked school/college essay, and should not have been rewritten.

Entrance Requirements: A level English Literature or English Language & Literature is essential. For French, German, Russian and Spanish an A level in the language is essential. For Celtic, Czech, Italian, Modern Greek or Portuguese an A level in the language is not required.

Past interview question: Is English a degenerate language that has lost its succinctness and precision?

"Working so closely with world-renowned scholars was the best thing about the course."

English & Modern Languages graduate

Not the course for you? At Oxford, both subjects can be studied on their own or in varying combinations with another subject such as **History, Classics, Linguistics** and **Philosophy**. You could also consider the **English** and **Modern & Medieval Languages** courses at Cambridge.

□ EMEL (European & Middle Eastern Languages)

EMEL has appoximately ten students per year which allows students to combine the study of a language taught in the Faculty of Modern Languages with modules in Arabic, Hebrew, Persian or Turkish. Whereas most Joint Honours remain separated, a real selling-point of this course is the 'bridging extended essay' that you complete in your third year (instead of a thesis). The aim of this is to combine your studies of both languages. For example, a Russian & Arabic student may choose to research Arabic countries which have adopted socialist or communist government in light of Russian influence.

Oxford has a wide range of facilities for students of EMEL: The Bodleian Library and Taylorian Institute have some of the largest collections devoted to modern European languages in the world, while there is also the Centre for Hebrew and Jewish Studies and the Oxford Centre for Islamic Studies which both house thousands of volumes. EMEL students come into contact with vast amounts of literature. They also spend their year abroad in a more exotic location, as they must spend the year submersing themselves in their Middle Eastern Language. Students are expected to travel a great deal out of term time in the first and second years. These experiences stand EMEL graduates in a strong position, with regularly successful applications into highly competitive areas of business, law and finance.

Duration of the course: 4 years

Admissions Test: All applicants with a language A level will be expected to take a language test at interview. The LAT (Linguistic Aptitude Test) may be required when studying a language from scratch, depending on the language chosen.

Written Work: Applicants must submit two pieces of written work usually in early November (in 2010, 10th November). At least one of them must be in the relevant modern language.

Entrance Requirements: For the Middle Eastern Language, Celtic, Czech, Italian, Modern Greek or Portuguese an A level in the language is not required. For French, German, Russian or Spanish, an A level in the language is required.

Past interview question: What is the greatest benefit of studying a Middle Eastern language?

"The most rewarding part of the course was the adventure of living with an entirely different culture and language for a year."

EMEL graduate

Not the course for you? Check out the **Modern Languages, History, Oriental Studies** and **English** courses at Oxford. The **Modern & Medieval Languages** and **History** courses at Cambridge may also be of interest.

☐ EP (Experimental Psychology)

The Oxford Experimental Psychology department is widely regarded as one of the leading Psychology departments in the UK. The course at Oxford is unusual because of its particularly scientific nature (hence 'Experimental'). There is a lot of statistics and neurophysiology in the first year and it helps, but is not essential, if you have taken Mathematics, Biology or Physics at A level. You are unlikely to be studying any Freud or doing much introspection. Psychology has been defined as the science of mental life and it is studied in Oxford through experiments and systematic observation.

Duration of the course: 3 years

Admissions Test: Applicants are required to take the Oxford TSA (Thinking Skills Assessment) usually in early November (in 2010, 3rd November).

Written Work: N/A

Entrance Requirements: At least one science or Mathematics A level is highly recommended.

Past interview question: Can a thermostat think?

"

The teaching quality was top notch because the tutors were all at the top of their research fields. There were also lots of opportunities to be involved with new research opportunities.

"

Experimental Psychology graduate

Not the course for you? Check out **Human Sciences, Psychology & Philosophy, Biological Sciences** or **Medicine** at Oxford. **PPS (Politics, Psychology & Sociology)** is offered at Cambridge and may also be of interest.

□ Fine Art

The Fine Art course offered at The Ruskin School of Drawing and Fine Art is a three year, studio-based course resulting in a BFA (Bachelor of Fine Art). The Ruskin BFA stands out because of its unique mix of practical and academic work, combination of traditional methods and cutting-edge techniques, and excellent teaching staff, many of whom are well-established contemporary artists in their own right. It is the perfect springboard for the next generation of modern artists.

Duration of the course: 3 years

Admissions Test: The interview includes a practical test, where applicants are required to create two pieces in a variety of media on a number of possible subjects.

Written Work: Applicants are required to submit a portfolio of original artwork. Applicants are also strongly recommended to bring further work to interview.

Entrance Requirements: A level Art is highly recommended.

Past interview question: What piece of art would you most like to own?

“I loved having visiting artists come up to Oxford. It gave me the opportunity to talk about my work with those I admired, and to hear their views.”

Fine Art graduate

Not the course for you? You might be interested in **History of Art** at either Oxford or Cambridge.

□ Geography

Geography is a multidisciplinary subject that includes elements taken from the arts, the social sciences and the natural sciences. It tackles major current issues, such as the transformation of global economy and culture, regional and global inequalities, ethnic segregation, urbanisation, planning, environmental change, natural hazards and many more. Students develop a lucid view of a world in flux and the ways in which physical and human environments inter-relate.

Duration of the course: 3 years

Admissions Test: N/A

Written Work: Applicants are required to submit two marked pieces of recent work produced as part of their geography course usually in early November (in 2010, 10th November).

Entrance Requirements: Geography A level is highly recommended.

Past interview question: What would happen to the climate of the UK if the earth spun in the opposite direction and the ocean currents and wind circulation all moved in opposite directions?

“

I most enjoyed my special options in second and third year. The field trip to Tunisia was a highlight (the best part about geography is seeing it in action, after all).

”

Geography graduate

Not the course for you? You might be interested in **Earth Sciences (Geology)** or **Human Sciences** at Oxford. Check out also the **Geography** and **Natural Sciences (Physical)** course at Cambridge.

□ History

History at Oxford is a course that gives students both chronological breadth and the chance to specialise in certain aspects of history, such as literature within the 16th century. The course requires the study of comparative European and British history and it is usual for students to cover economic, political, social and cultural history.

The tutorials are the main method of teaching and the emphasis is on independent learning, although lectures are available throughout the course. Students likely to thrive are those who enjoy reading efficiently and wisely and are keen to devise arguments with good use of supporting evidence. Students develop the skill of tackling large amounts of material, channelling their points into a cohesive structure and coming at topics they have never seen before from an interesting and logical angle.

Applicants should enjoy learning about new topics within history, like reading both sources and secondary literature, and be willing to go out on a limb and attempt to support complex arguments.

Duration of the course: 3 years

Admissions Test: Applicants will sit the HAT (History Aptitude Test) usually in early November (in 2010, 3rd November).

Written Work: One essay on a historical topic of A level or equivalent needs to be submitted usually in early November (in 2010, 10th November).

Entrance Requirements: History A level is highly recommended.

Past interview question: Would history be worth studying if it didn't repeat itself?

“

I feel that you need a strong individual strategy to crack the History course. When I began attending lectures beyond my examination topics and kept alert to my own interests, this was when I was able to learn about history in a dynamic and individual way.

”

History graduate

Not the course for you? History can be studied alongside **Politics, Economics,** and **Modern Languages. Theology, English, Classics** and **PPE (Philosophy, Politics & Economics)** could also be of interest.

□ History (Ancient & Modern)

One of the great advantages of the Ancient and Modern History degree is that students grapple with early historians such as Tacitus and Thucydides on a regular basis, and, as all other forms of writing history spring from them, students are in a great position to make the transition from A level to undergraduate history.

Due to the breadth of the time period, once rumoured to have been ostentatiously termed 'from the beginning to the present day', there are more options and a greater opportunity to develop a holistic understanding of what history is and how it is written. As the course develops, students will become increasingly aware that in order to read history it is imperative to understand how it is written.

In terms of the course options, this is the choice if they are interested in studying Roman and Greek history in conjunction with more 'modern' history. This combination is often illuminating in unexpected ways as issues such as democracy and imperialism span the centuries. This is not to say that this is a comparative history course, so it should not be thought that students will spend time comparing, say, the ways in which the Roman and British Empires controlled indigenous populations.

Duration of the course: 3 years

Admissions Test: Applicants are required to sit the HAT (History Aptitude Test) usually in early November (in 2010, 3rd November).

Written Work: One essay on a historical topic of A level or equivalent needs to be submitted usually in early November (in 2010, 10th November).

Entrance Requirements: History A level is highly recommended. A classical language, Classical Civilisation or Ancient History are also highly recommended.

Past interview question: What can we learn from Ancient Egypt?

The study of the Ancient World was something I cherished as an Ancient and Modern History student.

History (Ancient & Modern) graduate

Not the course for you? You can study just modern **History** or combine it with **Politics, Economics,** or a **Modern Language. Theology, English, Classics** and **PPE (Philosophy, Politics & Economics)** could also be of interest.

□ History & Economics

With roughly a dozen students studying the course every year, History and Economics is one of the smaller subjects at Oxford, and it tends to be the smallest History Joint Honours School. It is an intellectually stimulating course that allows students to consider real world issues from a variety of perspectives. Most importantly, the course gives students an opportunity to develop insights that the individual subjects aren't able to generate on their own.

Students benefit from a unique viewpoint offered by taking economic history papers. They also have plenty of opportunities to specialise in either of the two disciplines. As with most Joint History degrees, students can mix and match a number of papers and options, allowing them to design a course according to their interests.

One of the challenges of the course is to learn how to utilise the two different academic approaches of History and Economics. Students are asked to study different periods and societies in great detail. On the other hand, they have to be able to appreciate the greater forces that affected these people, applying the economist's analytical and quantitative methods.

Duration of the course: 3 years

Admissions Test: Applicants are required to take two tests: the HAT (History Aptitude Test) usually in early November (in 2010, 3rd November). They must take an Economics test (if shortlisted) at interview.

Written Work: Applicants are asked to submit two pieces of written work: one on History and one on Economics.

Entrance Requirements: History and Mathematics A level are highly recommended.

Past interview question: Consider the situation in Germany during the reunification: do you think that politicians had the right to distinguish between DDR-mark and D-mark?

“The British economic history paper was why I applied, and I loved it!”

History & Economics graduate

Not the course for you? You might be interested in **History** on its own, or with **Politics** or a **Modern Language. PPE (Philosophy, Politics & Economics)** or **E&M (Economics & Management)** may also be of interest. You could also check out the **History** and **Economics** courses at Cambridge.

□ History & English

A Joint Honours degree in History and English requires applicants to impress both faculties equally in order to receive one of the limited places. Students have to juggle the two disciplines individually over the three years. Despite their usually separate treatment, students are required to understand how History and English relate to and influence one another. History & English can be studied as separately or as cohesively as each student prefers, and the small number of students for this course allows a greater amount of freedom when choosing what to study.

Both faculties are the largest in Britain, and support students throughout the three years, whether their interests lie in the Medieval period, the Renaissance or later. The Bodleian Library, English Faculty and History Faculty offer an unrivalled variety of sources for students to choose from. Recent graduates from the course have entered into a variety of careers, including the media, law, teaching and finance.

Duration of the course: 3 years

Admissions Test: The HAT (History Aptitude Test) usually in early November (in 2010, 3rd November). The ELAT (English Literature Aptitude Test) is not required.

Written Work: A piece of written work on a historical topic, and two pieces of A level English school work are required usually in early November (in 2010, 10th November).

Entrance Requirements: A level English Literature or English Language & Literature is essential, History is highly recommended.

Past interview question: Students are interviewed separately by the two faculties. For past interview questions, see the History and English sections.

“What did I enjoy most about my course? I loved all of it!”

History & English graduate

Not the course for you? Check out the individual **History** and **English** courses at Oxford and Cambridge. **Classics, Modern Languages** and **Philosophy & Theology** at Oxford may also be of interest.

□ History & Modern Languages

History and Modern Languages is a stimulating and intense course. Although demanding, the Joint Honours degree provides a challenging, exciting and complementary breadth of study. This course would suit students who have a passion for the arts in general – language, history, literature, philosophy and linguistics – and who do not wish to be confined to one discipline.

One of the most interesting aspects of the course is the possibility it allows for students to combine their two subjects, especially in the final year. This leads to a deeper understanding of the way in which historical, political, social and religious developments impact on literature and philosophical thought. By way of example, students reading History & French may choose to examine the impact of the French Revolution on literature, while students reading History & Spanish may explore the literary expression of the Mexican Revolution and its aftermath.

Duration of the course: 4 years

Admissions Test: Applicants are required to sit the HAT (History Aptitude Test) usually in early November (in 2010, 3rd November). While there will also be a Modern Language test at interview, unless they intend to study the subject from scratch.

Written Work: An essay on a historical topic, a piece of work in the modern language, and one in English (see Modern Languages) is required usually in early November (in 2010, 10th November).

Entrance Requirements: History A level is highly recommended. For French, German, Russian or Spanish, the language at A level is essential. For Celtic, Czech, Italian, Modern Greek or Portuguese, the language at A level is not required.

Past interview question: Was Louis XIV a successful king?

“

I really enjoyed the combination of history and the study of literature in a modern language. Not only was it interesting, but the Joint Honours course was also a rewarding challenge.

”

History & Modern Languages graduate

Not the course for you? You might be interested in **History** on its own, or with **Politics, Economics** or **English.** You may like to consider **Modern Languages** as a Single Honours, or **English Literature.**

□ History & Politics

History & Politics is a fairly new degree, which had its first intake in 1999. The course provides the opportunity to study periods of history from 300AD to the 20th century, at both a general and a focused level. The politics spans institutions, theories and historical political events. With around forty to fifty students admitted to the course every year, it is a mid-size course, and the largest Joint School of History.

Duration of the course: 3 years

Admissions Test: All applicants are required to sit the HAT (History Aptitude Test) usually in early November (in 2010, 3rd November).

Written Work: Applicants need to submit an essay on a historical topic to A level or an equivalent level usually in early November (in 2010, 10th November).

Entrance Requirements: History A level is highly recommended. Sociology, Politics or Government & Politics are highly recommended.

Past interview question: Are there always winners and losers in politics?

"I enjoyed the freedom we were given to study subjects of our choice in depth, and the intellectual challenge of tutorials."

History & Politics graduate

Not the course for you? You might be interested in **History, PPE (Philosophy, Politics & Economics), Law, Philosophy, Archaeology & Anthropology** or **English.**

☐ History of Art

The History of Art degree at Oxford is less than a decade old. Although the course draws on a long and deep tradition, there are certainly some modern perspectives evident in the course structure. What is considered 'art' is usually limited to the art of the Western World, and to those artists and pieces discussed most regularly. The History of Art degree at Oxford branches into Eastern art, and examines what has been left out of the art history books in the past. This critical approach is perfect for an art-lover who does not want to study straight history.

The course at Oxford embraces its location, with regular contact with the Ashmolean, and an extended essay in the first year that discusses a piece of art or architecture in Oxford. In second year, students can continue to broaden their visual horizons with the study of pre-modern or non-Western art. Due to the small number of students on the course (currently twelve), students can tailor the course to suit their interests, and have plenty of help from tutors with their own specific research interests. Incredible trips to art galleries and exhibitions, in addition to excursions abroad, enhance the Oxford History of Art course.

Duration of the course: 3 years

Admissions Test: N/A

Written Work: Applicants need to submit an essay from their A level course usually in early November (in 2010, 10th November). They also need to submit a response of no more than 750 words to a piece of art or design that they have seen first hand.

Entrance Requirements: An essay-based subject at A level is highly recommended. History of Art, History, a Language or Art can be helpful.

Past interview question: Is the History of Art only a history of Western Art?

“

The relevance of History of Art in a town like Oxford made the course all the more rewarding.

”

History of Art graduate

Not the course for you? You might be interested in **History, Archaeology & Anthropology** or **Fine Art.** Cambridge also offers a traditional and prestigious **History of Art** course.

□ Human Sciences

Human Sciences is an extremely varied course. At its core is an interdisciplinary study of the fundamental issues and problems confronting contemporary human societies. The course aims to give students a thorough understanding of the interactions between biological and cultural factors in human evolution. Topics studied are pertinent to modern life, and often feature in the news. For example, recently the Human Sciences demography lecturer was called upon to comment on the proposed changes to Britain's immigration policy. Genetic issues surrounding obesity and psychiatric disease, frequently at the forefront of the news, are also analysed in lectures and tutorials. There are many more examples of this, some more specific to option subjects, such as health policies considered in the Health and Disease paper, and population issues in the Demography paper.

Duration of the course: 3 years

Admissions Test: N/A

Written Work: Applicants have the option of submitting a statement of 100 words outlining their reasons for wishing to study Human Sciences usually to be submitted in early November (in 2010, 10th November).

Entrance Requirements: No specific A level. A level Biology or Mathematics can be helpful.

Past interview question: What would the effects be if England's population was halved?

> "I loved how varied the course was – this made it challenging but it also meant you didn't get bored."
>
> **Human Sciences graduate**

Not the course for you? You might be interested in **Biological Sciences, Biomedical Sciences** or **Experimental Psychology.** At Cambridge, try looking at **PPS (Politics, Psychology & Sociology).**

□ Law (Jurisprudence)

Jurisprudence is the branch of philosophy concerned with the law and legal principles. Law at Oxford is both an immersion in this more theoretical area of study and a firm foundation for further legal training. The Oxford Law course counts as a qualifying Law degree for the Legal Practise Course (for solicitors) or the Bar Professional Training Course (for barristers), although there is no assumption that graduates from the course will go on to pursue a legal career.

As an undergraduate, you will be challenged to think in a deeply analytical way, approach problems from a logical position, and defend your thoughts, including written work, against criticism. You will be taught by leading figures in their field who will test your judgment and encourage you to explore a range of legal issues from new and interesting angles.

Most students who undertake a Law degree haven't studied the subject before, instead, what is far more important is to have an interest in the subject. A good tip for anyone considering taking Law is to do some work experience in the legal sector before the interview: this not only provides something to talk about in the interview but it also shows that the applicant has a genuine interest in the subject.

Duration of the course: 3 years

Admissions Test: All applicants are required to sit the LNAT (Law National Admissions Test) usually before November (in 2010, 1st November).

Written Work: N/A

Entrance Requirements: GCSE Grade C Mathematics is essential.

Past interview question: A man intends to poison his wife but accidentally gives the lethal draught to her identical twin. Murder?

"The specific legal knowledge I gained – for instance I can write a valid contract, and understand the criminal legal system and divorce law. Also, I feel I am able to debate and discuss much more effectively."

Law (Jurisprudence) graduate

Not the course for you? You might be interested in **PPE (Philosophy, Politics and Economics), History** and its Joint Honours, **English** or **Classics. Law** is also offered at Cambridge.

☐ Law with Law Studies in Europe

Law with Law Studies in Europe (Law with LSE) is also known as the Law (Jurisprudence) Course II. There are five different courses available under this umbrella term: Law with European Law, Law with French Law, Law with German Law, Law with Italian Law and Law with Spanish Law. In contrast to the standard Law Course I, it includes Law studies in Europe, allowing students to spend their third year studying in one of the following countries for a year: France, Germany, Spain, Italy or the Netherlands. The focus of study is the Law, not the language, of the chosen country.

Law at Oxford is a demanding but rewarding subject, both intellectually and in terms of enhanced career prospects. However, there is no assumption that graduates from the course will go on to pursue a legal career, even though the course counts as a qualifying Law degree for the Legal Practise Course (for solicitors) or the Bar Professional Training Course (for barristers).

Applicants unsuccessful in gaining a place on the Law Studies in Europe course are automatically considered for a place on the standard Law Course I.

Duration of the course: 4 years

Admissions Test: All applicants are required to sit the LNAT (Law National Admissions Test) usually before November (in 2010, 1st November).

Written Work: N/A

Entrance Requirements: Grade C GCSE Mathematics is essential. An A level in the relevant modern language is essential unless the applicant wishes to study Law with European Law.

Past interview question: Is International Law the first step to a single legal system, and would such a unified system be possible?

“The year abroad helped me to bring new perspectives to the intellectual questions surrounding difficult areas of Law that arose during my studies.”

Law with Legal Studies in Europe graduate

Not the course for you? You might be interested in **Law** on its own, or **Modern Languages** at Oxford or Cambridge.

□ Materials Science

Materials Science is the study of the advanced materials that modern society relies upon. This can include anything from lightweight composites, optical fibres, nanotechnology and silicon microchips to materials used in the medical sciences such as bone replacement materials, novel sensors and drug delivery systems. Emphasis is placed on relationships between the structure and properties of a material and how it is made. Research is also conducted into developing new materials to meet specific demands and devising processes for their manufacture.

The subject is truly multidisciplinary, spanning Physics, Chemistry, Engineering and Industrial Manufacturing processes. The Department of Materials at Oxford is highly rated, and the tutors are often world leaders in their respective fields. The one-on-one or one-on-two undergraduate teaching instills a real sense of privilege and support for those students studying the course.

Duration of the course: 4 years

Admissions Test: N/A

Written Work: N/A

Entrance Requirements: A level Mathematics and either Physics or Chemistry are essential. AS level Physics and Chemistry are highly recommended. Further Mathematics and Design & Technology (Resistant Materials) can be helpful.

Past interview question: What are the electronic properties of nanotubes?

“

The most enjoyable year was almost certainly the fourth year, with flexibility to research nearly anything and to experience a year in academia.

”

Materials Science graduate

Not the course for you? Try checking out **Engineering, Physics,** or **Materials, Economics and Management** at Oxford, or take a look at the **Economics** and **Engineering** courses at Cambridge.

□ MEM (Materials, Economics & Management)

MEM (Materials, Economics & Management) combines the knowledge garnered from the study of Materials Science with a thorough grounding in Economics and Management.

Materials Science is the study of the advanced materials that modern society relies upon. This can include anything from lightweight composites, optical fibres, nanotechnology and silicon microchips to materials used in the medical sciences such as bone replacement materials, novel sensors and drug delivery systems. The Department of Materials at Oxford is highly rated, with many world experts offering tuition to undergraduate students.

In addition, both the Department of Economics and the Said Business School also benefit from outstanding international reputations. It is the aim that the combined course will provide a foundation for future work in, for example, technical management, management consultancy, or the financial services sector, especially in the financial appraisal of technology.

Duration of the course: 4 years

Admissions Test: N/A

Written Work: N/A

Entrance Requirements: A level Mathematics is essential and either Chemistry or Physics is highly recommended.

Past interview question: How would you control pollution from traffic?

“

The management element – I really love management as a subject because it's so relevant to working in business.

”

MEM graduate

Not the course for you? Try checking out **Engineering, Physics, Materials Science,** or **PPE (Philosophy, Politics and Economics),** or take a look at the **Economics** and **Engineering** courses at Cambridge.

□ Mathematics

While A level Mathematics does provide students with the basic techniques needed to study the applied subjects, Mathematics taken at degree level is quite different to what students may have studied previously.

A degree in Mathematics uses mathematical techniques to model a whole variety of real-life situations, for example, considering how a leopard gets its spots. In addition, by encouraging students to look at how these techniques have developed from traditional systems, a clearer understanding of the foundations of Mathematics can be gained. A degree in Mathematics will develop many skills, such as logical argument, communication, analysis and problem solving, and it will provide an excellent grounding for most post-university careers.

Oxford offers two degrees: a three year BA and a four year MMath. The essential difference between these two courses is that the four year course offers the chance to take a deeper look at mathematics and become even more specialised. There is also a chance to write a dissertation in the fourth year that comprises one third of that year's work. Oxford does not distinguish between the three and four year course at the point of application – all students have to apply for the fourth year at the start of the third year, though this is just a formality if the student is performing to a reasonable standard.

Duration of the course: 3 or 4 years

Admissions Test: All applicants must take the Oxford MAT (Mathematics Aptitude Test) usually in early November (in 2010, 3rd November).

Written Work: N/A

Entrance Requirements: A level Mathematics is essential. A level Further Mathematics or a science are also highly recommended.

Past interview question: How do you predict a Pythagorean triple?

“I enjoyed the third and fourth years the best as we had free reign in what options we could choose.”

Mathematics graduate

Not the course for you? **Mathematics** can also be studied jointly with **Philosophy, Statistics** and **Computer Science.** You may also enjoy **Computer Science** on its own, or **Physics, Engineering** or even **E&M (Economics & Management).**

□ Mathematics & Computer Science

Oxford offers two courses in Mathematics and Computer Science, a three year BA degree and a four year Masters degree. There is no distinction between them on applying and the first three years of the Masters follow the BA course so there is no need to decide whether to take three or four years of study until the start of the third year.

The Computer Science course at Oxford concentrates on bridging theory and practice, including a wide variety of hardware and software technologies and their applications. It has to be said that a great part of the course is theoretical, and some students find it too abstract, having expected a course which has more to do with writing programmes than reasoning about programmes. However, it turns out that this theoretical approach is very useful, putting the student in a position of understanding the underlying principles of programming, an invaluable basis from which to solve a great variety of programming problems.

Duration of the course: 3 or 4 years

Admissions Test: All applicants must take the Oxford MAT (Mathematics Aptitude Test) usually in early November (in 2010, 3rd November).

Written Work: N/A

Entrance Requirements: A level Mathematics is essential. Further Mathematics or a science are also highly recommended.

Past interview question: Why do you think people buy lottery tickets when the chances of winning are extremely small?

"

My tutors were wonderful. They were experts in their fields, had written the textbooks, and yet still had time to answer my questions.

"

Mathematics & Computer Science graduate

Not the course for you? You might be interested in **Mathematics** on its own, or with **Philosophy** or **Statistics. Computer Science** is also offered on its own, while **Engineering** and **Physics** are similar courses. You could also take a look at the **Engineering** course at Cambridge.

□ Mathematics & Philosophy

The combination of Mathematics & Philosophy may seem an odd one to some people, but the subjects fit very well together. The basis of Mathematics - set theory and logic - raises very interesting philosophical questions about the nature of mathematics, which can be explored in the philosophical side of the course. Students also acquire strong analytical skills from solving mathematical problems which they can then employ when studying the Western philosophical tradition. Both subjects train students to be critical, logical, and inquisitive, which makes this degree both stimulating and challenging, and an excellent foundation for many post-university careers.

Duration of the course: 3 or 4 years

Admissions Test: All applicants must take the Oxford MAT (Mathematics Aptitude Test) usually in November (in 2010, 3rd November).

Written Work: Applicants must submit two essays usually in early November (in 2010, 10th November). These need to show clear and well-structured argument, but are not expected to be on philosophical topics.

Entrance Requirements: A level Mathematics is essential. Further Mathematics A level is highly recommended.

Past interview question: Is Mathematics a language?

“The challenge of it – there is very little drudgery and dull learning of facts in Mathematics & Philosophy, with the exception of memorising the odd proof for exams.”

Mathematics & Philosophy graduate

Not the course for you? **Mathematics** can also be studied on its own, or in combination with **Statistics** and **Computer Science.** You may also enjoy **Computer Science** on its own, or **Physics, Engineering** or even **E&M (Economics and Management).** Take a look at the **Mathematics** and **Engineering** courses at Cambridge as well.

□ Mathematics & Statistics

Oxford offers two courses in Mathematics & Statistics, a three year BA degree and a four year Masters degree. There's no distinction between them in applying, and as the first three years of the Masters follow the BA course, there is no need to decide whether to take three or four years of study until the start of the third year.

The BA and MMath Mathematics and Statistics combine the strengths of the traditional Oxford Mathematics degrees with the ability to pursue probability and statistics in depth.

The Maths & Statistics courses follow the same route as a straight Maths degree for the first year and the first term of the second year, so it is easy to switch between the two courses up until then. There's no distinction between the application criteria either, although students may be asked an extra question about Statistics in the interview.

Duration of the course: 3 or 4 years

Admissions Test: All applicants must take the Oxford MAT (Mathematics Aptitude Test) usually in early November (in 2010, 3rd November).

Written Work: N/A

Entrance Requirements: A level Mathematics is essential. A level Further Mathematics is highly recommended.

Past interview question: Prove 'e' is irrational.

"Although it took me a while to familiarise myself with the maths software, I found my computational skills developed dramatically over time."

Mathematics & Statistics

Not the course for you? You might be interested in **Mathematics** on its own, or **Physics** or **Economics.** Cambridge also offers **Mathematics** and **Economics** courses.

□ Medicine

While some medical schools choose to introduce students to clinical medicine right from the start of the course, at Oxford there is a distinction between pre-clinical and clinical phases. The three pre-clinical years focus the student on developing basic medical scientific knowledge to a high level, leaving the three clinical years to developing clinical skills. The two phases are separate and students can choose to remain in Oxford for the clinical course or move to another hospital, most likely in London. The aim of the course is to produce doctors with good scientific knowledge who have had the training needed to pursue a career either in hospitals or in general practice, also with the ability to evaluate research and make their own original contributions.

Duration of the course: 4 years

Admissions Test: All applicants must take the BMAT (BioMedical Admissions Test) usually in early November (in 2010, 3rd November).

Written Work: N/A

Entrance Requirements: Applicants must have A level Chemistry and Biology, and/or Physics and/or Mathematics.

Past interview question: How have doctors' lives changed in the last 30 years?

“

I enjoyed the tutorials the most. To be constantly challenged, week in and week out about something in which the tutor is a renowned expert is truly humbling.

”

Medicine graduate

Not the course for you? **Biomedical Sciences** is very similar, while **Biological Sciences, Chemistry** and **Human Sciences** are also related. You could also check out the **Medicine** course at Cambridge.

□ Modern Languages

There are two main branches to the Oxford Modern Languages degree. Firstly, the course is structured to allow students to attain spoken fluency, as well as the ability to write essays and produce translations both into and out of the foreign language. There is also the opportunity to study linguistics. Secondly, the course has a clear focus on literature, and over the four year course students will study a wide range of literary texts in their chosen language or languages. Literature, as well as being studied for its own sake, is a gateway to a deeper understanding of the culture from which it originates.

This dual focus makes the course challenging, stimulating and rewarding. The skills required for translation, for example, are very different from those needed for writing literary essays, and students must juggle both these tasks on a weekly basis. For this reason, Oxford linguists develop a wide range of transferable skills along with competence in their language(s).

Duration of the course: 4 years

Admissions Test: Applicants are required to sit a 30-minute language test (mainly focusing on grammar) for each of the languages they intend to study, though not in languages they intend to study more or less from scratch. Applicants for beginners' Russian and those wishing to study linguistics in their first year must take the LAT (Linguistics Aptitude Test).

Written Work: Applicants must submit one piece of marked classwork in each language which they plan to study (though not in languages they intend to study from scratch), and one piece of marked writing in English (perhaps on literature, or history).

Entrance Requirements: For Celtic, Czech, Italian, Modern Greek, Polish or Portuguese, an A level in the language is not required. For French, German, Russian or Spanish, an A level in the language is required. For beginners' Russian an A level in the language is not required. It is not usually possible for students to students to study two languages from scratch.

Past interview question: If English is the worldwide business language, why don't we just abolish all other languages?

"I loved the variety. The course combines the study of the language itself with literature, culture and philosophy – understanding what makes a country 'tick'."

Modern Languages graduate

Not the course for you? **Modern Languages** can also be studied jointly with **Linguistics, English, Classics** or **History.** Alternatively you might be interested in **Oriental Studies, English Language** and **Literature** or **Philosophy** & **Theology.**

□ Modern Languages & Linguistics

There are two main branches to the Oxford Modern Languages with Linguistics degree. The first is the study of the chosen modern language. This follows exactly the same syllabus as the study of any other modern language at Oxford with an emphasis on spoken fluency, ability to write essays and produce translations, as well as a clear focus on literature. Linguistics is the study of our language faculty: one of our most complex and fascinating abilities. Very much an interdisciplinary field, Linguistics combines knowledge and methods from areas as diverse as Biology, Physics, Psychology, Philosophy, Sociology and Anthropology and looks at every aspect of the production and perception of all kinds of language. There is a strong emphasis on the importance of experimentation and the scientific method within Linguistics, making it an ideal subject to combine with Modern Languages for somebody who does not wish to entirely abandon science on leaving school.

Duration of the course: 4 years

Admissions Test: Applicants who want to read Modern Languages & Linguistics or those wanting to read any combination of languages including Beginners' Russian or Polish will be required to sit the LAT. Candidates wishing to read a language sole may also be required to sit the LAT. Check Oxford's Modern Languages Faculty website for more details.

Written Work: Applicants must submit one piece of marked classwork in the language which they plan to study (though not in a language they intend to study from scratch), and one piece of marked writing in English (especially anything involving linguistic analysis).

Entrance Requirements: For French, German, Modern Greek, Spanish or Russian, an A level in the language is required. For Italian and Portuguese an A level in the language is not required.

Past interview question: Why do some languages have genders when others don't?

“

I loved the cross-fertilisation between rigorous and often quite technical analysis of language with the more romantic investigations of literature and culture.

”

Modern Languages & Linguistics graduate

Not the course for you? **Modern Languages** can also be studied on its own, or with **English, Classics, History** or **Philosophy.** Alternatively you might be interested in **Oriental Studies** or **English Language & Literature,** or the **Linguistics** or **Modern Languages** courses at Cambridge.

□ Music

Music at Oxford offers a wide variety of options and choices in order to suit every individual. Every student studies the same key areas in music in first year: Music History, Analysis, Techniques of Composition and Keyboard Skills. Students can then opt to do Performance, Extended Essay or Composition Portfolio. In second and third years, students can tailor the course to suit their preferences, and can opt to take a variety of specialist papers. In the past, students have studied everything from 14th century poet-composer Guillaume de Machaut to the Beatles!

Oxford musicians are taught by leaders in their field. The fact that there are on average only sixty students per year means everyone gets to know each other very well, regardless of college. It also means that tutors dedicate a generous proportion of their time to each student's musical education. Oxford also grants free music tuition for each musician. If performing is the key point of interest, students should be aware that the Music course at Oxford requires them to spend a great deal of time writing and researching essays and that performance is never larger than a fifth of their degree.

Duration of the course: 3 years

Admissions Test: Applicants will be asked to perform a prepared piece on their instrument of choice at interview.

Written Work: Written work must be submitted usually in early November (in 2010, 10th November). If the student is studying harmony and counterpoint, or if the student is a composer, then he or she will also be invited to submit examples of this work for interviewers to see.

Entrance Requirements: A level Music is required. Keyboard ability to ABRSM Grade V or above is highly recommended.

Past interview question: Can the listener and their attitude change the music they hear?

“

My dissertation was on an area that has not been written about a great deal, and I really felt that I was contributing to scholarship.

”

Music graduate

Not the course for you? Cambridge also offers a more performance-based **Music** course.

□ Oriental Studies

'Oriental Studies' is an umbrella term that encompasses courses in Egyptology & Ancient Near Eastern Studies, Arabic, Chinese, Hebrew & Jewish Studies, Japanese, Persian, Sanskrit and Turkish. This section details the Japanese course as an example. The course is broadly divided into two parts: the study of the Japanese language, and the study of the history and culture of Japan. In this respect, the course is rather unusual. It is not merely based upon one discipline but draws upon many to give a wide understanding of the country and its culture. This also means that the course is fairly demanding, in that essay work is expected on top of language study. However, the workload is by no means unmanageable and there is plenty of time for extracurricular activities.

Duration of the course: 4/5 years

Admissions Test: Applicants are usually required to sit a Language Aptitude Test during the interview period.

Written Work: Applicants are required to submit two pieces of written work on two separate subjects of their choice usually in early November (in 2010, 10th November 2010).

Entrance Requirements: A language at A level can be helpful, but no specific requirements.

Past interview question: What do you see as the future for the Japanese economy?

“

The language lessons were brilliant and stood me in good stead for my travels to Japan.

”

Oriental Studies graduate

Not the course for you? You might be interested in **Modern Languages** or **History** at Oxford or Cambridge. **Theology** is also offered with **Oriental Studies.**

□ Philosophy & Modern Languages

The Philosophy & Modern Languages course at Oxford combines two very different but complementary disciplines. It is taught as Joint Honours so students are members of two different faculties and have access to the full range of lectures, papers, tutors and libraries for each individual subject. Students can choose whether they want to weight their final degree towards either Philosophy or their Modern Language, or they can choose to split the papers evenly. Students can also choose to study papers in either subject that overlap across the two disciplines.

For example, a student studying Philosophy and French could take four papers in each subject, but select options that allow them to apply the work studied and skills obtained in one discipline to the other. By way of example, a student could study Sartre's literature and plays in French and his philosophical works in Philosophy, or delve into Wittgenstein's philosophy of language and the philosophy of aesthetics, both of which complement the study of French literature. The combinations students choose are entirely up to them and some choose to keep them completely separate.

Duration of the course: 4 years

Admissions Test: Applicants are required to sit a one hour philosophy test at interview. Some languages, though not those taken from scratch, will also be tested at interview, in a 30-minute language test.

Written Work: Applicants are required to submit two pieces of written work on two separate subjects of their choice.

Entrance Requirements: For French, German, Russian or Spanish, an A level in the language is essential. For Celtic, Czech, Italian, Modern Greek or Portuguese an A level in the language is not required.

Past interview question: What do you think Voltaire meant by *Il faut cultiver notre jardin?*

“The academic independence of my thesis was the best part of the degree, I loved the freedom I had to explore the areas I found most interesting.”

Modern Languages & Philosophy graduate

Not the course for you? You might be interested in other **Modern Languages** combination. **Philosophy** is also available with **Theology, Physics, Mathematics,** as part of **PPE (Philosophy, Politics & Economics)** and **Psychology.**

☐ PPE (Philosophy, Politics & Economics)

The combination of Philosophy, Politics and Economics (known as PPE) forms a very popular and extremely diverse degree. 'PPE-ists' come from all kinds of backgrounds, including many parts of the world, and go on to do all kinds of important jobs in government, administration, business, academia and many more fields. It's about being trained how to think and approach arguments in a confident and rigorous way, analysing how things work, asking why people think the way they do, and explaining how systems relate to theoretical principles. All three branches of the course are studied in the first year, with most students choosing to drop one of the three in their final two years.

It's a great subject to study at Oxford because it combines these analytical tools with real-world evidence and case studies. PPE deals with both timeless human debates and modern day problems of economics and politics. Time and again, students find headline news that can be applied to their essays, such as ethical debates or political/economic crises. Study PPE, and the world will begin to make sense.

Duration of the course: 3 years

Admissions Test: All applicants must take the Oxford TSA (Thinking Skills Assessment) usually in early November (in 2010, 3rd November).

Written Work: N/A

Entrance Requirements: No specific A level requirements. History and Mathematics can be useful.

Past interview question: Is it moral to hook up a psychopath (whose only pleasure is killing) to a reality-simulating machine so that he can believe he is in the real world and kill as much as he likes?

“

I was able to study extensively a wide range of subjects but did not feel that the depth with which I studied was any less than that experienced by friends at other universities who studied only one of those subjects.

”

PPE graduate

Not the course for you? Cambridge offers either **Economics** or **Politics** as a distinct degree or a Joint Honours degree in **PPS (Politics, Psychology and Sociology).** If it is economics that really drives you, you might want to take a look at **E&M (Economics & Management)** at Oxford.

□ Philosophy & Theology

Philosophy and Theology is a subject that tackles the big questions. In fact, the three years of the course will almost certainly see students covering life, the universe and everything in between. One for the abstract thinkers out there, the course gives them the best of both quite different worlds. Students look at the Theology side of things with a philosophical perspective, bringing critical thinking to the study of God and religion, while covering Philosophy with a theological bent – debating arguments for and against God's existence. The course touches upon many key thinkers in both spheres and develops a solid critical appreciation of the debates surrounding religion and philosophy.

Students develop analytical skills, and the ability to reason logically and clearly, as well as literary and historical critical skills. They also write and read out more than their share of essays, so they'll get pretty good at structuring a written argument.

Duration of the course: 3 years

Admissions Test: Applicants must sit a one hour written philosophy test at interview.

Written Work: Applicants need to submit two essays usually in early November (in 2010, 10th November).

Entrance Requirements: No specific requirements. An A level in Religious Studies can be helpful.

Past interview question: Determinism: do we have free choice? Can a machine have free will?

"There are some quite arcane options in the further reaches of the Philosophy and Theology course prospectus. These turned out to be absolutely fascinating."

Philosophy & Theology graduate

Not the course for you? Cambridge also offers a Single Honours **Theology** course. **Philosophy** can also be read with **Modern Languages, Maths, Physics, Psychology,** and as part of **PPE (Philosophy, Politics & Economics).** Additionally, **English, History, Classics** or **Ancient History** may be of interest.

□ Physics

Physics at Oxford is a rewarding course that requires hard work and a willingness to embrace applying new mathematical, computational, experimental, physical and theoretical concepts at a fast pace. University-level Physics takes the best bits of mathematics and tries to make sense out of the universe.

Learning predominantly takes the form of problem sheets, usually worked through independently, and discussed in tutorials, which may take place in small groups. In labs, students get to apply theory to practice and in lectures they gain crucial exposure to new concepts and talk over problems with fellow undergraduates. The lectures make up the bulk of the teaching, with between three and four hours a day, especially in the first year.

The emphasis in the first year is on directed learning and as the course develops you are given more freedom to explore concepts that excite you. For example, fourth years tend to spend the majority of their time in labs with a post-graduate research team working on projects related to diverse material, such as particle Physics.

Duration of the course: 3 or 4 years

Admissions Test: Applicants must sit the Physics Aptitude Test usually in early November (in 2010, 3rd November).

Written Work: N/A

Entrance Requirements: A level Physics and Mathematics are essential. The inclusion of a mathematics mechanics module is highly recommended. Further Mathematics can be helpful.

Past interview question: I'm bouncing a marble. What is happening to the particles at the top of the marble?

"

I really valued the emphasis on problem solving and now feel confident in overcoming difficult challenges in the real world, whether they are professional or academic.

"

Physics graduate

Not the course for you? You might be interested in **Physics** with **Philosophy,** or **Mathematics, Engineering** or another science. **Natural Sciences** at Cambridge will also appeal.

□ Physics & Philosophy

What particles and forces do we believe the world is made of, at the most fundamental level? What laws do we think govern its behaviour? Why do we think this – and why did we once have different theories? What can we know about the world anyway? Why might our most basic physical theories - Einstein's theory of relativity and quantum mechanics - not be consistent? What might be the implications? Physics & Philosophy is the course for students with a strong inquisitive and analytical mind, who refuse to be placed in a box of either 'Arts' or 'Science'.

You learn the theories of Physics - and the Maths on which they are based - to an advanced technical level, on a par with students of straight Physics. However you also take your abstract analytical skills to a new level, grappling with concepts in Philosophy that have kept the greatest philosophers pondering for centuries. You read both historical and modern philosophical views, and are able to bring forward and debate your own ideas in essays and tutorials. Options in both Physics and Philosophy - with the chance to write a dissertation, if you wish - also allow you to take the course in the direction that interests you most. Through this mechanism you can look more closely at subjects you've already covered or take the opportunity to broaden your studies, for instance into Atmospheric Physics, the thoughts of the Ancient Greeks, or more modern philosophers like Sartre, Heidegger and Nietzsche.

Duration of the course: 4 years

Admissions Test: Applicants must sit the Physics Aptitude Test usually in early November (in 2010, 3rd November).

Written Work: N/A

Entrance Requirements: A level Physics and Mathematics are essential. The inclusion of a Mathematics Mechanics module is highly recommended. Further Mathematics and an arts subject can be helpful.

Past interview question: How would one go about travelling through time?

“

In your fourth year there is the option of replacing one Philosophy paper with a dissertation – I found this provided me with an excellent opportunity to further pursue areas which I am interested in.

”

Physics & Philosophy graduate

Not the course for you? Physics can be studied on its own, and **Philosophy** in combination with **Modern Languages, Theology, Mathematics, Psychology.** You may also be interested in **Engineering** or **PPE (Philosophy, Politics & Economics).**

□ PP (Psychology & Philosophy)

Roughly equal number of courses are taken in both Psychology and Philosophy Honours subjects. Students are thus able to take advantage of the facilities and teaching of both faculties. A particular challenge for students on the course is to reach a high standard in the somewhat different ways of arguing, and to be able to appreciate material which differs in form between the subjects. Each subject may also demand slightly different styles of writing, which naturally develops the student's skills and flexibility.

The Oxford Experimental Psychology department is widely regarded as one of the leading psychology departments in the UK. The course is particularly scientific (hence 'Experimental') with a strong emphasis on statistics and neurophysiology.

Similarly, the Oxford Philosophy Faculty, which is the largest philosophy department in the UK, has a renowned worldwide reputation with many fellows of international standing. Of particular note for the Psychology and Philosophy course is the Philosophy department's active interest in the philosophy of mind and the philosophy of science.

Duration of the course: 3 years

Admissions Test: All applicants must take the Oxford TSA (Thinking Skills Assessment) usually in early November (in 2010, 3rd November).

Written Work: N/A

Entrance requirements: One or more science or Mathematics at A level is highly recommended.

Past interview question: I can see both of my hands in front of me. Does this prove their existence?

"

I enjoyed the diversity of the course. Managing my time to cope with both a science and a humanities subject was both challenging and rewarding.

"

PP graduate

Not the course for you? Psychology can be studied on its own as **Experimental Psychology** and **Philosophy** can be studied in combination with **Modern Languages, Theology** and **Mathematics.** You may also be interested in **PPE (Philosophy, Politics & Economics)** or **PPS (Politics, Psychology and Sociology)** at Cambridge.

☐ Theology

Theology was one of the first subjects offered at Oxford University, and while its status may be a little diminished since the glory days of the Middle Ages, it still has plenty to offer a modern student. It trains you to think critically and analytically, and it deals with huge issues – however secular Britain feels, the world is still shaped by the forces of religion. The course concentrates mainly on the origins and development of Christian theology, but it can appeal to students from any faith background. To engage with all the different aspects of the course, you need all sorts of skills: historical, philosophical, literary-critical and languages.

Duration of the course: 3 years

Admissions Test: N/A

Written Work: Two pieces of marked written work, preferably on Religious Studies, otherwise on a related subject.

Entrance Requirements: A level Religious Studies is recommended.

Past interview question: What is your preferred solution to the synoptic problem in the New Testament?

"

My dissertation was the high point of the course. It felt like a real adventure to uncover information for myself and dig deeper into an area which fascinated me.

"

Theology graduate

Not the course for you? Oxford also offers **Theology** with **Philosophy** or **Oriental Studies.** Additionally, **English, History, Classics** or **History (Ancient & Modern)** may be of interest.

□ Theology & Oriental Studies

This new Joint Honours degree complements the study of Christianity (mainly undertaken in the Theology Faculty) with the study of Buddhism, Hinduism, Islam and Judaism (mainly undertaken in the Oriental Studies Faculty). Students will develop a much broader understanding of the history and nature, and also the similarities of the great world religions. Applicants will need to demonstrate linguistic skills, the ability to analyse historical and literary texts critically, and an understanding of the histories and cultures of the different religions.

The Theology Faculty is one of the leading Christian faculties in the world, and when combined with the Oriental Studies Faculty, has over 270 members and excellent libraries. Graduates of Theology & Oriental Studies can expect to be able to choose from a wide range of careers. Graduates with oriental languages are currently in high demand and are among the most successful applicants in employment.

Duration of the course: 3 years

Admissions Test: Applicants may be asked to sit a Language Aptitude Test at interview.

Written Work: Two marked essays usually in early November (in 2010, 10th November). For Oriental Studies, applicants should submit a piece of work in English from an A level or equivalent course. The essay for Theology should be from part of your Religious Studies course or, if that isn't possible, on a related subject.

Entrance Requirement: No specific A levels, although an A level language and Religious Studies can be helpful.

Past interview question: Students are interviewed separately by the two faculties. Check out the interview questions in the Theology and Oriental Studies sections.

“

I loved the fact that I could develop an interest in Islam over the course of my degree. Also it was a privilege to study in such a beautiful city under academics who are leading figures in their field.

”

Theology & Oriental Studies

Not the course for you? Oxford also offers **Theology** with **Philosophy.** Additionally, **English, History, Classics** or **History (Ancient & Modern)** may be of interest.

2. Choosing a college

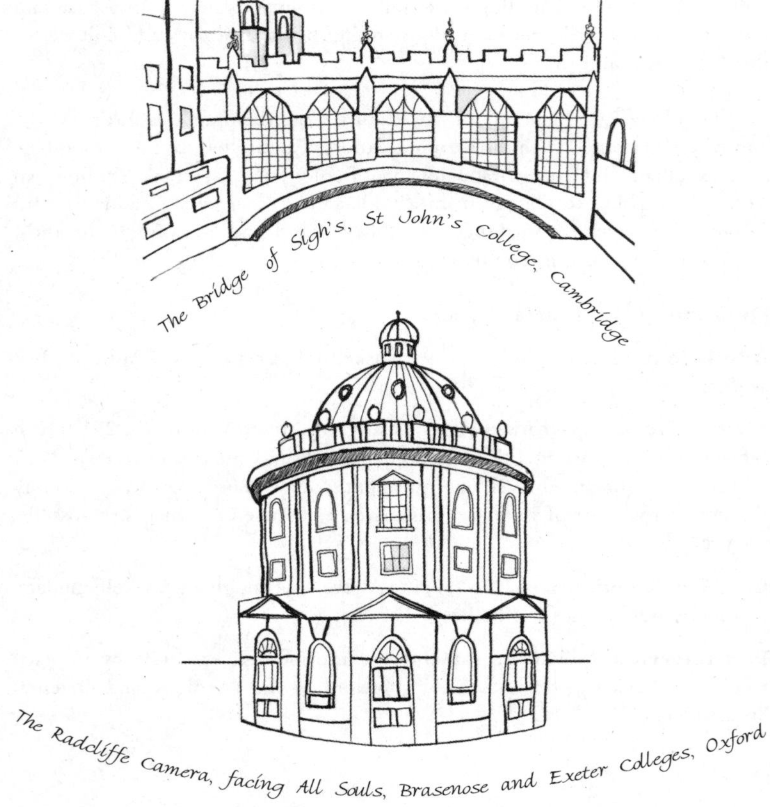

The Bridge of Sigh's, St John's College, Cambridge
The Radcliffe Camera, facing All Souls, Brasenose and Exeter Colleges, Oxford

Party animal or drama queen? Sporting hero or Prime Minister in the making? We take a look at the differences between colleges and how you can go about finding the one that's right for you.

With over sixty colleges between Oxford and Cambridge, it can be hard to know what to look for when making your choice. The college is where the majority of teaching at Oxford (tutorials) and Cambridge (supervisions) takes place. While each faculty has a library that focuses on specialisation within the subject, colleges have their own libraries with books on a wide range of topics.

In addition to the academic side of things, a lot of your social life may take place in your college. College 'entz' (entertainment) reps will organise (usually twice-termly) parties called 'bops' in the college bar alongside other events such as arts weeks and theatre productions. You will live in the college grounds for at least one year, and possibly for your entire degree. If you are really lucky, you may even snag the ultimate luxury - an en-suite bathroom.

The college is the institution that will reward you with a travel grant or book award, but will also remember you well when it is time to send you a bill at the end of each term - to the dread of many students! You'll eat there, represent your college in intercollegiate events and competitions (if it takes your fancy) and it'll go right there at the top of your CV when you've graduated. Colleges are communities, which shape your time at university, and for many students, they keep a special place in their heart long after leaving. Some students even go back and exercise their right to get married in the college chapel. As one recent graduate mused, 'my college gave me a teeny, but perfect room, Jurisprudence tutorials under the willow tree, and all-important boat club dinners.'

So...how do you choose?

You might consider choosing a college to be a superfluous addition to the application process. In reality, it can be one of the best parts. Try thinking about your future life as a student and what you want out of your time at university - imagine the societies you could join, the beautiful grounds and buildings you could surround yourself with and the kind of community you want to live in.

Having spoken to lots of 2009's applicants, it's clear that everyone has their own point of view on how to choose a college. One successful Cambridge applicant we spoke to believes that applicants should pick the one that they feel is right for them, while in contrast, one successful Oxford applicant stresses the importance of checking the competitiveness of the chosen college for the subject the student wishes to study.

Speaking to a number of recent Oxbridge graduates, the reasons they chose their individual colleges vary greatly. Emma, who graduated from Trinity College, Oxford, came to the conclusion that its location between the lecture hall and the centre of town made it the perfect college for her. Nick chose Corpus Christi at Cambridge because he felt the small, close-knit community feel would make a refreshing change after years at a rather large northern state school. As for John, who graduated from Oxford, he didn't actually choose his college. He was pooled by the university and ended up spending four happy years at Lady Margaret Hall reading Classics.

When it comes to choosing a college, the key is to remember that Oxford and Cambridge look for the best students, regardless of whether they have applied to a college directly or submitted an open application. While each college has its own personality, it's important to remember that colleges look at students as individuals, regardless of their educational, socio-economic or personal background. They look for applicants who are going to thrive in the one-to-one teaching environment that the collegiate system offers.

To help you work out which college is for you or whether you will make an open application, here are a few questions that can help you reach that decision:

Does the college offer my course?

This is the fundamental first step to choosing a college. There are a number of colleges that do not have supervision/tutorial provision for every course. You may have fallen in love with Emmanuel College's stunning grounds and the ducks that you met on your open day, but if you are applying for Land Economy then alas it is not meant to be. College websites are there to guide you on these matters and our college profiles on the next pages will give you more food for thought.

Will I need to sit an admissions test?

At Cambridge, whether you have to sit an admissions test depends on the college to which you apply. For example, if you are applying for Natural Sciences at Cambridge, at Peterhouse you will be required to sit the Cambridge TSA (Thinking Skills Assessment). In contrast, Jesus College does not require this test and makes decisions based on interviews alone, whereas King's College sets an essay. You can find out more about admissions tests in chapter five.

Would I like to spend the next few years of my life here?

What is important to you academically and personally? Is the college located centrally? How big is it? How rich is it? How academic is it? Think about your own personality, interests and ambitions. Do you want to be the next hot-shot hack or rugby superstar? Do you want to wave the socialist flag from the dreaming spires or lead a team to create the best Oxbridge summer ball yet? From here, you can move on to more practical contemplations. Do you thrive in a small, close-knit community, like Nick, or would you prefer a larger sporty college such as Keble College, Oxford? Do you like to laze by the river in the sun or would you prefer to be nearer to the lecture hall and have an extra five minutes in bed?

Which college is ripe for your picking? We've put together some fun questions to ask yourself, to get you thinking. **Tick the sentence** that best describes you and then make a shortlist of colleges that match your preferences. (Our college profiles in the next section can help start you off).

1. **Size & Community:** The average Oxbridge college has around 400 undergraduates. However, some are a lot larger than that, whilst others are a lot smaller. With this in mind, which statement describes you best?

   ☐ I like to be a big fish in a small pond; I thrive on social pressure

   ☐ I like the comfort of being nestled in a cosy, close-knit community

   ☐ I'm a modern day Goldilocks; nothing too big, nothing too small. Just right in fact

   ☐ I like to be a small duck skimming an expansive lake so that I can choose plenty of friends, but also hide in the weeds occasionally if things get too much

2. **Environment:** If you look out of a window, do you prefer to survey sweeping landscapes or contained courtyards?

   ☐ I'm more of an indoor, feet-up kind of person

   ☐ If there's a gorgeous garden, I'll happily sit in it

   ☐ There's nothing better than a bracing walk, fresh air and trees

3. **Architecture:** Does the idea of studying in a brand new college appeal to you or appal you? Would you prefer old quads and traditional cloisters or cutting-edge design and modern-day comfort?

   ☐ Ancient splendour

   ☐ Modern glamour

   ☐ I don't mind

4. **Location:** Your college is going to be the focus of your life for three or four years. Do you want to be right in the thick of it, or prefer to be a little more secluded from tourists?

   ☐ Bright lights (in the city centre)

   ☐ One step removed (5 minutes' walk)

   ☐ Keep-fit commute (10 minutes' walk)

   ☐ I don't mind

Once you've had a little think, have a look at the college profiles on the proceeding pages, as well as the individual college websites and alternative prospectuses to help you match your preferences to real colleges. If you're a small duck, partial to sitting in a pretty garden, enveloped by some of central Cambridge's finest historic architecture, then you might find Emmanuel and Gonville and Caius Colleges rather enticing. Alternatively, if you love nothing better than to bask in bounteous green spaces, far from Oxford's throbbing crowds, then St Hilda's or Worcester might tempt you.

There's lots of information out there. Take time to do some research. The choice really is yours.

How likely am I to get in?

Both Oxford and Cambridge publish their application statistics on their respective websites, which means, with a little bit of research, every student can find out which college/course options are the most competitive.

In September 2008, The Times School Gate blog published two posts on tactical applications to Cambridge and Oxford. The author John O'Leary, editor of *The Times Good University Guide*, mentioned that prospective applicants really should do their research when choosing a college - the ratio of successful-to-unsuccessful applicants as well as the number of pooled applications can vary drastically from college to college.

The two blog posts drew a number of comments from readers, including Cambridge's own Director of Undergraduate Admissions Geoff Parks, who stressed that employing a tactical approach will not increase your chances of success. The article had pointed out that in 2007, Murray Edwards College (then New Hall) had only 111 applications in total but had actually made 145 offers. More than 100 of those who had received offers came via the pool (more about pooling later). Parks pointed out that the analysis in the blog was flawed, commenting that those 44 applicants who were made offers, were actually chosen from among an additional 222 open applicants who were allocated to the college. Therefore, while on the surface the college looked less competitive, in reality, the average success rate was 13.2% (44/333). The remaining 101 students who were made offers had applied to other colleges, and as Parks pointed out, no student who applied to New Hall was made an offer by another college.

In contrast, Parks draws attention to Pembroke College, Cambridge, pointing that the average success rate in 2007 was almost double (25.1%) that of New Hall. Of the 749 students who applied to the college, 143 were made offers and an additional 45 were made offers by other colleges.

Many Oxford and Cambridge graduates we spoke to still hold the belief that some colleges are more competitive than others. The fact that a smaller number of places are available for particular course/college combinations can be one reason why a college ends up looking more competitive than another. If you look at the statistics on the Cambridge University website from 2006 to 2009, the average success rate for students applying to read Law at King's Cambridge (which offers between 3 and 4 places) is 10%, while for Clare it is 13% and for St John's and Trinity it is 19%. In contrast, at Jesus it is 31% and at Gonville and Caius 24%, where they have between 8 to 11 and 10 to 13 places available respectively.

Over the course of researching this book, we have met a number of successful Oxbridge graduates who believe that they were offered a place because they applied to a college which is perceived to be less competitive than the average. One PPE graduate, James, founder of Oxbridge Applications, believes that his statistical approach significantly increased his chance of success. For every success story however, there are other applicants who have applied similar tactics to no effect.

The key point to remember is that with or without statistical analysis, your application will be set in the wider context of the application process. James worked hard for his place. He wrote a strong personal statement, produced excellent written work, performed well in the admissions test, practised talking about his subjects in a face-to-face, oral environment, communicated well at interview and finally attained the grades he required to meet his conditional offer.

What if I simply cannot decide?

You can, of course, opt to make an open application to the university, where the university itself decides to which college they send your application. If this is what you decide to do, then be assured - they are all brilliant places, and the faculty may send you somewhere you would never have dreamed of applying, a stroke of fate which becomes the best thing that ever happened to you. Cambridge states on their website that 'Applicants from the UK/EU are allocated to colleges which happen in that year to have had fewer applications per place in the subject than the colleges generally,' and therefore if you are thinking of making an open application, you might find it helpful to check out the previous year's college statistics for your subject, to see which colleges traditionally have less applicants per place. This might serve as a guideline as to which college you might be sent to – but as ever, there are no guarantees that it will be that one.

According to Oxford's website, 20% of applicants make an open application, leaving the admissions office computer to make the decision. Once the computer has selected your college, however, you will not be able to change it. While the admissions tutors will not ask you why you chose a certain college, your enthusiasm for studying your chosen subject at a particular college will shine through if you've made a rational and articulate decision about it. For example, if you know a certain college has an Egyptology library, or a very active literary society, or another has a tutor aligned with your own interests in geography, you may well be spurred on in your interview performance.

In short, you wouldn't make a choice about a new school or a new job lightly; you would want to know where it is, what sort of activities it offers and also whether you think you would fit in there. The same philosophy applies to selecting a college at Oxford or Cambridge. If you do decide to make an open application, it should be a positive decision - a conclusion, after careful thought, that you want the university/faculty to make the decision for you.

Remember, pooling happens. Keep an open mind.

Hundreds of students each year are redistributed throughout the different colleges after making their applications. Oxford may send you to a college other than your 'first choice' and Cambridge often 'pools' applicants.

Pooling refers to a process whereby your interview with your first choice college does not result in an offer, but you are eligible to be interviewed a second time at another college. Although it sounds like a 'cattle market' approach, swapping students here and there, it is a fair process, designed to ensure that any student who is worthy of a place receives an offer. If, in one year, a college receives a significant number of strong applications, and another college receives fewer, there is a chance that those brilliant candidates will be pooled to another college.

At Oxford, tutors exchange information on applicants to make sure the best are offered places. This means that if you reach the interview stage, as well as being interviewed at your chosen college (or one that was allocated to you if you made an open application), another college might also want to invite you to interview. They may offer you a place, or you may still be offered a place by the one you initially selected/were allocated in the first instance.

Cambridge has a different approach, operating a Winter Pool, and an excellent guide to pooling can be found on its website. In short, the Pool exists to ensure strong candidates who either make open applications or do not get into their first choice of college worthy of an offer do not miss out.

In December, you will be notified if you have been placed in the Pool by Cambridge and there is nothing that you need then do. The bureaucratic machinery will kick in and guide you through the process. If another college wishes to re-interview you, they will contact you early in the New Year, most likely by telephone. If you are called up for another interview, the university advises that you find out a little more about the college as well as who might be interviewing you. In 2010, Pool interviews took place in mid-January and by the 31st of January all applicants had been informed as to whether they had been successful or not. Cambridge openly publishes statistics regarding how many applicants have applied to one college and have received offers from other colleges through the pool. In 2009, Downing College received 80 Economics applications. The college made five offers, but an additional three applicants were given offers by other colleges through the pool. In the 2009 Winter Pool, 3,185 applicants were pooled, of which 850 were made offers (610 received an offer without returning for an interview, the remainder following an additional interview). That year, the average success rate for a 'pooled applicant' was therefore 26.68%.

The main thing to remember is that pooling does not make you a second-class interviewee. Indeed it can be quite the reverse. One state school student we spoke to applied to read Medicine at Cambridge. She was plopped into the Winter Pool and after several interviews, was offered a place at one of Cambridge's top colleges, noted for its distinctive academic excellence, high-achieving undergraduates and a regular fixture in the top third of the Tomkins table.

It is important to be optimistic about the college you may attend. When all is said and done, you are applying to Oxbridge to study, rather than simply to live in a certain college. Life at Oxbridge really is what you make it, and sometimes being pooled works out as an incredible stroke of luck that leads to a brilliant university experience.

If at first you don't succeed...

Applying to Oxbridge is a difficult and demanding task and due to the intense competition for places, some very bright, interesting and well-prepared applicants do not get their offer. This can be very disappointing and frustrating – especially given the amount of work the application process can require.

While there are no official statistics on how many students re-apply to Oxford and Cambridge each year, both universities accept re-applications. At the same time, they also advise that applicants think carefully before giving up a place at another good university to re-apply (particularly in this increasingly competitive market for university places). Many applicants worry however that if they do re-apply, they will be discriminated against. There is absolutely no evidence to suggest this, and the fact that year on year there are a number of students who successfully re-apply, indicates that this fear is unfounded.

On its website, Magdalene College, Cambridge states that the 'College is happy to consider second-time applicants without prejudice.' Similarly, Trinity College say that there is no problem with re-applications but adds, 'our standard advice is always that applicants should try another college the second time around so that candidates and interviewers do not find themselves repeating the previous year's experience.'

So are re-applicants successful? In short, the answer is yes and no. Just as there are no guarantees for first-time applicants, it's just as competitive if you are applying again. As to why some applicants are successful second time round, there are a number of different reasons. For many, it is simply the case that initially, they chose the wrong course. A number of applicants we have spoken to admit to not having thought through their application. While Experimental Psychology or Philosophy might have sounded like interesting options, in the cold light of day (the interview), they soon realised they were on the wrong track.

For some it was the admissions test that got the better of them and, for others it was simply the case that they felt, first time round, that their application did not reflect their potential and wanted to give it another shot. Indeed, re-applicants have in their favour the simple fact they have been through the application process before and know what to expect. They have their grades, and so the university can see that they have excelled academically and on the whole, most re-applicants tend to be more academically mature – not only as they are one year older and have completed the school syllabus, but also because they have had to learn through the first year rejection that even if you are brilliant on paper (and have consistently achieved academically since the first day at school), when it comes to Oxbridge, there are no guarantees and very motivated and gifted students are rejected. For some, if can be a most humbling experience. As one high-flying graduate recalls, 'I was an utter nightmare at the age of 17! I waltzed into the interview, thinking the university would be begging to offer me a place. Needless to say, I was rejected. The reality of not succeeding was the wake-up call I needed. I took a gap year, grew up and re-focused. Looking back, I am so pleased that Oxford turned me away initially. I was immature and would not have valued highly enough the education I went on to receive.' This high-flying gentleman graduated from Oxford with a First.

If you are thinking of re-applying, we have put together three things to consider:

1. Is Oxbridge definitely for me?

Oxbridge isn't for everyone. Some people thrive under the academic pressure, whilst others get on better if they are given more time to digest the information they have received, get more chance to talk about it in large seminar groups and think about it in their own time. Another reason to look elsewhere may be that the course you are looking for or the modules you are most interested in aren't on offer at Oxford and Cambridge.

2. Is the course right for me?

It's all too easy to fall into the trap of doing a course because it fits in with what you are doing at school, but university degrees are very different to their A level or IB equivalents. Have you really done your research and thought laterally about what you are most interested in when you come to pick your degree course? If you do not want to study Medicine and are passionate about animal and human biology, why not look into Biological Sciences at Oxford? If you cannot decide between your love of Physics and Chemistry, why not research Physical Natural Sciences at Cambridge?

3. Is the college right for me?

For some applicants, choosing a college, as we've just covered, can be one of the hardest parts of the application. Does the college you are applying to always take applicants for your subject? How many places does it have for your subject each year?

If you've thought about all these things and you still want to re-apply, it's best to start afresh. You need to see your re-application as a completely new application.

Ask your teacher whether your initial university and college choice sent the school any feedback from your interview or ring up the college you applied to and find out if they can send you a record of the admissions tutors' feedback. Read carefully through what is said to see if there is anything you could work on.

Start your personal statement from scratch and get your teacher to write you a new reference. Do some more reading and try to fix up some more relevant work experience so you will have even more strings to your bow. If you have to submit written work, your work one year on is likely to be much more mature and will really reflect your learning, and so refrain from handing in last year's work because you think it will be less hassle. If it was the admissions test you struggled with, then practice (our admissions tests chapter can help you). Finally, unless you can't imagine yourself anywhere else, give yourself a fresh start and apply to a different college.

And just remember - if you are thinking about re-applying, even some of Oxbridge's most famous alumni weren't successful on their first application: Margaret Thatcher only got her place at Somerville College, Oxford because another student dropped out (albeit the first time that she applied).

So which college will it be?

You've done our quiz – now pick up your pencil and tick the colleges that catch your eye (we suggest a shortlist of three to five).

☐ Christ's College

Founded: 1448

Size: Medium (430 undergraduates, 150 postgraduates)

Academic Ranking: 2010 Tompkins Table = 12/29

Does not offer: Veterinary Medicine

Words that best describe it: 'friendly', 'supportive', 'central', 'welcoming', 'green'

Suitable for: Those in search of academic excellence in the heart of Cambridge

Pros:
- ✓ Central
- ✓ Extensive gardens
- ✓ Not too big, not too small
- ✓ Good clubs and societies

Cons:
- ✗ The sixties architecture of New Court

☐ Churchill College

Founded: 1958

Size: Large (440 undergraduates, 210 postgraduates)

Academic Ranking: 2010 Tompkins Table = 3/29

Does not offer: Land Economy, Theology & Religious Studies

Words that best describe it: 'friendly', 'informal', 'recreational', 'open', 'sporty'

Suitable for: Those looking for an escape from Cambridge's formalities

Pros:
- ✓ Everyone lives on site
- ✓ Dedicated theatre/cinema
- ✓ On-site playing fields

Cons:
- ✗ The architecture is not in the traditional style of Cambridge

☐ Clare College

Founded:	1326
Size:	Large (440 undergraduates, 210 postgraduates)
Academic Ranking:	2010 Tompkins Table = 8/29
Does not offer:	The College accepts applications for all courses
Words that best describe it:	'musical, 'informal', 'welcoming, 'popular', 'fun'
Suitable for:	History buffs wanting the picture postcard experience
Pros:	✓ Great Chapel crypt music venue ✓ Strong extra-curricular options ✓ Ancient architecture ✓ Decent external accommodation
Cons:	✗ Its beauty is a little intimidating

☐ Corpus Christi College

Founded:	1352
Size:	Small (260 undergraduates, 220 postgraduates)
Academic Ranking:	2010 Tompkins Table = 13/29
Does not offer:	Architecture, Education, Land Economy, Veterinary Medicine
Words that best describe it:	'friendly', 'small', 'historic', 'convivial'
Suitable for:	Those looking for a small community
Pros:	✓ The Corpus Christi Playroom ✓ The Parker Library ✓ The outdoor swimming pool ✓ The location
Cons:	✗ The academically-weighted room ballot

☐ Downing College

Founded: 1800

Size: Medium (410 undergraduates, 300 postgraduates)

Academic Ranking: 2010 Tompkins Table = 15/29

Does not offer: The College accepts applications for all courses

Words that best describe it: 'spacious', 'convenient', 'friendly', 'beautiful', 'supportive', 'sporty'

Suitable for: Sports players, sports fans

Pros:
✓ A sporting powerhouse
✓ Huge, rolling lawns
✓ Plenty of space

Cons:
✗ You have to sign guests into the bar

☐ Emmanuel College

Founded: 1584

Size: Large (480 undergraduates, 210 postgraduates)

Academic Ranking: 2010 Tompkins Table = 1/29

Does not offer: Certain Education courses, Land Economy

Words that best describe it: 'fun', 'beautiful', 'central', 'open-minded', 'academic'

Suitable for: Those who want to work hard and play hard

Pros:
✓ The famous duck pond
✓ The outdoor swimming pool
✓ Active music and drama societies
✓ The bar
✓ The unique laundry service

Cons:
✗ Limited cooking facilities

□ Fitzwilliam College

Founded:	1869
Size:	Large (475 undergraduates, 275 postgraduates)
Academic Ranking:	2010 Tompkins Table = 22/29
Does not offer:	The College accepts applications for all courses
Words that best describe it:	'relaxed', 'unpretentious', 'friendly', 'fun'
Suitable for:	Those involved in university-level activities
Pros:	✓ State-school friendly ✓ Lovely grounds ✓ Brand-new library and computer centre ✓ 250-seat auditorium
Cons:	✗ A little out of the way

□ Girton College

Founded:	1869
Size:	Large (503 undergraduates, 201 postgraduates)
Academic Ranking:	2010 Tompkins Table = 21/29
Does not offer:	Education, History of Art
Words that best describe it:	'distant', 'sprawling', 'pleasant', 'close-knit', 'unpretentious', 'easy-going'
Suitable for:	People who enjoy cycling
Pros:	✓ Huge grounds ✓ Sports facilities all on site ✓ Indoor heated swimming pool ✓ Tasty food
Cons:	✗ A bit of a trek from the centre of Cambridge

☐ Gonville & Caius College

Founded:	1348
Size:	Large (475 undergraduates, 230 postgraduates)
Academic Ranking:	2010 Tompkins Table = 11/29
Does not offer:	The College accepts applications for all courses
Words that best describe it:	'traditional', 'supportive', 'academic', 'energetic', 'sporty'
Suitable for:	Energetic types who want to work and play
Pros:	✓ Stephen Hawking studied here ✓ Central Location ✓ Strong boat club
Cons:	✗ Compulsory Hall most nights

☐ Homerton College

Founded:	1730
Size:	Huge (600 undergraduates, 600 postgraduates)
Academic Ranking:	2010 Tompkins Table = 26/29
Does not offer:	Architecture, Medicine, Veterinary Medicine,
Words that best describe it:	'friendly', 'open', 'inventive', 'unpretentious', 'warm'
Suitable for:	Slightly more relaxed characters
Pros:	✓ Very large ✓ Sports facilities all on-site ✓ Beautiful gardens ✓ Academic pressure at a minimum
Cons:	✗ Not what you might call 'centrally located'

☐ Jesus College

Founded:	1496
Size:	Medium (489 undergraduates, 270 postgraduates)
Academic Ranking:	2010 Tompkins Table = 16/29
Does not offer:	The College accepts applications for all courses
Words that best describe it:	'friendly', 'historic', 'beautiful', 'secluded'
Suitable for:	People who like old buildings without a side-helping of tourists, fans of sculpture
Pros:	✓ The architecture ✓ Five minutes from the centre of town ✓ Sports facilities are all on-site ✓ Lots of statues
Cons:	✗ The kitchen fixed charge is expensive

☐ King's College

Founded:	1441
Size:	Medium (400 undergraduates, 280 postgraduates)
Academic Ranking:	2010 Tompkins Table = 14/29
Does not offer:	Education, Land Economy, Veterinary Medicine
Words that best describe it:	'open', 'different', 'fun', 'impressive', 'accessible'
Suitable for:	Those looking for an 'alternative' experience
Pros:	✓ The architecture ✓ The 'King's Affair' (King's May Ball alternative) ✓ The location ✓ Mingles (large parties, held at the end of the autumn and spring terms)
Cons:	✗ The tourists

□ Magdalene College

Founded:	1428 or 1542, depending on who you ask
Size:	Small (345 undergraduates, 239 postgraduates)
Academic Ranking:	2010 Tompkins Table = 5/29
Does not offer:	The College accepts applications for all courses
Words that best describe it:	'small', 'old', 'welcoming', 'close-knit', 'supportive'
Suitable for:	Agoraphobic prospective applicants and traditionalists
Pros:	✓ Plenty of river bank ✓ A plethora of 'Cambridge-style' traditions ✓ Close-knit community ✓ Great central location
Cons:	✗ A small community can mean gossip spreads like wildfire

---

□ Murray Edwards College

Founded:	1954
Size:	Small (360 undergraduates, 99 postgraduates)
Academic Ranking:	2010 Tompkins Table = 23/29
Does not offer:	Certain Education courses, Philosophy
Words that best describe it:	'modern', 'dynamic', 'inspiring', 'diverse', 'girly', 'low-key'
Suitable for:	Women who want a quieter, cleaner place to study
Pros:	✓ Luxurious 2nd and 3rd year accommodation ✓ Beautiful lawns you can sit on ✓ Free parking for students ✓ The non-central location makes for a quieter home
Cons:	✗ The cycle ride up Castle Hill

☐ Newnham College

Founded: 1871

Size: Medium (400 undergraduates, 150 postgraduates)

Academic Ranking: 2010 Tompkins Table = 25/29

Does not offer: Education

Words that best describe it: 'sociable', 'safe', 'pretty', 'comfortable', 'peaceful', 'convenient'

Suitable for: Those in need of an escape

Pros:
✓ The gardens (which you are allowed to sit in)
✓ Proximity to many humanities departments
✓ On-site sports facilities
✓ The food

Cons:
✗ There is no one to clean your room for you

☐ Pembroke College

Founded: 1347

Size: Small (400 undergraduates, 295 postgraduates)

Academic Ranking: 2010 Tompkins Table = 10/29

Does not offer: Education, Geography

Words that best describe it: 'friendly', 'relaxed', 'central', 'inclusive', 'beautiful'

Suitable for: Aspiring thesps and aesthetes

Pros:
✓ Location bang in the middle of Cambridge
✓ The drama scene
✓ Opportunities to go abroad with the college in the holidays
✓ The lovely gardens

Cons:
✗ Not politically active

☐ Peterhouse College

Founded:	1284
Size:	Small (255 undergraduates, 125 postgraduates)
Academic Ranking:	2010 Tompkins Table = 7/29
Does not offer:	Education, Geography, Land Economy, Politics, Psychology & Sociology, Veterinary Medicine
Words that best describe it:	'intimate', 'close-knit', 'relaxed', 'supportive', 'old', 'quaint'
Suitable for:	Those looking for a small community
Pros:	✓ Candlelit dining ✓ Deer Park ✓ Good accommodation
Cons:	✗ Small community can get a bit claustrophobic

☐ Queens' College

Founded:	1448
Size:	Large (490 undergraduates, 350 postgraduates)
Academic Ranking:	2010 Tompkins Table = 17/29
Does not offer:	Certain Education courses
Words that best describe it:	'large', 'friendly', 'relaxed', 'sociable', 'extracurricular'
Suitable for:	Those that are out-going, looking for a community-feel
Pros:	✓ The famous Mathematical Bridge ✓ Entertaining rumours about the history of said bridge ✓ Sports facilities and societies ✓ The bar ✓ The Fitzpatrick Theatre
Cons:	✗ Can be a little boisterous at times

☐ Robinson College

Founded:	1979
Size:	Medium (375 undergraduates, 120 postgraduates)
Academic Ranking:	2010 Tompkins Table = 19/29
Does not offer:	Certain Education courses
Words that best describe it:	'unpretentious', 'open', 'diverse', 'supportive', 'modern'
Suitable for:	Those looking for a less traditional experience
Pros:	✓ Modern accommodation ✓ Great food ✓ Beautiful gardens ✓ Lake
Cons:	✗ The modern architecture is not to everyone's liking

☐ St Catharine's College

Founded:	1473
Size:	Medium (435 undergraduates, 220 postgraduates)
Academic Ranking:	2010 Tompkins Table = 9/29
Does not offer:	Architecture, Education, History of Art
Words that best describe it:	'open', 'supportive', 'engaging', 'central'
Suitable for:	Those in search of a friendly, central experience
Pros:	✓ Central ✓ Good accommodation ✓ Good facilities for sports and the arts
Cons:	✗ Poor self-catering facilities

□ St John's College

Founded:	1511
Size:	Large (530 undergraduates, 300 postgraduates)
Academic Ranking:	2010 Tompkins Table = 20/29
Does not offer:	The College accepts applications for all courses
Words that best describe it:	'big', 'beautiful', 'fun', 'grand', 'sporty', 'cosmopolitan'
Suitable for:	Those who want to be the centre of attention
Pros:	✓ Very large ✓ Plenty of funding ✓ Beautiful gardens ✓ The May Ball ✓ Sporty, dramatic AND musical
Cons:	✗ Can get slightly overwhelming at times

□ Selwyn College

Founded:	1882
Size:	Small (360 undergraduates, 130 postgraduates)
Academic Ranking:	2010 Tompkins Table = 6/29
Does not offer:	The College accepts applications for all courses
Words that best describe it:	'sociable', 'close-knit', 'academic', 'supportive'
Suitable for:	Those looking for a close-knit community
Pros:	✓ Proximity to many humanities departments ✓ Fabulous new accommodation block ✓ Known for its friendly atmosphere ✓ Spacious
Cons:	✗ A little out of the centre

☐ Sidney Sussex College

Founded:	1596
Size:	Small (360 undergraduates, 190 postgraduates)
Academic Ranking:	2010 Tompkins Table = 18/29
Does not offer:	Education
Words that best describe it:	'central', 'friendly', 'cosy', 'close-knit'
Suitable for:	Those involved in university-level activities
Pros:	✓ The student-run bar ✓ The location ✓ Houses all of its first-years together ✓ Currently updating some of its oldest facilities
Cons:	✗ Often overlooked in favour of more famous colleges

☐ Trinity College

Founded:	1546
Size:	Large (670 undergraduates, 330 postgraduates)
Academic Ranking:	2010 Tompkins Table = 2/29
Does not offer:	Education, Veterinary Medicine
Words that best describe it:	'grand', 'traditional', 'sociable', 'rich', 'impressive'
Suitable for:	Big cheeses
Pros:	✓ An academic reputation par excellence ✓ Huge library ✓ Accommodation in college for the duration
Cons:	✗ Too imposing for some

□ Trinity Hall

Founded:	1350
Size:	Small (370 undergraduates, 240 postgraduates)
Academic Ranking:	2010 Tompkins Table = 4/29
Does not offer:	Certain combinations with Education
Words that best describe it:	'idyllic', 'small', 'central', 'sociable', 'sporty'
Suitable for:	Those looking for riverside calm
Pros:	✓ Central ✓ Beautiful architecture and grounds ✓ Modern library and sports facilities ✓ Good opportunities for musicians
Cons:	✗ The size – it can be a little too intimate at times

☐ Balliol College

Founded: 1263

Size: Large (390 undergraduates, 320 postgraduates)

Academic Ranking: 2008/09 Norrington Table = 14/30

Does not offer: Archaeology & Anthropology, Biochemistry, Classics & English, Earth Sciences (Geology), Experimental Psychology, Geography, History of Art, Human Sciences, Materials Science, MEM (Materials, Economics & Management), Mathematics & Statistics, Music, Philosophy and Modern Languages, Philosophy & Theology, Psychology & Philosophy, Theology, Theology & Oriental Studies

Words that best describe it: 'unpretentious', 'liberal', 'energetic', 'high-achieving'

Suitable for: Those who operate a little left-of-centre

Pros:
✓ The tortoise
✓ The grass you can sit on
✓ The sports societies
✓ The bar

Cons:
✗ The lack of Formal Hall

☐ Brasenose College

Founded: 1509

Size: Medium (360 undergraduates, 210 postgraduates)

Academic Ranking: 2008/09 Norrington Table = 26/30

Does not offer: Archaeology & Anthropology, Biomedical Sciences, Classics & Oriental Studies, Computer Science, Earth Sciences (Geology), EEM (Engineering, Economics & Management), History & English, History of Art, Human Sciences, Materials Science, MEM (Materials, Economics & Management), Mathematics & Computer Science, Oriental Studies, Philosophy & Theology, Theology, Theology & Oriental Studies

Words that best describe it: 'old', 'stately', 'warm', 'easygoing'

Suitable for: Relaxed sorts, traditionalists

Pros:
✓ Like living in a castle
✓ Plenty of extracurricular societies
✓ Central location

Cons:
✗ One or two obnoxious drinking societies

□ Christ Church College

Founded: 1525

Size: Large (440 undergraduates, 230 postgraduates)

Academic Ranking: 2008/09 Norrington Table = 12/30

Does not offer: Archaeology & Anthropology, Biomedical Sciences, Classics & English, Computer Science, Earth Sciences (Geology), History & Economics, History & English, Human Sciences, Materials Science, MEM (Materials, Economics & Management), Mathematics & Computer Science

Words that best describe it: 'prestigious', 'grand', 'proud', 'beautiful', 'traditional'

Suitable for: Those looking for a BIG experience, future Prime Ministers

Pros:
✓ The history
✓ The accommodation
✓ The funding and grants
✓ Brideshead Revisited
✓ Christ Church Meadows

Cons: ✗ The tourists

□ Corpus Christi College

Founded: 1517

Size: Small (250 undergraduates, 105 postgraduates)

Academic Ranking: 2008/09 Norrington Table = 4/30

Does not offer: Archaeology & Anthropology, Biological Sciences, Classics & Modern Languages, Classics & Oriental Studies, Computer Science, Earth Sciences (Geology), Economics & Management, Engineering Science, EEM (Engineering, Economics & Management), English & Modern Languages, European & Middle Eastern Languages, Fine Art, Geography, History & Economics, History & Modern Languages, History of Art, Human Sciences, MEM (Materials, Economics & Management), Modern Languages, Music, Oriental Studies, Philosophy & Modern Languages, Philosophy & Theology, Theology, Theology & Oriental Studies

Words that best describe it: 'friendly', 'supportive', 'intellectual', 'quaint', 'compact'

Suitable for: Those who want to win University Challenge

Pros:
✓ Strong academic performance
✓ Good accommodation for a small college
✓ Wonderful library
✓ Central location

Cons: ✗ The small size can get a bit claustrophobic

☐ Exeter College

Founded: 1314

Size: Small to medium (345 undergraduates, 205 postgraduates)

Academic Ranking: 2008/09 Norrington Table = 18/30

Does not offer: Archaeology & Anthropology, Biological Sciences, Classics & Oriental Studies, European & Middle Eastern Languages, Experimental Psychology, Geography, History & Economics, History & Modern Languages, History & Politics, History of Art, Human Sciences, Materials Science, MEM (Materials, Economics & Management), Oriental Studies, Philosophy & Theology, Psychology & Philosophy, Theology, Theology & Oriental Studies

Words that best describe it: 'central', 'open-minded', 'chilled', 'beautiful', 'close-knit', 'relaxed'

Suitable for: Those looking for an idyllic central college

Pros:
✓ Central
✓ Strong musical tradition
✓ WiFi in the college gardens

Cons:
✗ A bit cramped

☐ Harris Manchester College

Founded: 1889 (full college status granted in 1996)

Size: Small (85 undergraduates, 110 postgraduates)

Academic Ranking: 2008/09 Norrington Table = 30/30

*Harris Manchester College only accepts mature students (over 21s)

Does not offer: Archaeology & Anthropology, Classics & English, Economics & Management, English Language and Literature, English & Modern Languages, Experimental Psychology, History & Economics, History & English, History & Politics, History of Art, Human Sciences, Law (Jurisprudence), Law with Law Studies in Europe, Mathematics & Philosophy, Oriental Studies, Philosophy & Modern Languages, PPE (Philosophy, Politics & Economics), Philosophy & Theology , Psychology & Philosophy , Theology, Theology & Oriental Studies

Words that best describe it: 'friendly', 'liberal', 'mature', 'homely', 'small'

Suitable for: Mature students looking for a loving family

Pros:
✓ The food (the best kept secret in Oxford)
✓ The close-knit community
✓ The lack of tourists
✓ Caters well to the needs of older students

Cons:
✗ Low profile (not a Christ Church or a Magdalen)

□ Hertford College

Founded: 1282 (achieving full college status in 1874)

Size: Medium (400 undergraduates, 190 postgraduates)

Academic Ranking: 2008/09 Norrington Table = 6/30

Does not offer: Biomedical Sciences, Classical Archeology & Ancient History, Classics, Classics & English, Classics & Modern Languages, Classics & Oriental Studies, Computer Sciences, Earth Sciences (Geology), European & Middle Eastern Languages, Experimental Psychology, Fine Art, History (Ancient & Modern), History & English, History of Art, Materials Science, MEM (Materials, Economics & Management), Mathematics & Computer Science, Mathematics & Statistics, Philosophy & Theology, Physics & Philosophy, Theology, Theology & Oriental Studies

Words that best describe it: 'democratic', 'unpretentious', 'central', 'social', 'relaxed'

Suitable for: Progressive types

Pros:
- ✓ Relaxed yet still academically successful
- ✓ The Hertford Bridge (popularly known as the Bridge of Sighs)
- ✓ Student-run bar

Cons:
- ✗ Food not amazing

□ Jesus College

Founded: 1571

Size: Medium (350 undergraduates, 170 postgraduates)

Academic Ranking: 2008/09 Norrington Table = 17/30

Does not offer: Archaeology & Anthropology, Biochemistry, Biomedical Sciences, Classical Archaeology & Ancient History, Classics & Oriental Studies, Computer Science, Earth Sciences (Geology), Fine Art, History (Ancient & Modern), History of Art, Human Sciences, Materials Science, MEM (Materials, Economics & Management), Mathematics & Computer Science, Oriental Studies, Physics & Philosophy, Theology, Theology & Oriental Studies

Words that best describe it: 'small', 'close-knit', 'welcoming', 'sleepy', 'central'

Suitable for: Sports fans

Pros:
- ✓ Very competitive sports teams
- ✓ Gentle atmosphere
- ✓ Lovely buildings
- ✓ Very central

Cons:
- ✗ External accommodation is quite far away from college

☐ Keble College

Founded: 1584

Size: Large (420 undergraduates, 200 postgraduates)

Academic Ranking: 2008/09 Norrington Table = 13/30

Does not offer: Biochemistry, Classics, Classics and English, Classics and Modern Languages, Classics and Oriental Studies, Earth Sciences (Geology), EEM (Engineering, Economics & Management), English and Modern Languages, European & Middle Eastern Languages, Experimental Psychology, Fine Art, History & Economics, History & English, History of Art, Human Sciences, Materials Science, MEM (Materials, Economics & Management), Music, Oriental Studies, Physics & Philosophy, Psychology & Philosophy, Theology & Oriental Studies

Words that best describe it: 'friendly', 'buzzing', 'gothic', 'fun', 'traditional'

Suitable for: Those looking for extra-curricular experience

Pros:
✓ The proximity to the Science Area
✓ The unique architecture
✓ The lack of tourists
✓ The O'Reilly Theatre

Cons:
✗ A tad too far from the city centre bustle

☐ Lady Margaret Hall

Founded: 1878

Size: Large (400 undergraduates, 180 postgraduates)

Academic Ranking: 2008/09 Norrington Table = 21/30

Does not offer: Archaeology & Anthropology, Classics & Oriental Studies, Computer Science, Earth Sciences (Geology), Geography, History & Economics, History & English, History of Art, Human Sciences, Materials Science, MEM (Materials, Economics & Management), Mathematics & Computer Science

Words that best describe it: 'pretty', 'friendly', 'scenic', 'relaxed', 'lively'

Suitable for: Those looking to get away from it all

Pros:
✓ The accommodation
✓ The gardens
✓ The atmosphere

Cons:
✗ The location

□ Lincoln College

Founded: 1427

Size: Small (320 undergraduates, 290 postgraduates)

Academic Ranking: 2008/09 Norrington Table = 8/30

Does not offer: Archaeology & Anthropology, Biological Sciences, Classics, Classics and English, Classics and Modern Languages, Classics and Oriental Studies, Computer Science, Earth Sciences (Geology), Economics & Management, EEM (Engineering, Economics & Management), English & Modern Languages, European & Middle Eastern Languages, Experimental Psychology, Fine Art, Geography, History & Economics, History & English, History of Art, Human Sciences, Materials Science, MEM (Materials, Economics & Management), Mathematics & Computer Science, Mathematics & Philosophy, Oriental Studies, Philosophy & Theology, Physics & Philosophy, Psychology & Philosophy, Theology, Theology & Oriental Studies

Words that best describe it: 'friendly', 'small', 'busy', 'close-knit', 'high-achieving'

Suitable for: Those looking for a sociable community

Pros:
✓ The accommodation
✓ The food
✓ The bar
✓ The location

Cons:
✗ The size

□ Magdalen College

Founded: 1458

Size: Big (420 undergraduates, 200 postgraduates)

Academic Ranking: 2008/09 Norrington Table = 3/30

Does not offer: Earth Sciences (Geology), Economics & Management, EEM (Engineering, Economics & Management), Geography, History & Economics, History & English, History of Art, Materials Science, MEM (Materials, Economics & Management), Oriental Studies, Philosophy & Theology, Theology, Theology & Oriental Studies

Words that best describe it: 'big', 'inspiring', 'beautiful', 'surprising', 'challenging'

Suitable for: Movers and shakers

Pros:
✓ Live in all three years
✓ Lots of space
✓ Great music and drama scenes
✓ Your own deer park

Cons:
✗ Envy from the rest of the university

☐ Mansfield College

Founded: 1886

Size: Small (220 undergraduates, 80 postgraduates)

Academic Ranking: 2008/09 Norrington Table = 28/30

⋆Mansfield offers a smaller number of courses, detailed below⋆:

Does offer: Engineering Science, EEM (Engineering, Economics & Management), English Language & Literature, Geography, History, History & English, History & Politics, Human Sciences, Law, Law with Law Studies in Europe, Materials Science, MEM (Materials, Economics & Management), Mathematics, Mathematics & Philosophy, Mathematics & Statistics, Oriental Studies, PPE (Philosophy, Politics & Economics), Philosophy & Theology, Physics, Theology

Words that best describe it: 'unpretentious', 'small', 'friendly', 'accommodating', 'relaxed'

Suitable for: Humble types

Pros:
✓ Friendly community
✓ Access-oriented
✓ Close to the science facilities and the parks

Cons:
✗ Not one of the richer colleges

☐ Merton College

Founded: 1264

Size: Small (315 undergraduates, 300 postgraduates)

Academic Ranking: 2008/09 Norrington Table = 2/30

Does not offer: Archaeology & Anthropology, Biochemistry, Biomedical Sciences, Classics & Oriental Studies, Earth Sciences (Geology), Engineering Science, EEM (Engineering, Economics & Management), Experimental Psychology, Fine Art, Geography, History of Art, Human Sciences, Materials Science, MEM (Materials, Economics & Management), Oriental Studies, Philosophy & Theology, Physics & Philosophy, Psychology & Philosophy, Theology, Theology & Oriental Studies

Words that best describe it: 'small', 'central', 'academic', 'pretty'

Suitable for: Academics and extremely high-achievers

Pros:
✓ Great teaching and tutorial support
✓ Cheap food and rent
✓ Central location

Cons:
✗ Over-indulgence in extra-curricular activities is not encouraged

☐ New College

Founded: 1379

Size: Large (420 undergraduates, 220 postgraduates)

Academic Ranking: 2008/09 Norrington Table = 5/30

Does not offer: Archaeology & Anthropology, Classical Archaeology & Ancient History, Classics & English, Earth Sciences (Geology), Geography, History & English, History of Art, Materials Science, MEM (Materials, Economics & Management), Oriental Studies, Philosophy & Theology, Theology, Theology & Oriental Studies

Words that best describe it: 'social', 'big', 'active', 'diligent', 'supportive', 'fun'

Suitable for: Social types

Pros:
✓ Large student body
✓ Beautiful and spacious surroundings
✓ Celebrated musical tradition

Cons:
✗ Limited cooking facilities

☐ Oriel College

Founded: 1326

Size: Small (300 undergraduates, 160 postgraduates)

Academic Ranking: 2008/09 Norrington Table = 24/30

Does not offer: Archaeology & Anthropology, Biological Sciences, Classics & Oriental Studies, Earth Sciences (Geology), Economics & Management, EEM (Engineering, Economics & Management), European and Middle Eastern Languages, Experimental Psychology, Fine Art, Geography, History & English, History & Politics, History of Art, Human Sciences, Law with Law Studies in Europe, Materials Science, MEM (Materials, Economics & Management), Mathematics & Philosophy, Mathematics & Statistics, Oriental Studies, Psychology & Philosophy, Theology & Oriental Studies

Words that best describe it: 'sporty', 'small', 'old', 'traditional', 'central', 'warm-hearted'

Suitable for: Rowing and sports enthusiasts

Pros:
✓ Excellent facilities for sports
✓ One of the top rowing colleges
✓ Central location

Cons:
✗ Food not the tastiest

☐ Pembroke College

Founded: 1624

Size: Medium (365 undergraduates, 140 postgraduates)

Academic Ranking: 2008/09 Norrington Table = 23/30

Does not offer: Archaeology & Anthropology, Biomedical Sciences, Classical Archaeology & Ancient History, Classics, Classics & English, Classics & Modern Languages, Classics & Oriental Studies, Computer Science, Earth Sciences (Geology), EEM (Engineering, Economics & Management), Fine Art, Geography, History (Ancient & Modern), History of Art, Human Sciences, Materials Science, MEM (Materials, Economics & Management), Mathematics & Computer Science, Mathematics & Statistics, Physics, Physics & Philosophy

Words that best describe it: 'inclusive', 'busy', 'sporty'

Suitable for: Sporty types (especially those interested in rowing)

Pros:
✓ Well-funded JCR
✓ Relaxed atmosphere
✓ Distinguished alumni

Cons: ✗ Expensive rent

☐ The Queen's College

Founded: 1341

Size: Large (345 undergraduates, 130 postgraduates)

Academic Ranking: 2008/09 Norrington Table = 10/30

Does not offer: Archaeology & Anthropology, Classical Archaeology & Ancient History, Computer Science, Earth Sciences (Geology), Engineering Science, EEM (Engineering, Economics & Management), Geography, History & English, History of Art, Human Sciences, Theology

Words that best describe it: 'cosy', 'friendly', 'down-to-earth', 'old-fashioned'

Suitable for: Laid back

Pros:
✓ Beautiful architecture
✓ Relaxed student body
✓ Central location

Cons: ✗ Small college bar

☐ St Anne's College

Founded: 1879

Size: Large (445 undergraduates, 235 postgraduates)

Academic Ranking: 2008/09 Norrington Table = 20/30

Does not offer: Archaeology & Anthropology, Biomedical Sciences, History & English, History of Art, Human Sciences, Oriental Studies, Physics & Philosophy, Theology, Theology & Oriental Studies

Words that best describe it: 'sociable', 'relaxed', 'down to earth', 'spacious'

Suitable for: Chilled-out untraditional types

Pros:
✓ Large site
✓ Good food
✓ Lack of regimented traditions

Cons:
✗ Not the prettiest of colleges

☐ St Catherine's College

Founded: 1963

Size: Large (500 undergraduates, 220 postgraduates)

Academic Ranking: 2008/09 Norrington Table = 16/30

Does not offer: Archaeology & Anthropology, Classical Archaeology & Ancient History, Classics, Classics & English, Classics & Modern Languages, Classics & Oriental Studies, Earth Sciences (Geology), History (Ancient & Modern), Philosophy & Theology, Theology, Theology & Oriental Studies

Words that best describe it: 'social', 'friendly', 'sporty', 'vibrant', 'peaceful', 'modern'

Suitable for: Those looking for a modern touch.

Pros:
✓ Excellent facilities for sports and the arts
✓ Good food
✓ Biggest college bar in Oxford

Cons:
✗ The architecture's a total marmite affair – you either love it or you hate it

☐ St Edmund Hall

Founded: c. 1278

Size: Large (405 undergraduates, 160 postgraduates)

Academic Ranking: 2008/09 Norrington Table = 27/30

Does not offer: Archaeology & Anthropology, Biological Sciences, Classical Archaeology and Ancient History, Classics, Classics & English, Classics & Modern Languages, Classics & Oriental Studies, Computer Science, European & Middle Eastern Languages, History (Ancient and Modern), History & English, History of Art, Human Sciences, Mathematics & Computer Science, Oriental Studies, Philosophy & Theology, Theology, Theology & Oriental Studies

Words that best describe it: 'sociable', 'small', 'sporty', 'intimate', 'relaxed', 'central'

Suitable for: Sporty types

Pros:
✓ Sports
✓ Location
✓ Social life

Cons:
✗ Food is not great

☐ St Hilda's College

Founded: 1893

Size: Medium (400 undergraduates, 140 postgraduates)

Academic Ranking: 2008/09 Norrington Table = 29/30

Does not offer: Archaeology & Anthropology, Biomedical Sciences, Classics & English, Classics & Modern Languages, Computer Science, Earth Sciences (Geology), EEM (Engineering, Economics & Management), Fine Art, History & Economics, History of Art, Human Sciences, Materials Science, MEM (Materials, Economics & Management), Mathematics & Computer Science, Philosophy & Theology, Theology, Theology & Oriental Studies

Words that best describe it: 'relaxed', 'friendly', 'spacious', 'inviting', 'fun', 'supportive'

Suitable for: Those wanting a bit of riverside charm

Pros:
✓ Excellent music facilities
✓ Spacious gardens
✓ Very close to University sports complex

Cons:
✗ Lacks the traditional 'Oxford' trimmings (cloisters, quads, etc.)

☐ St Hugh's College

Founded: 1886

Size: Large (400 undergraduates, 225 postgraduates)

Academic Ranking: 2008/09 Norrington Table = 22/30

Does not offer: Classical Archaeology & Ancient History, Classics & Oriental Studies, Geography, History & Economics, History of Art, Materials Science, MEM (Materials, Economics & Management), Oriental Studies, Philosophy & Theology, Theology, Theology & Oriental Studies

Words that best describe it: 'spacious', 'unpretentious', 'chilled-out', 'friendly', 'calm'

Suitable for: Those looking for a bit of tranquillity

Pros:
✓ Large grounds
✓ Well stocked library
✓ Tranquil setting

Cons:
✗ Quite far out

☐ St John's College

Founded: 1555

Size: Large (400 undergraduates, 212 postgraduates)

Academic Ranking: 2008/09 Norrington Table = 1/30

Does not offer: Earth Sciences (Geology), EEM (Engineering, Economics & Management), Materials Science, MEM (Materials, Economics & Management), Theology & Oriental Studies

Words that best describe it: 'friendly', 'rich', 'big', 'academic', 'diverse', 'high-achieving'

Suitable for: Academic high-achievers

Pros:
✓ Location
✓ Resources
✓ Reputation

Cons:
✗ Entrance is highly competitive

☐ St Peter's College

Founded: 1929

Size: Medium (350 undergraduates, 95 postgraduates)

Academic Ranking: 2008/09 Norrington Table = 25/30

Does not offer: Biomedical Sciences, Classical Archaeology & Ancient History, Classics, Classics and English, Classics and Modern Languages, Classics and Oriental Studies, Computer Science, Engineering Science, EEM (Engineering, Economics & Management), European & Middle Eastern Languages, Experimental Psychology, Fine Art, History (Ancient & Modern), Human Sciences, Materials Science, MEM (Materials, Economics & Management), Mathematics & Computer Science, Oriental Studies, Psychology & Philosophy

Words that best describe it: 'open', 'friendly', 'grounded', 'central', 'caring', 'cosy'

Suitable for: Those looking for an alternative, light-hearted Oxford experience

Pros:
✓ Location
✓ Cheap food
✓ Unpretentious

Cons:
✗ No undergraduate cooking facilities

☐ Somerville College

Founded: 1879

Size: Medium (400 undergraduates, 80 postgraduates)

Academic Ranking: 2008/09 Norrington Table = 19/30

Does not offer: Archaeology & Anthropology, Biomedical Sciences, Earth Sciences (Geology), Economics & Management, EEM (Engineering, Economics & Management), Fine Art, Geography, History & Politics, History of Art, Human Sciences, Materials Science, MEM (Materials, Economics & Management), Oriental Studies, Philosophy & Theology, Theology, Theology & Oriental Studies

Words that best describe it: 'friendly', 'open minded', 'homely', 'supportive', 'untraditional'

Suitable for: Those looking to avoid Oxford clichés

Pros:
✓ The library
✓ The community spirit
✓ Located in a trendy area

Cons:
✗ Less than brilliant food

☐ Trinity College

Founded: 1554-5

Size: Small (300 undergraduates, 100 postgraduates)

Academic Ranking: 2008/09 Norrington Table = 11/30

Does not offer: Archaeology & Anthropology, Biological Sciences, Biomedical Sciences, Classical Archaeology & Ancient History, Computer Science, Earth Sciences (Geology), European & Middle Eastern Languages, Experimental Psychology, Fine Art, Geography, History & Economics, History & English, History of Art, Human Sciences, Mathematics & Computer Science, Music, Oriental Studies, Psychology & Philosophy, Theology & Oriental Studies

Words that best describe it: 'spacious', 'inclusive', 'friendly', 'warm', 'beautiful', 'open'

Suitable for: Those looking for beautiful surroundings

Pros:
✓ Exquisite gardens
✓ Central location
✓ High quality food

Cons:
✗ Poor self-catering options on the main college site

☐ University College

Founded: 1249

Size: Medium (366 undergraduates, 208 postgraduates)

Academic Ranking: 2008/09 Norrington Table = 7/30

Does not offer: Archaeology & Anthropology, Biological Sciences, Economics & Management, EEM (Engineering, Economics and Management) Fine Art, Geography, History & Economics, History & English, History of Art, Human Sciences, Materials Science, MEM (Materials, Economics & Management), Philosophy and Theology, Theology, Theology & Oriental Studies

Words that best describe it: 'relaxed', 'fun', 'diverse', 'welcoming', 'cosy'

Suitable for: Those looking for a close-knit community.

Pros:
✓ Relaxed atmosphere
✓ Central location
✓ Distinguished history

Cons:
✗ Bit of a squish

□ Wadham College

Founded: 1610

Size: Large (460 undergraduates, 130 postgraduates)

Academic Ranking: 2008/09 Norrington Table = 9/30

Does not offer: Archaeology & Anthropology, Biomedical Sciences, Computer Science, Earth Sciences (Geology), Fine Art, Geography, Materials Science, MEM (Materials, Economics & Management), Music, Philosophy & Theology, Theology, Theology & Oriental Studies

Words that best describe it: 'alternative', 'open', 'political', 'sociable', 'friendly', 'unpretentious'

Suitable for: Those looking for a diverse and progressive community

Pros:
✓ Relaxed atmosphere
✓ Light and airy bar
✓ Politically involved student body

Cons:
✗ Accommodation is not guaranteed for the duration of your studies

---

□ Worcester College

Founded: 1714

Size: Large (420 undergraduates, 190 postgraduates)

Academic Ranking: 2008/09 Norrington Table = 15/30

Does not offer: Archaeology & Anthropology, Biomedical Sciences, Human Sciences, Materials Science, MEM (Materials, Economics & Management), Oriental Studies, Theology & Oriental Studies

Words that best describe it: 'beautiful', 'friendly', 'relaxed', 'sociable', 'welcoming', 'sporty'

Suitable for: Those looking for a sociable community

Pros:
✓ The accommodation
✓ The food
✓ The lake
✓ The sports and music facilities

Cons:
✗ Less well known internationally

What is a Permanent Private Hall or PPH?

PPHs are smaller than Oxford colleges, and while they offer a limited number of courses, they offer a unique Oxford experience. Students at PPHs have the same access to University and Faculty Libraries. They were originally founded by different Christian denominations, but stuedents are not required to be of that denomination to apply (only sympathetic). The following five PPHs accept undergraduate admissions:

Blackfriars (founded 1221) only accepts mature students (those over 21) and admits a large number of American students – usually 'Visiting Students'- which creates a diverse mixture of young people. It offers Theology, Theology & Philosophy, PPE (Philosophy, Politics & Economics), and Classics (very occasionally). Blackfriars hosts the occasional party, and is located centrally on St Giles – the main street into North Oxford, near the popular Little Clarendon Street.

Regent's Park (founded 1927) is the largest PPH, with over 200 undergraduate, graduate and visiting international students. Slightly hidden away on Pusey Street (off St Giles) it has a small college feel and boasts an unusual Art Deco dining hall. It is definitely worth a look en route to all the bustle of Jericho. Regent's Park accepts applications from both male and female students of any age, and offers the broadest range of subjects: Classical Archaeology & Ancient History, Classics, Classics & English, English Language and Literature, Geography, History, History (Ancient & Modern), History & Politics, Law (Jurisprudence), Philosophy & Modern Languages, PPE (Philosophy, Politics and Economics), Philosophy & Theology, and Theology.

St Benet's Hall (1879) is, like Blackfriars, located fairly centrally on St Giles. It only admits a small handful of (male) students each year, and offers a wider range of subjects than most other PPHs: Classics, Classics & Oriental Studies, History, History and Politics, Oriental Studies, PPE (Philosophy, Politics & Economics), Philosophy and Theology, Theology, and Theology & Oriental Studies. St Benet's is notorious for their Sunday lunches and termly parties, where friends (male and female) are invited into the large town house, garden and croquet lawn.

St Stephen's House (1876) offers only Theology and Philosophy and Theology to mature students (over 21s) who apply. It was founded in the fervour of the Oxford Movement, and is situated outside the town centre, on the main Iffley Road which heads east out of Oxford. The PPH boasts their students' involvement in sport, as the main University Sports Centre can be found just opposite.

Wycliffe Hall (1877) is top of the PPH Norrington table (with a Norrington score of 67.27% it is the academic equal of colleges such as Pembroke and Oriel). It also only admits mature students (over 21s), and accepts applications for Theology and Theology & Philosophy. Wycliffe boasts one of the best Theology libraries in the University, and is situated towards North Oxford (similar distance to St Anne's).

3. The personal statement

How to start, how to finish (!) and how to make it personal.

Students are expected to excel at every stage of the admissions process – and the personal statement is one of these stages. It is important, however, not to overestimate the weight placed on the personal statement as a selection tool – a brilliant personal statement alone is not enough to secure success if you do not have the academic grades, admissions test score and strong performance at interview to match.

Today, you would be hard pressed to find an admissions tutor who truly believes that a personal statement is the exclusive work of an applicant. It is common knowledge that many students receive some form of outside help, be it from a teacher, parent, or sibling. Further, there are a number of excellent books on the market too, providing applicants with essential advice and guidance, many of which are available in schools' own libraries. (Our top pick is *40 Successful Personal Statements: For UCAS Application* by Guy and Gavin Nobes). That said, an overwhelming majority of students we spoke to were asked about aspects of their statement in their interview, which clearly indicates that what you write does matter. When it comes to writing it, you should view everything you say as a potential springboard for discussion at interview. In most cases, the personal statement serves as a foundation for insightful questions, with students asked to elaborate on something they have written about, be it a book, work experience, particular areas of academic interest, or an extended project (completed as part of your A level studies or EPQ).

One applicant we spoke to this year had written about her love for the theatre, and the admissions tutor asked her about her interest and the latest production she had seen. Another was asked why they had chosen a particular quote in their personal statement, another about a building they had mentioned and one applicant was asked to select what academic topic from their personal statement they wanted to discuss at interview.

Of course, no two Oxbridge interviews are the same and there are many applicants who are not questioned on any aspect of their personal statement. This often annoys applicants, who leave the interview shocked and frustrated that they were not asked a single thing from a statement they spent hours agonising over! One former headmaster told us, having spoken to some state schools in his local area, that what makes it slightly difficult is that the application process now demands greater attention, but there are so many different opinions on how the personal statement is used, and that ultimately it seems to come down to who interviews you. It can therefore be hard to know that what you are advising a pupil is definitely right.

In many ways, this is part of the beauty of the Oxbridge application process – it really is there to test the applicant, and to get them thinking for themselves. There are no guarantees or set answers, and if you decide to set yourself on the Oxbridge application path, you need to embrace the unknown.

Some teachers and students assume that those applying for hard-science based courses will not be asked about their personal statement, however, having spoken with some of last year's successful applicants, this was not always the case. Certain students applying for Mathematics and Physics were asked about the books they had read and to elaborate on ideas and topics they had mentioned in their statement. You should therefore write your personal statement thinking that there is a chance you will be asked about it. In addition, do consider the writing of a personal statement in the context of the rest of your university application. The preparation that goes into researching and writing it will ultimately help you to become more comfortable with your subject – which will only help to make your application stronger.

There is no formula for writing the 'perfect' personal statement – part of what makes it successful is how you convey your personality, interests and potential. It is your chance to outline your abilities, motivations and achievements, and is a key opportunity to show why these will make you a fantastic undergraduate on your chosen course. It's essential that your personal statement reflects your personality and writing style – admissions tutors want to see whether you are someone whom they would want to spend the next three or four years teaching. Also remember this is a piece of written work you are showing your potential future tutor, so you will want to make it good! Do remember to make it 'personal.' As Jane Bennett-Rees, a former Schoolteacher Fellow at Magdalene College, Cambridge and now Lecturer of Mathematics at King's College London, says, 'Your personal statement should come from the heart. Why do you love Maths? What is it about this subject that really grabs you?' Remember, admissions tutors have seen thousands of personal statements (and can tell if it is the work of someone else), but they have not seen yours.

'But I am just not good with words!'

Ah! Such words of exasperation were uttered by one applicant we spoke to last year. Rest assured that you are not alone. Most applicants find starting the personal statement tricky! A good way to start can be to ask yourself a series of thought-provoking questions to help you focus your thoughts and ideas, and get your creative juices flowing.

We've put together some questions you might want to ask yourself. One of the many attributes that Oxbridge admissions tutors look for in successful applicants is an ability to think independently, so before rushing off to ask someone what they think is your greatest achievement, try to jot down your own thoughts first (you can always talk them through with someone who knows you afterwards).

What really excites you about studying your chosen course/s at university and why? (Remember, you may not be applying to the same course at every university).

What do you think is your greatest academic achievement to date and why, both inside and outside of the classroom?

What do you think makes a good undergraduate for your chosen course and why do you think you would make an excellent candidate?

What part of your current studies has most inspired you and why?

What books or articles have you recently read? (The same questions can be applied to work experience and extra-curricular activities).

What did you enjoy about them? What do you feel you learned from reading them? (Think about what challenged you, or whether anything surprised you). Did you agree or disagree with the author/s? Did the particular book/article make you want to learn more about a certain subject? If so, what exactly?

If you are applying for a course that you have not studied at A level, for example Law or Philosophy, it's important to show that you have an understanding of the subject and the course. Admissions tutors want to see that you have made an effort to get to grips with it and that you know what you are committing yourself to.

You might want to ask yourself: What is your understanding of your chosen course? What have you read and/or done to help further your understanding of this chosen course? How do you think your current academic subjects, support your chosen course and will help to excel at university?

While you obviously won't be able to include everything in your personal statement (you only have 4,000 characters, including spaces, or 47 lines – whichever comes first), asking yourself these questions can help to clarify your motivations for choosing your university course and your understanding of it. Your personal statement really needs to show that you want to study the course and that you would thrive in an academic environment.

So how to do I fit everything in?

Relevance is key – trying to talk about everything can lead to not talking about anything in enough detail. You can also assume a certain level of knowledge in the reader. For example, you can assume that the reader knows about the Duke of Edinburgh Award Scheme, so you do not need to tell them what this is.

Your personal statement must show your ability to organise your thoughts clearly and concisely. The structure of your personal statement will determine how easy it is for the reader to understand and process the points you are making. Think of your personal statement as an essay – with a beginning, middle and end. You begin by introducing your hypothesis that you will make a good student of the subject you are applying for. You then provide evidence for your hypothesis in the form of a series of well-explained examples. You may end the statement by revisiting your hypothesis and concluding that the evidence you have given proves it to be true.

While, as we said earlier, there is no set formula when it comes to writing the statement, a good basic template is as follows:

First paragraph

An introduction as to why this subject is the one that inspires and motivates you enough to want to spend the next three or four years of your life (potentially more) studying. You need to support your points with personal examples, and avoid falling into the trap of broad clichés. Everyone wants to study history because the past informs the present, but why does that matter to you? What have you read, seen, experienced that's made you realise it's essential that you study history? Think creatively about the opening sentence – you want your introduction to capture the reader's attention. You want it to reflect why you stand out.

Second paragraph

An honest account of the specific academic areas of interest you have and any extra-curricular activities you have undertaken to explore your subject in greater depth. This is where you can convey your commitment, dedication and enthusiasm for your subject both within and outside of the classroom. Use this section to discuss areas of your own interest – one the best ways to make your personal statement, 'personal'. Medical and law applicants may want to draw on their work experience, an Archaeology student on a school trip or dig. You need to show you have an understanding of the subject and that have the right skills and abilities to excel in undergraduate studies. Constantly keep in mind what an admissions tutor would look for in a personal statement for your chosen course. Demonstrate your ability to analyse experiences, not just tell a story. The first and second paragraphs should take up approximately three quarters of the statement.

Third paragraph

Here you can shift to extra-curricular activities not directly related to your course, however, a word of advice – please do not slip into listing your achievements. This is not just about saying how amazing you are at everything. This is about revealing why your activities would make you an interesting applicant for the admissions tutors to get to know and teach for the next few years. Think about what you have done – how has it helped you to develop as an individual. If you are applying for Maths, have you reached the Olympiad round of the UK Mathematical Challenge or have you just been crowned chess Grand Master? Think how your achievements reflect your personality, talent and intellect, and help strengthen your application for that particular subject.

Fourth paragraph

A good conclusion, as with the opening sentence, will refer directly to what you have said in your statement without repeating it. Like a good essay, returning to and building on the opening sentence works well.

You will not get your personal statement right first time, which is okay; something like this will take time. The process of re-drafting is important as it allows you to link the different elements of your statement together so give yourself plenty of time to go back to it, but at the same time know when to stop. Many a promising personal statement has been spoiled by excessive tinkering. Have the confidence to say – it's done!

And finally...here are some handy top personal statement tips from a former admissions tutor:

"

1. Be Honest. NEVER suggest knowledge that you haven't got, or refer to a book you haven't read. By mentioning something in your personal statement, you are inviting the interviewer to bring it up in interview. Be sure you are prepared for this possibility.
2. Remember this is a PERSONAL statement. Write what you want the reader to hear about you, not what you think they want to hear, otherwise it will ring false.
3. Keep the emphasis on your academic interests, achievements and goals. While the universities are interested in your extra-curricular activities and want to see the whole person, the primary concern is your academic motivation and potential and this should occupy most of the statement.
4. Avoid over-use of superlatives. It is believable that you are 'fascinated' and 'committed' to your subject but not 'completely fascinated' and 'utterly committed'.
5. There is a fine line between sounding confident and sounding arrogant. To say: 'I am a talented and determined student and am confident that I will succeed academically,' sounds arrogant. To say: 'I hope that I can build on my present achievements and develop academically' sounds modestly confident.
6. Avoid being too 'informal'. Making jokes is dangerous and likely to strike the wrong note, sound over-confident and fail to impress.
7. Avoid just listing books read or places visited without showing the relevance of each. One clear reference to the specific benefit that one book has brought you is worth more than a long list of books that you happen to have read.
8. It is not essential to say what you may want to do after your degree, however if it is related to the subject, for example a career in academia, you may want to add this in.
9. Beware of being too anecdotal. By all means write about personal, relevant experiences, but balance this with a degree of objectivity.
10. Try to make the statement as fluent as possible. It is likely to be the first impression the university has of you before interview. You want them to see that you can write with clarity and precision.

"

And remember, while the personal statement can take a good deal of your time, do keep reminding yourself that this is the chance to write about a very interesting subject, that no one else will be writing about - YOU!

4. The Oxbridge application process

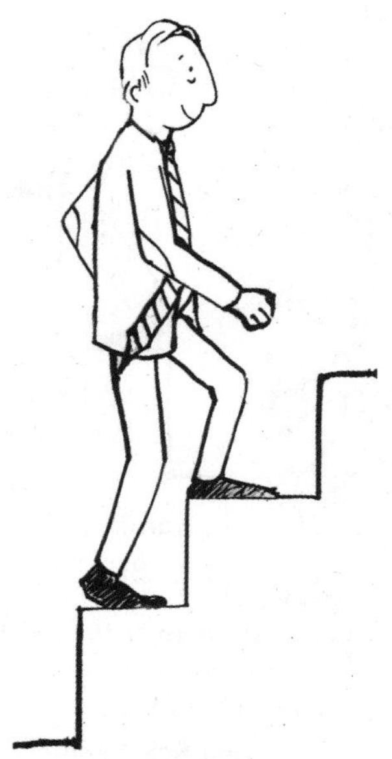

A step-by-step guide (literally).

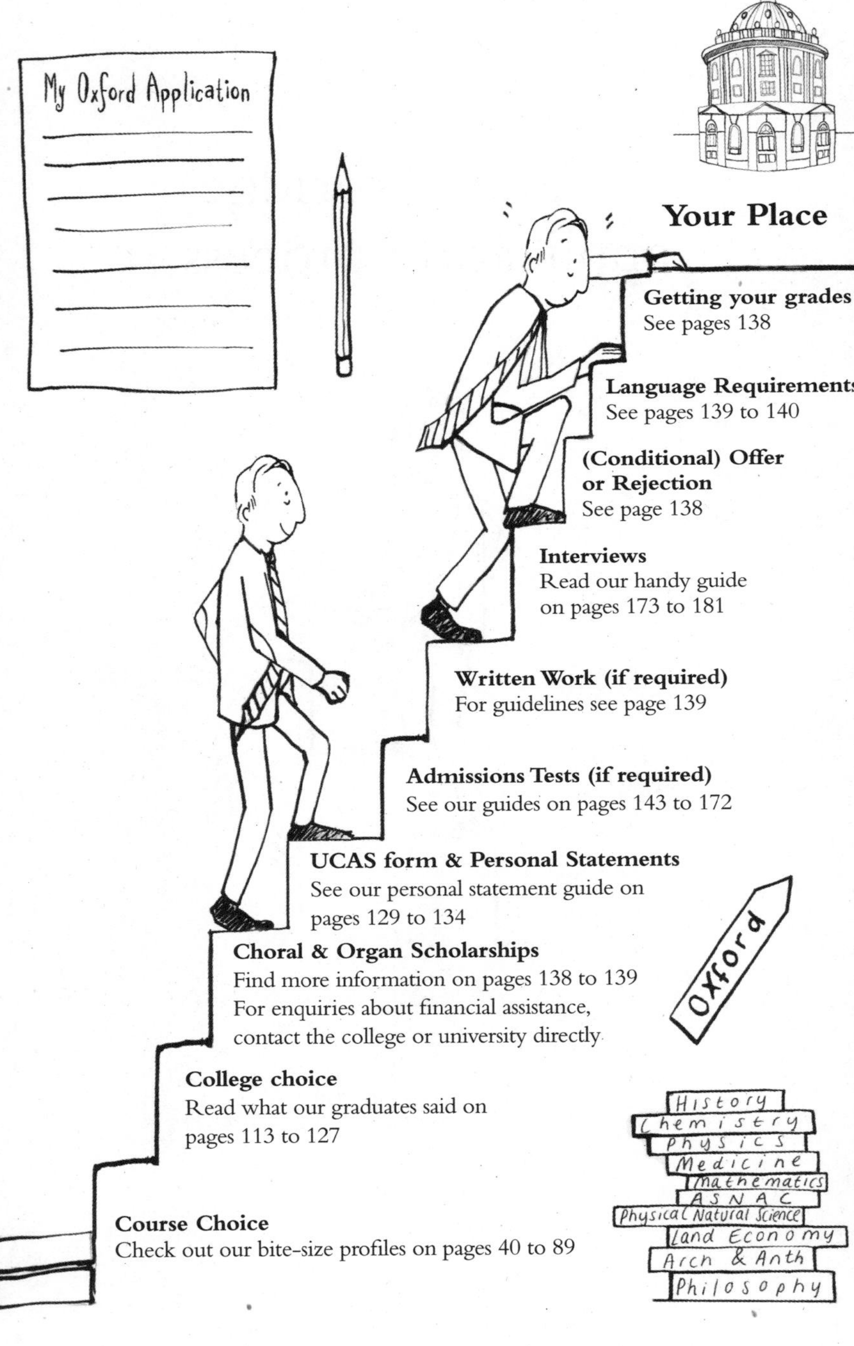
My Oxford Application
Your Place
Getting your grades
See pages 138
Language Requirements
See pages 139 to 140
(Conditional) Offer
or Rejection
See page 138
Interviews
Read our handy guide
on pages 173 to 181
Written Work (if required)
For guidelines see page 139
Admissions Tests (if required)
See our guides on pages 143 to 172
UCAS form & Personal Statements
See our personal statement guide on
pages 129 to 134
Choral & Organ Scholarships
Find more information on pages 138 to 139
For enquiries about financial assistance,
contact the college or university directly
College choice
Read what our graduates said on
pages 113 to 127
Course Choice
Check out our bite-size profiles on pages 40 to 89
Oxford
History
Chemistry
Physics
Medicine
Mathematics
ASNAC
Physical Natural Science
Land Economy
Arch & Anth
Philosophy

Your Place

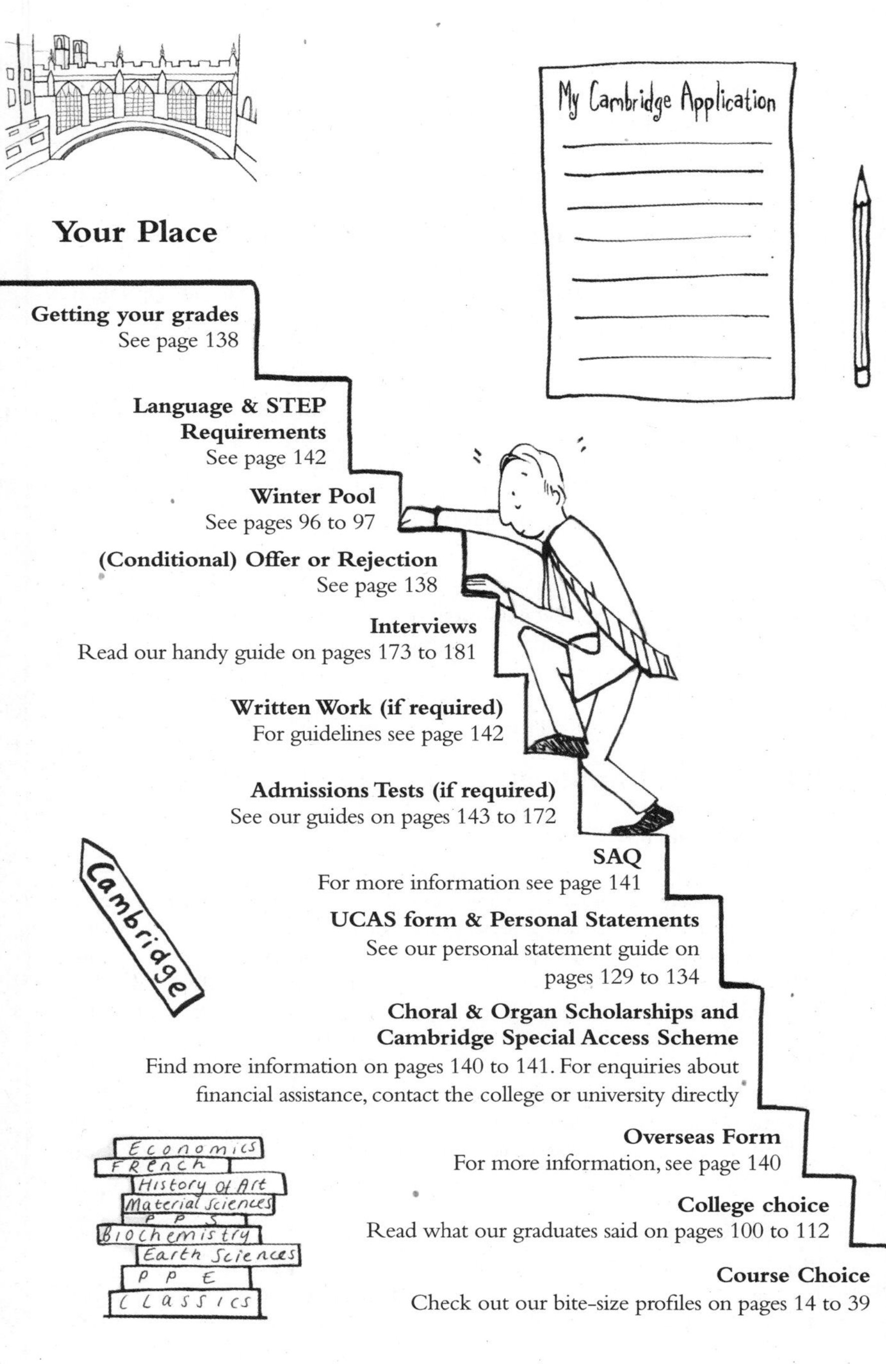

Getting your grades
See page 138

Language & STEP Requirements
See page 142

Winter Pool
See pages 96 to 97

(Conditional) Offer or Rejection
See page 138

Interviews
Read our handy guide on pages 173 to 181

Written Work (if required)
For guidelines see page 142

Admissions Tests (if required)
See our guides on pages 143 to 172

SAQ
For more information see page 141

UCAS form & Personal Statements
See our personal statement guide on pages 129 to 134

Choral & Organ Scholarships and Cambridge Special Access Scheme
Find more information on pages 140 to 141. For enquiries about financial assistance, contact the college or university directly

Overseas Form
For more information, see page 140

College choice
Read what our graduates said on pages 100 to 112

Course Choice
Check out our bite-size profiles on pages 14 to 39

While Oxford and Cambridge share many steps in the application process, some aspects are dealt with differently. Our guide below runs through some specific details and where to find out more information.

UCAS Form

Applicants to Oxford and Cambridge must submit their UCAS form by 15th October. On the form, you need to specify which college and course you wish to apply to. Universities will not be told which other universities you are applying to. You can find the UCAS form on the website: www.ucas.ac.uk

Offer

After your interview, the college or department will send you a letter letting you know the outcome of your application. If you have been successful, the letter will make you an offer and these usually have academic conditions attached e.g. A level results or STEP requirements.You will receive your offer sometime between mid-December and 31st January.

Grades

You must achieve the grades set out in your conditional offer in order to secure your place. If you do miss your grades by a couple of marks, or if special circumstances affected your performance, get in contact with your College as soon as possible to see whether they might still be able to accept you.

The Oxford application process

Organ Scholarship

The deadline for the Organ Scholarship Application Form is 1st September. Auditions usually take place in Oxford from 22nd to 24th September. Academic interviews happen at the same time, so you should be ready to submit your written work when you apply as it will be requested soon afterwards. Organ scholarship offers and academic places are then confirmed before the UCAS deadline. You must accept any scholarship offer you are made by a college, even if it was not your first choice. Offers will then be made formally through UCAS. Organ Scholars can apply to both Oxford and Cambridge and to more than one college but must specify only one choice on their UCAS form. For more information on which colleges are offering scholarships and the form, see the Oxford website page: www.ox.ac.uk/admissions/undergraduate_courses/how_to_apply/scholarships/organ.html

Choral Scholarship

The deadline for the Choral Scholarship Application Form is 1st September. Choral trials usually take place on 20th and 21st September. Those who are successful are not guaranteed an academic place. Both successful and unsuccessful applicants should submit their UCAS application in the usual way. Unsuccessful applicants for the choral scholarship may still gain an academic place. If you are unsuccessful with your application for a choral scholarship, but receive an academic offer, there may be an opportunity when you arrive to re-apply to a particular choir. For more information on which colleges are offering scholarships and the form, see the Oxford website page: www.ox.ac.uk/admissions/undergraduate_courses/how_to_apply/scholarships/choral.html

Overseas Interviews

International applicants apply through UCAS in the same way as any other student and have the same deadline of 15th October. If your application is shortlisted you will be invited to interview. All applicants for Medicine and Fine Art must attend the interview if they would like their application to be considered. Applicants for all other subjects must attend the interview if they live in Europe, but can choose to interview by telephone, video conference, or over the internet if they live outside of Europe. Oxford's website has some useful information explaining the application process for overseas applicants: www.ox.ac.uk/admissions/undergraduate_courses/international_students/interviews.html

Written work

Depending on which course you are applying to, you may have to submit written work. The deadline for Oxford is usually 10th November. Written work must be:

- No longer than 2000 words
- Produced as part of normal school work
- Marked by your teacher
- Typed or (legibly) hand-written
- Submitted with a covering sheet which can be downloaded here: http://www.ox.ac.uk/admissions/undergraduate_courses/how_to_apply/written_work/written_work.html

Your written work should be of a high standard and on a subject that you are reasonably well informed on, as your essay may form the basis of your interview. Oxford is as interested in how you are taught and how you respond to feedback so don't be too dismayed if you have made mistakes. You can see Oxford's guidelines on written work at: www.ox.ac.uk/admissions/undergraduate_courses/how_to_apply/written_work/index.html

English Language Requirements

All non-native English-speaking applicants must pass an English language test to the standard required by Oxford by 31st August of the year that you want to start your course. There are several different tests that Oxford will accept. You only need to satisfy one of the following requirements.

- IELTS – overall score of 7.0 with at least 7.0 in each of the four components)
- TOEFL (paper-based): overall score of 600 with a Test of Written English score of 5.5
- TOEFL (internet-based): overall score of 100
- Cambridge Certificate of Advanced English (CAE): grade A
- Cambridge Certificate for Proficiency in English (CPE): grade B
- International Baccalaureate Standard level (SL) : score of 5 in English
- European Baccalaureate: score of 70% in English

If you have been in full time education in the English language throughout the most recent two years before the application deadline and you remain so, you will not have to sit the test. Oxford's website has some useful information for their English Language Requirements: www.ox.ac.uk/admissions/undergraduate_courses/courses/courses_and_entrance_requirements/english_language.html

The Cambridge application process

Cambridge Overseas Application Form

International applicants must submit their UCAS application form to UCAS by the relevant deadline (depending on which country they would like to be interviewed in). Applicants who are living in countries outside the EU (including Switzerland and Norway) must complete and submit a COAF, that must be received by the relevant admissions office in Cambridge by the relevant deadline. To find out what your deadline is and where to send your form see the information included on the COAF. Deadlines vary from 1st August to 15th October. The COAF can be found on the Cambridge Admissions website or by contacting the college you wish to apply to. You will need to make a payment of £25 in order to proceed, so make sure you do this in plenty of time. Cambridge provides very thorough information to complete the form, which you can find with the form. The COAF can be found here: www.cam.ac.uk/admissions/undergraduate/apply/forms/coaf.pdf.

Organ Scholarships

The deadline for the Organ Scholarship Application Form is 1st September. Auditions are usually held in Cambridge from 19th-22nd September. Cambridge requires you to enclose a copy of your personal statement (or working draft) with your Organ Scholarship Application Form. Academic interviews happen at the same time, so you should be ready to submit your written work (if required) when you apply as it may be requested soon afterwards. Organ scholarship offers and academic places are then confirmed before the UCAS deadline. You must accept any scholarship offer you are made by a college, even if it was not your first choice. Offers will then be made formally through UCAS. In some cases, applicants may be asked to return in December for a further interview. Organ Scholars can apply to both Oxford and Cambridge and to more than one college but must specify only one choice on their UCAS form. For more information on which colleges are offering scholarships and the form, see the Cambridge website page: www.cam.ac.uk/admissions/undergraduate/musicawards/organ.html

Choral Scholarships

The deadline for the Choral Scholarship Application Form is 4th September. Auditions are usually held from 27th–30th September. Cambridge requires you to enclose a copy of your personal statement (or working draft) with your Choral Scholarship Application Form. King's and St John's Colleges hold academic interviews at this time, and some colleges hold academic screenings, but most choral award applicants have a separate academic interview in December, once they have completed their UCAS application. Those who are successful are not guaranteed an academic place. Both successful and unsuccessful applicants should submit their UCAS application in the usual way. Unsuccessful applicants for the choral scholarship may still gain an academic place. For more information on which colleges are offering scholarships and the form, see the Cambridge website page: www.cam.ac.uk/admissions/undergraduate/musicawards/

Cambridge Special Access Scheme

The scheme is designed for applicants whose predicted grades are lower than Cambridge requirements due to personal or social disadvantages, but who have the potential and the motivation to successfully follow a course at Cambridge. The deadline for the form is 15th October. You must return it to the college you are applying to or the Cambridge Admissions Office if you are making an open application. You are eligible for the scheme if few people from your school go on to higher education, your family has little or no tradition of study for a degree or your education has been severely disrupted for health or personal problems. You can find the form and more information on Cambridge's website: www.cam.ac.uk/admissions/undergraduate/apply/csas.html

The Supplementary Application Questionnaire (SAQ)

The SAQ deadline will most likely be the 22nd October, but keep checking the Cambridge Undergraduate Admissions website. The form is designed to collate information about applicants and make sure it is complete and consistent. It also gathers information that is not asked on the UCAS form but is helpful when assessing applications, such as individual module marks in AS and/or A levels. You will receive an email with the details you need to complete the SAQ form. The information about the SAQ and deadline dates can be found here: www.cam.ac.uk/admissions/undergraduate/apply/saq.html

Written work

Depending on the course you are applying for you may be asked to submit written work. This may be one or two pieces. There is no official word count for the written work. It is best to contact the college you wish to apply to for their guidelines. Written work must be:

- Produced as part of normal school work
- Marked by your teacher

Your written work should be of a high standard and on a subject that you are reasonably well informed on, as your essay may form the basis of your interview. Cambridge is as interested in how you are taught and how you respond to feedback so don't be too dismayed if you have made mistakes. Cambridge has more information on their website, which you can find here: www.cam.ac.uk/admissions/undergraduate/apply/tests.html

STEP Requirements

Sixth Term Examination Papers in Mathematics consists of three papers, which give Cambridge additional information to A level grades. The questions test your insight, originality, grasp of broader issues in your subject and the ability to apply what you know to more complex or unusual situations. STEP is used by colleges as part of a conditional offer. Some colleges may require it for other courses in addition to Maths such as Computer Science, Engineering or Natural Sciences. Your application to take STEP should be organised through your school or college. You can find out more at www.stepmathematics.org.uk or by contacting the STEP support team at Cambridge on 01223 558455.

English Language Requirements

If English is not your first language and you are not educated in English you will need to obtain one of the following formal qualifications. The deadline to present the certificate to Cambridge is 31st August of the year you want to start your course.

- GCSE in English Language/IGCSE English Language (as a first language): grade C
- IELTS: with at least a 7.0 in each component
- Cambridge Certificate in Advanced English: grade A
- Cambridge Certificate of Proficiency in English: grade A or B
- For EU students, a high grade in English taken as part of a leaving examination (eg. Baccalaureate or Abitur)

To find out more, have a look at Cambridge's website: www.cam.ac.uk/admissions/undergraduate/international/requirements.html

5. Admissions tests

Where, what, why…and how to prepare.

"The time constraints...
The fact you could not revise for it...
It was so hard to understand what the questions were actually asking...
Fear of the unknown..."

These are just some of the concerns expressed by some of last year's applicants as to what were, in their opinion, the most difficult aspects of the Oxbridge admissions tests.

Over the past few years, admissions or 'aptitude' tests have become an increasingly important part of the application process for a number of subjects at Oxford and Cambridge. Admissions tests have been introduced to help the university differentiate between applicants, in subjects for which a high number of students apply. They also help to differentiate between the rising number of students who obtain top As, and now A*s at A level and equivalent. The tests also give tutors the opportunity to assess an applicant's ability, thought process and academic potential on paper, much like the interview does in an oral context.

As a number of the tests are relatively new, such as the Cambridge Law Test, applicants may find the 'unknown' factor a rather nerve-wracking part. Compared with normal school exams at A level or equivalent, where there are numerous past papers to go through and guidelines on how they are marked, applicants are unclear about how admissions tests are used in the selection process.

When it comes to approaching the admissions tests, regardless of which subject you are applying for, it is important to remember that the tests, like the interview, are not designed to trap you. They have been carefully written to test key abilities – logical, independent and analytical thought. The tutors want to see how you tackle questions and problems that are very different from your normal school work. They are testing your academic potential and intelligence – not your existing knowledge about a particular topic or subject.

Mark Shepherd is a practising lawyer, author of *Mastering the National Admissions Test for Law*, and has conducted a number of Oxbridge Applications' seminars for students on the LNAT. He believes it is impossible to underestimate the benefit of being familiar with the format of the test. Over 90% of over three hundred applicants we spoke to rated their admissions test difficult or very difficult. The majority of applicants found that practising the types of questions that they might face in the test helped to build up their confidence – which in turn, they felt, led to a stronger performance when it came to the real thing. A number of teachers we have spoken to suggest students look at the A level Critical Thinking exam papers to help them prepare for some tests, most notably the Thinking Skills Assessment, required for a number of subjects at both Oxford and Cambridge (albeit with a slightly different format at each university).

When it comes to preparing for the admissions tests, much like other exams, every applicant will approach the process slightly differently. What matters, however, is that you prepare in the way that makes you feel the most confident – so that when it comes to the real test, nerves do not get the better of you.

On the following pages we have put together our research and top tips on tackling the admissions tests - test by test.

Our top tips (from those who have sat the tests and succeeded!):

Know the test you need to take

This will allow you to consider what you will have to do in order to prepare effectively beforehand.

Know the structure and format of the test

This will enable you to work on your examination technique. Think about your strengths and weaknesses in relation to the test and how you can improve upon these. Think about the timing of the test and how you usually react to time pressure. Plan your approach. It is very important to know how you will navigate your way through the paper. Familiarity with the structure will help you to relax in the test itself.

Practise the core skills required in the test

Most of the tests are about analysis rather than factual knowledge. Think about this. Avoid doing reams of unstructured preparation because good sense and planning are more important. Should you practise analysing language/pieces in the newspaper/numeracy/questions employing GCSE Physics?

Remember the bigger picture

It's all too easy to compartmentalise parts of the application process – the personal statement, the admissions tests and the interview. Admissions tutors want to see how you think, whether you are going to thrive in the one-to-one supervision/tutorial environment. They want to see genuine academic motivation and potential at all stages of the process – so try to keep that thought in your head.

Our next section goes into details about a number of admissions tests, including advice from successful applicants on what they would do if they had to do it all again. We've included as many tests as we could, but we do advise that you always check the individual test and university websites for all the latest test updates, including dates, timings, deadlines and structure of the tests.

The BMAT (BioMedical Admissions Test)

Test format
The BMAT is a two hour pre-admission test in three sections.

Section 1 (60 minutes): Aptitude and Skills (9 marks)
There are 35 multiple choice questions with four possible answers. The test is designed to examine numeracy, verbal reasoning, problem-solving and data analysis.

Section 2 (30 minutes): Scientific Knowledge and Application (9 marks)
There are 27 multiple choice questions with five possible answers. This section is designed to test science and maths knowledge up to and including GCSE Double Science and Maths.

Section 3 (30 minutes): Writing Task
You have to pick one question out of a choice of four and write a short essay. This tests your ability to construct an argument in a logical and coherent way and use evidence to support your points.

(Tests are marked on a scale of 0 – 5 for content and A, C or E for quality of written English. Tests are double marked and moderated to read an average score - for example if a test was awarded 2C by one examiner and 1E by another the final grade would be 1.5D).

Do I have to sit it?
You do if you are applying to Cambridge, Imperial, Oxford, The Royal Veterinary College or UCL for a Biomedical Science course (Medicine, Biomedical Sciences, Pharmacology and Veterinary Medicine).

When do I have to register?
You can register at any time between 1st September and 30th September.

How do I register?
Through a test centre - most likely your school. If you are an international student or if you are applying as an individual, you need to register with another test centre.

When do I sit it?
You usually sit the BMAT in early November. In 2010, you must take the test on 3rd November at 9am.

When do I get my results?
You usually receive your results in late November (in 2010, on 24th November).

In 2009, the average BMAT score for 2009 was 4.7, 4.7 and 7.6. (The essay section was scored differently and marked out of 15).

Although the BMAT does include a section on science (section 2), the different sections together are really testing your ability to handle large amounts of information quickly and efficiently. Solid logic and ability to reason are far more important than 'knowledge'.

Kirsty successfully applied to read Medicine at Cambridge in 2009. Like many applicants who sit the BMAT, the most difficult thing she found about the test was the timing. 'You get so little time for each question, it is so hard to get the timing right so that you finish the paper.' Many applicants feel that there is simply not enough time to finish the paper to the best of their ability.

While of course you should aim to complete the whole test, as timing is tight, the first two sections are multiple choice with no negative marks, (in other words, you cannot decrease your score for incorrect answers), so you should really try to aim to get every single box ticked before the end of the exam. That way, even if you have to make an educated guess, (or simply a last-minute tick of any one box) there could be a good chance your answer is correct.

With regard to section 1, medical students we spoke to from both Oxford and Cambridge advised that it can be helpful to draw diagrams to assist you instead of solving problems in your head. Jotting something down on paper can be a simple yet highly effective way to work through a question.

They also advise looking out for text-based critical thinking problems, otherwise known as 'best answer questions', where many possible answers could be correct, but only one is the most appropriate. Some applicants find this a particularly difficult aspect of the test, as these questions require real attention to detail and concentration and can take a little longer to work through. This can be a little stressful when you are conscious of time constraints.

A great way to practise these types of questions, and the BMAT as a whole, is to work through past papers so that you know the style of questions beforehand. 'I was fortunate to receive quite a lot of support for the BMAT from school,' says Kirsty, 'and my teachers gave me a lot of really helpful information. They said that we should be aiming for marks above 50% in the multiple choice sections and at least a 9 in the essay. My brother is a medic at Oxford and sat the BMAT two years earlier, so he was well-placed to give me some tips. He said that I should focus on the first two sections as this is what universities look at, but I think that Oxford and Cambridge use it differently.'

Section 2 is the science section. 'If I had to do the BMAT again,' Kirsty says, 'I would brush up on some simple Physics formulae from GCSE as I got stuck on a few really simple questions.' This is echoed by another successful applicant who also applied to read Medicine at Cambridge. He found the science components of section 2 of the BMAT to be particularly difficult, especially as he had not taken Physics at A level. 'I was advised the BMAT would test up to GCSE level only, but I felt that the standard of the exam was much higher, although that could also have been because it had been over a year since I had looked at any of my revision notes.'

In section 2, when it comes to working through the questions, a useful tip is to look out for shortcuts. If a complicated calculation is given, but there is a hidden common denominator, being able to spot this will help you to answer the question quickly and accurately. Indeed, as was said by one admissions test consultant who helps students prepare for admissions tests: 'Often if you can find that shortcut, you can save minutes – which in the BMAT, (and all the admissions tests, in fact) is a very long time!' To help you to become more adept at finding those shortcuts, practise simple mental arithmetic - to keep that part of your brain working quickly and efficiently and then try to spot these shortcuts in practice papers.

Section 3 is the essay section, and you need to show that you can structure a good argument in a logical way, drawing on specific examples and evidence to support your points. You need to find a balance between writing concisely and ensuring that you bring in detailed evidence to back up your arguments. Once again, going through questions from past exam papers, and mock tests online can help when it comes to preparing for this section.

'It may sound silly,' as Kirsty says, 'but one of the most important things when it comes to the BMAT is to stay calm! The test is pretty intense, and you don't have time to re-read the question, or be able to plan out your essay as you would like if you had more time. The key thing is not to panic, keep a cool head and remember all the students taking the test will be anxious, just as you may be. The BMAT is a test, different from all school exams, and once you accept that you are going to find parts of it challenging, that should actually (and somewhat ironically) put you at ease.'

The Cambridge Language Test

Test format

The Cambridge Language Test is a 45 minute test in which applicants have to read a passage in English (of approximately 300 to 350 words) and write a short essay (200 to 250 words) in the target language, answering two questions on the passage. You only have to do the test in one language that you have been studying at school. If you are applying for two languages, both of which you studied at school, you can choose which language to answer in.

Do I have to sit it?

You will have to sit the Language Test if you are applying for Modern & Medieval

Languages. Most Cambridge Colleges use this test, but check with the college you want to apply to whether they will set their own test.

When do I have to register?

You are automatically registered to take the Language Test when you apply through UCAS to a college and course which requires it. The college will arrange for you to sit the test.

When do I sit it?

You sit the Language Test when you go up for interview.

When do I get my results?

Results are not published, they are reviewed by the college you applied to.

Many applicants we spoke to find the hardest aspect of the Cambridge Language Test is the fact that there is a limit to the amount of practice you can do beforehand, and therefore you feel unprepared. Claudia, who successfully applied for French & Italian at Cambridge and sat the Language Test, believes the test has been designed so that it is very hard to prepare for it. Having spoken to a number of Cambridge graduates, there are a few fundamental things you can do to help you stand out.

The test is both a straightforward comprehension exercise showing you have understood the information in the article, and then a more complex composition. Some of last year's applicants actually found the English passage rather challenging. A key thing to remember however is that those individuals marking the test will be looking at good grammar, accuracy and self expression. 'The nature of the test is that you can make the standard as high or as low as you want', says Claudia. 'The tutors aren't too interested in what you know, which is why applicants should not worry if the passage that they are presented with is on a topic for which they do not have a strong vocabulary. It's all too easy to forget tutors do actually want to teach you when you come up! You are not supposed to have all the answers now.

In this test, what they want to see is how you use what you know. That being the case, my advice is to be brave and don't be afraid to be yourself in the more personal questions. My top tips would be to try to make your work as interesting as possible – illustrate your ability to use diverse sentence structures and interesting phrases and demonstrate how you can manipulate the language you know to fulfil your needs.' Claudia's advice is echoed by a number of other successful applicants and graduates. 'You should try to make your answers as interesting as possible to ensure that you stand out from the crowd. You need to look at the links in the texts and synthesise it all together rather than just explaining exactly what is being said.'

'At the same time,' says Claudia, 'like any test, it is really important that you don't make silly mistakes, so make sure you have time to read your work through really thoroughly so that you catch any errors.' And, a final tip, in the weeks before your admissions test and interview, brush up on your verb endings, agreements and tenses. Our research shows this proves far more fruitful than trying to second guess what topic might come up and learning reams of specialist vocabulary you may never need to know.

The Cambridge Law Test

Test format

The Cambridge Law Test is a one hour test in which candidates have to answer one question out of a choice of three different options:

Essay questions

You are given a statement of opinion which you will have to consider and discuss. You will be asked to give reasons for your answer. This assesses your ability to give opinions in a coherent, structured and balanced way.

Problem questions

You are given a statement of law which you then have to apply to different factual situations. This assesses your ability to understand and apply the statement and explain your reasoning.

Comprehension questions

You are given a passage of text which you have to summarise and then answer questions on. This assesses your ability to understand the text and present balanced, structured arguments.

Up until 2009, Cambridge Law applicants were required to sit the LNAT. The test was changed partly because a study, commissioned by Cambridge's Faculty of Law and colleges at the university, found that the numerical scores awarded to applicants in the multiple choice section of the LNAT did not necessarily correlate to a student performing significantly better in Cambridge's Tripos exams. As a result, the university came to the conclusion that it would be more appropriate to create and manage a university law test, excluding a multiple choice section and at no extra cost to applicants.

Do I have to sit it?

You do if you are applying to Cambridge for Law at any of the Colleges except Churchill, Hughes Hall, St. Edmund's and Wolfson, which set their own tests at interview.

When do I have to register?

You are automatically registered for the Cambridge Law Test by applying for undergraduate law at most colleges in Cambridge.

When do I sit it?
All candidates called for interview will sit the Cambridge Law Test during the interview period in Cambridge. If you are from overseas and you are not coming to interview in Cambridge, you can sit the test in a test centre. Contact Cambridge for more information.

When do I get my results?
Results are not published. Your script goes directly to the college you applied to.

While the Cambridge Law test was new for 2009, and therefore something of an 'unknown,' there are things you can do so that you feel more prepared for the real thing. The test is designed to assess your ability to create a coherent, structured argument on paper – much like the interview does in an oral context. Admissions tutors want to see how prospective applicants engage with material they have not seen before, and how they identify key themes and analyse the information provided to form a convincing, logical and sound argument.

'I think the most difficult thing is not knowing what type of questions you will be able to answer', says one recent Cambridge Law graduate we spoke to. She continued: 'Without a doubt you have to work quickly and concisely, as you might run out of time – much like the LNAT. Admissions tutors want to see budding law brains in action, they want applicants to conclusively argue their point.'

'Having looked at some of the sample papers provided for by the university, I can see how easy it could be for an applicant to get to the end and realise that their conclusion is weak,' says one Law graduate, 'but due to the time constraints, you cannot to go back and change your line of argument - once you've made a decision you have to stick to it!'

A key thing to remember, as always, is that there is no right or wrong answer. What matters is that an applicant supports their argument – fully, and to the end, even though the conclusion might be different to the one you had originally set out to reach. You should be prepared to encounter unforeseen problems as this is a very different test to your normal in-school examinations.

While no prior knowledge of the Law is required, and the university clearly states this, one Cambridge Law graduate we spoke to believes, just as is the case at interview, a good knowledge of current affairs (particularly in the area of the Law) is helpful. Having an understanding of what is going on in the world around you will help applicants to back up their argument with strong, pertinent examples. Most prospective applicants should be brushing up on their current affairs before the interview anyway, and so preparation for the test and interview go hand in hand! To read Law, it is essential applicants have the ability to see two (or more) sides to a discussion, and to argue from a detached point of view. When there are two situations that are similar but slightly different, a strong Law undergraduate should be able to recognise this and explain how they differ and discuss how to approach them. Where two situations are the same, applicants should be able to analyse these accordingly. Admissions tutors want to see applicants starting to think in this way, and if students keep this in mind when it comes to approaching this test (and the LNAT), it can help put the questions being asked into context.

The Classics Language Aptitude Test

Test Format

The Classics Language Aptitude Test (CLAT) is a one hour test, divided into three sections.

Section A (25 marks) requires candidates to answer questions on the structure and grammatical rules of existing languages, deducing the answers by analysing patterns in the language.

Section B (50 marks) requires candidates to translate and compose sentences in an invented language, building on the rules that they can deduce through the analysis of the language's structure.

Section C (25 marks) requires candidates to answer questions on linguistic features of the English language and explain the reasoning behind their answer.

Do I have to sit it?

You do if you are applying to Oxford to read Classics II (Latin or Greek only, not having previously studied the subject) Classics & Modern Languages, Classics II & English and Classics II & Oriental Studies.

When do I have to register?

You are automatically registered when you apply to Oxford to read a subject which requires the CLAT. If you are still at school the paper will be couriered to the school and you will sit the paper there. If you are no longer at school you need to find another test centre and nominate someone to communicate with the university.

When do I sit it?

You usually sit the Classics Language Aptitude Test in early November. In 2010, applicants must take the test on 3rd November.

When do I get my results?

Results are not published. Your script goes directly to the college you applied to. The CLAT was only extended to Classics (Course II) for 2010, but it is a similar test to the test for Classics II. This was previously sat at interview.

The test is designed to ascertain your ability to pick up language skills, and to recognise patterns and rules in languages. It's designed for Classics applicants who haven't studied Greek or Latin, to give the tutors an idea of how easily and confidently you'd be able to pick up ancient languages, since at least one of Greek and Latin has to be studied for all four years of the undergraduate degree.

One graduate we spoke to, who applied to read Classics & German at Oxford in 2009 sat a similar Classics Language Aptitude test at interview and remarked that the hardest thing about the test for him was the timing. 'The test was difficult because it is only an hour long, and there's an awful lot of information to digest in that time, even before you can begin to answer the questions! Being faced with unfamiliar and invented languages can be a bit daunting, and articulating your answers in a linguistic way can be challenging if you don't have much experience of learning a language. That said, everyone sitting the test is in the same boat, and if you find a certain aspect of the test hard, the chances are most applicants will too.'

A good way to prepare is to look at the specimen papers provided by the university, which are freely available on the website. This will help to familiarise yourself with the test format and structure, as it is unlike any test you will have encountered before. Some applicants find it helpful to get non-verbal reasoning books which train you to look for patterns. Don't worry if the test goes horribly wrong, it's just one part of the application/interview process, and you'll have an interview with a member of the language faculty after the test, where you'll review your answers together.

Toby advises not to panic at the unfamiliar languages: 'The test is designed to see how you look for rules and patterns, not how much vocabulary you can pick up in an hour. And more than anything,' Toby advice is to 'try to enjoy it: if you look at the test you'll see it's quite light hearted, and the tutors are just trying to get to know your mind rather than to torture you!'

And while this is by no means prescriptive reading for this test, Sarah, who read Medieval and Modern Languages at Oxford, suggests that applicants required to sit an Oxbridge language test, might find dipping into Steven Pinker's *'The Language Instinct'* useful, as this gets you thinking about the use of language. 'I first read Pinker's book when I was applying to read languages at university', says Sarah. 'I was initially quite sceptical about just how interesting a book ostensibly about grammar could be, but after a couple of paragraphs I was hooked. Pinker, a Harvard Psychologist by trade, asks whether language - and with it grammar - is in fact a universal instinct as natural and unique to us as web-weaving is to a spider. Pinker illustrates his theories with fascinating examples - why do children who are born speaking their parents' grammatically informal pidgin impose their own grammatical rules on it and turn it into a creole? Why does deaf babies' spontaneously invented sign-language always have a true grammar? Why do children never make certain seemingly obvious mistakes when they are learning to speak? Pinker's book made me re-examine the way I and everyone around me used language. What's more, it introduced me to other languages, which work completely differently to those I know and which still fascinate me today. In short, it got me thinking laterally about language, and I know this helped my understanding of my chosen course before, during and after my interview.'

The ELAT (English Literature Admissions Test)

Test Format

The ELAT is a 90 minute test in which students must write one essay comparing and contrasting two or three passages out of a choice of six. These texts are a mixture of poetry, prose, fiction and possibly non-fiction and are linked by a common theme.

Do I have to sit it?

You do if you are applying to Oxford for English Language & Literature, English & Classics (Course I and II) and English & Modern Languages.

When do I have to register?

You will be registered by your school or college. Check with your examinations officer when they are registering their students.

How do I register?

Through a test centre – most likely your school. To be certain, check with your examinations officer.

When do I sit it?

You usually sit the ELAT in early November. In 2010, you must take the test on 3rd November at 9am.

When do I get my results?

You will receive your results in early January. For tests taken in 2010 results will be released on 14th January 2011.

The ELAT tests your ability to synthesise unseen passages together and come up with a well-organised answer which contains interesting insights into the passages. There is definitely no right approach, or even a correct way of going about it. One of the hardest things applicants find about the test is the ability to formulate a logical, coherent argument in the limited time available. As one successful applicant from 2009 said, 'finding something useful and intuitive to say in the time, with little direction in the question was particularly challenging.'

'I was a little bit intimidated when I found out that the ELAT is marked by two different examiners', says David, who applied to read English at Oxford in 2009. 'I had no idea that you are judged on the combined mark – it suddenly felt a little less like a simple admissions test and more like a full blown exam! I also hadn't realised that it would be so decisive in determining who was invited for interview.' David continues, 'quite a few of us at my school took the test and, although we all had really similar AS level grades, we found out when we were told our marks, that everyone who got above about 42 was invited to interview and everyone who got below it was rejected without interview. I think we would all have worked a bit harder had we known.'

A good way to prepare for the ELAT is to look at sample papers, mock tests and also to brush up on the practical criticism skills, which you are already developing as part of your current studies. Good English applicants will be perceptive and open minded and in the ELAT, applicants need to show they can make links between extracts and present their ideas clearly.

As an undergraduate, tutors want English applicants to possess good analytical writing skills, an appreciation of language and textual analysis and the ability to place literary works in their historical and social contexts by doing outside reading. The ELAT is just one aspect of the application process, where prospective applicants need to demonstrate they have the potential to develop these analytical skills. It is essential therefore, that applicants do not just write commentary on the texts. You have to make sure you have an interesting and well-supported argument.

Another aspect of the test that applicants struggle with is to know which passages to pick, so that they work together as well as individually. One applicant recalled how, after sitting the test, he was worried because he had only looked at two of the passages, when everyone else he knew looked at three. 'This did not seem to matter in the end however, as I was still offered a place – this just shows there really is no right way of approaching the test!'

Our advice therefore to anyone taking the exam would be: don't be afraid to choose the texts you want to write about – you don't get fewer marks for a text which you think is easier. Also, as one Oxford English graduate says, 'once you've had a good idea, make sure you stick to it and ensure you pursue and continue to analyse your perceptive ideas to a logical conclusion.'

The HAT (History Aptitude Test)

Test format

The HAT is a two hour test in which you have to answer four questions based on two extracts.

Question one

This question is based on a piece of historical writing. The question has three parts, the first two of which are based on the piece of writing. These parts are designed to assess your understanding of the ideas and arguments and your ability to analyse the extract. The third part usually goes beyond the piece of writing and asks you to write a short essay on a specific topic within any period of history with which you are familiar.

Question two

The second question is usually based on a primary source, the contents of which you are asked to interpret without knowing the context. There is usually only one part to this section, which means you will be expected to write between one and two sides.

Do I have to sit it?

You do if you are applying to Oxford to read Modern History, History (Ancient & Modern), History & Economics, History & English, History & Modern Languages or History & Politics.

When do I have to register?

You are automatically registered for the HAT test when you apply to Oxford for any degree course involving History.

How do I register?

If you are applying through your school you should be able to sit it there. If you are applying as an individual you will need to register with a test centre.

When do I sit it?

You usually sit the HAT in early November. In 2010, on 3rd November at 9am.

When do I get my results?

Results are not published, but the scripts are marked internally by the college you are applying to.

The HAT tests your intelligence and your analytical skills as a historian rather than your knowledge of any particular historical period. It is very different to what you learn at school, which is why many students find it challenging. You have to find the theory from the evidence rather than being taught the theory and looking at evidence to support it. It's testing the most basic and natural skills of a historian, and while that might seem a little daunting, it actually makes it a really interesting test. Candidates are advised by the rubric to spend about a third of the examination time on reading, thinking and planning, and the rest of the time writing. Question one, which has three parts, should take about twice as much time as question two but the first two parts of question one only account for 30% of the marks so you should spend no longer than 30 minutes on them (including thinking and planning time).

Each question is based around a source, given in the paper. Question one is worth 70 marks and is broken into three parts, (each question worth 10, 20, 40 marks respectively) and the second is a 30 mark essay question. When it comes to answering question one, candidates should ensure they read the question thoroughly, paying special attention to the specific terms of the question. If you are asked to analyse a phrase or idea, it's important you spend enough time focused on this. A top tip from the historians we spoke to is to avoid extensive quotation from the extracts, if you have been asked to explain a particular statement. It will waste valuable time, and will not strengthen your argument. You should use your own words as much as possible – the examiners want to see how you think and express yourself, not how well you can paraphrase a source.

Once you have identified interesting ideas and themes in the source, a good applicant will ensure they argue their points, to a strong conclusion. Just as in your History A level or equivalent, the examiners want to see your ability to analyse a source critically, and not simply give a descriptive account of its content. This is exactly what they look for at interview, and it's the same skill that you employ in your personal statement. Admissions tutors don't want to read a list of things, they want the hows and the whys – they want to know what this is telling us, what it reveals, and why your points mean you are answering the question.

In the last part of question one, applicants will be asked to relate issues raised in the source to an example derived from their own historical knowledge. This is arguably the part that many applicants find difficult, as many applicants say that finding a topic from their own studies and relating it to a source can be hard. This part is designed to test your ability to think laterally, but also your ability to then analyse and structure a sound argument. The important thing is not to panic here, as an applicant from last year commented: 'the question was more geography-based than anticipated, which was a little off-putting at first, but once I took the time to really think about it, it actually ended up being ok. Think about what you have learned to date, and don't let nerves get the better of you.'

You may be asked, for example, to assess the development and/or effects of a unifying national or community identity in a society or period with which you are familiar or you might be asked to discuss a proposed relationship between economic decline and political unrest. The key thing to remember is that every fact or point you make about your chosen period must be strictly relevant. In the case of the latter, the French Revolution might be a good period on which to focus. If, however, your analysis strays from the 'let them eat cake' side of things into 'Tyrant' Maximilien Robespierre's fanaticism, you will begin to lose marks. This is not the time to show off how much you know, it's about deploying what you do know to form the meat of your theoretical argument.

Katie applied for History & German at Oxford and sat the HAT test in 2009. She says that in many ways 'to succeed in the HAT you have to approach it using different skills to those with which you would tackle your A level or equivalent History exam'. To do well, Oxford historians we have spoken to advise that you need to start by thinking philosophically about what history is and how it functions, as well as the role of the historian. 'I knew that the HAT test was an important part of the application process and that I needed to do well to get an interview', says Katie. 'Our teacher told us earlier this year (2010) that the bottom third were not invited to interview in 2009. I am glad I didn't know this when I took the test! I suppose it just reinforces the need to work hard.'

A good way to practise for the HAT is to look at past papers. Oxford's History Faculty currently has past papers freely available online including those from 2008 and 2009, coupled with an outline of the marking scheme. They have also produced a fantastic 'HAT, dos and don'ts' fact sheet, which can be found here: http://www.history.ox.ac.uk/prosundergrad/applying/documents/HAT-dosanddonts.pdf

At the start of the factsheet, Oxford explains that they have put this sheet together as they are aware some applicants receive extra help from their school when it comes to the HAT and so this sheet is there to help everyone beforehand. A good way you can prepare for the test is to practise applying the types of questions you might be asked to other sources. 'I asked my teacher to give me some unseen sources to look at which I found very helpful', says Katie. 'I also attended a seminar on the test, which helped to break it down. It was reassuring to hear someone talking about the test, and how you might approach certain questions. It helped to build up my confidence.'

In the final essay question, another piece of advice from historians is to ensure your answer is about the text in front of you. This is not the time to explore your own areas of interests – that's for the personal statement and extra reading! What you must do is ensure you use the information that's there. You need to explore your findings thoroughly, and make sure you do not stray from this. You need to analyse fully the extract in front of you. Spot interesting things, and then use your budding historical mind to answer the question. Just as is the case with your History A level or equivalent, avoid descriptive waffle. Tutors want to see that you can construct a strong argument and support your points wholeheartedly. An ability to analyse a source in this way demonstrates not only sharp analytical skills but also a real sense of passion and interest in history. 'Write clearly', says successful applicant Katie and 'don't be afraid to think independently – this is your chance to show your academic potential. Good luck!'

The LAT (Linguistic Aptitude Test)

Test Format

The Linguistic Aptitude Test (LAT) is a 30 minute test in which you have to answer grammatical and comprehension questions on a language invented for the test. You are given some basic rules on the grammar and translation of the invented language, for example, word order and articles to begin with and the rest you must deduce from the language.

Do I have to sit it?

You do if you are applying to Oxford to read Linguistics, Modern Greek, Italian, Portuguese, Russian & Spanish sole, or if you are doing any of these languages in conjunction with either Polish or Beginners Russian.

When do I have to register?

You are automatically registered when you apply to Oxford to read a subject which requires the LAT. If you are still at school the paper will be couriered to the school and you will sit the paper there. If you are no longer at school you need to find another test centre and nominate someone to communicate with the university.

When do I sit it?

You usually sit the Linguistics Aptitude Test in early November. In 2010, on 3rd November.

When do I get my results?

Results are not published. Your script goes directly to the college you applied to.

The LAT has only recently been extended to Modern Languages, but it is the same as the test taken for Linguistics in previous years. In short, it tests how well you can understand the building blocks of language; how you can find patterns in what seems like nonsense and then piece together a language, identifying the rules that hold it together as you go along.

While at first it can seem like an impossible task, it can actually be really fun once you've cracked the code. 'I think the hardest thing about the test', says one student who we spoke to, 'is being confronted by an unfamiliar language – especially if it has a different structure to the languages you are familiar with. I was really lucky in that I took German A level so I was familiar with the case system. People who hadn't learnt about cases as part of Latin, German or Russian A level found it much harder to spot the patterns in the sentences and to understand why the words were changing.' As with all admissions tests, the time limit is tough. It takes a while to get your head around the new language and there are a lot of questions to answer on it. It can therefore be helpful to practise analysing languages you know and also those with which you are unfamiliar. You'll be able to find exercises to work through in any good linguistics text book. 'I found the best way of preparing for the Linguistics Aptitude Test', says one applicant 'is to understand the real bones of language – why certain languages behave in one way and other languages do not. To do this you definitely need to understand the parts of the sentence, so I would brush up on cases.'

Finally, the most important thing is not to panic! Read the sentences a couple of times before you extrapolate any theories and make sure you get the basics right first – the test gets harder as it goes on. And just remember, if you find an element of the test difficult, so will many, if not most, applicants.

The LNAT (National Admissions Test for Law)

Test format
The LNAT is a two hour test for Law broken up into two sections.

Section A
This is a multiple choice section containing 42 questions for which you have 95 minutes. You are required to read 12 passages, each of which is followed by either three or four multiple choice questions (an increase from previous years in which the tests have comprised 30 questions in 80 minutes).

Section B
This is an essay section for which you have 40 minutes. You must write one essay from a choice of of up to five titles. Your essay should be between 500-600 words (no more than 750) and should demonstrate your ability to construct a logical and coherent argument in a succinct and focused way.

Do I have to sit it?
You do if you are applying for an undergraduate law course at Birmingham, Bristol, Durham, Glasgow, KCL, Nottingham, Oxford or UCL

When do I have to register?
You can register at any time from 2nd August to 15th October if you are applying for Oxford or 15th January if you are applying to another university.

How do I register?
You need to register online and book a slot at your Test Centre. Your teacher can register you with your consent.

When do I sit it?
Any time from 1st September to 1st November, if you are applying for Oxford. The deadline for other universities is 20th January.

When do I get my results?

The results of the muliple choice section and copies of your essay are passed directly to the relevant universities once you have sat the test. You will receive confirmation of your multiple choice results later (normally by 30th January if you have taken the test before 15th January deadline).

The LNAT is mostly testing your argument and analytical skills. You need to be able to think in a critical way, but also make sure that you can structure your thoughts well. Broadly speaking, the first part may be said to test your ability to process and digest the information presented in a text, and the second section to test your ability to formulate and structure, coherent and persuasive arguments.

'The difficult thing for most people,' notes Mark Shepherd, author of *Mastering the National Admissions Test for Law*, 'is the fact that the LNAT is something of an unknown quantity. Very often applicants have little or no idea what to expect when they come to sit the test. This doesn't immediately sound like it should be a problem given that the test comprises what sounds like a fairly innocuous combination of a reading comprehension and an essay section, but neither are directly comparable to those which might be encountered elsewhere in one's studies. The multiple choice questions, for example, place a heavy premium on analysis rather than factual understanding, whilst the required essay is often on a broad subject yet within very tight length and time constraints.'

'The hardest thing for me,' says one successful 2009 applicant we spoke to 'was that it was the first exam I took which I couldn't revise for. It isn't knowledge based so you can't really learn anything for it, but I knew it was important to do well in it.' In truth, there is little you can actually 'revise' in terms of content. However, as Shepherd points out, it is 'very easy to be lulled into a false sense of security by the fact that the LNAT does not demand any specific factual knowledge, but it is impossible to overestimate the benefit of being familiar with the format of the test. In particular, the multiple choice section contains a style of questions which are unfamiliar to most people and it is only after having done a few sample test papers that you really start to develop an understanding of what is actually being asked. This is particularly important given the time pressure that candidates are under in the test itself. The time that can be saved by knowing in advance what you're looking for is often the difference between finishing the test and leaving some questions unanswered.'

Successful applicants we spoke to found it was helpful to look over past papers. The LNAT website (www.lnat.ac.uk) is particularly helpful. As one applicant commented, 'you need to be really focused to the point where you're almost on a higher plane of concentration.' Familiarity with the test is therefore invaluable.

'I knew that the multiple choice section of the LNAT would be used as a tool for sorting who was invited to interview and who wasn't, so I aimed to do really well in that section,' says Josh who applied to read Law at Oxford in 2009. 'Most people got between 10 and 20. I achieved 22 in the end and I had thought that, with that sort of score, I was pretty much guaranteeing myself an interview, but another friend who got 21 didn't actually get an interview. At the same time a girl in my class who achieved a low score had been invited up in December.'

Josh's experiences show that the LNAT is just one aspect of the application process. Like many applicants, Josh found the multiple choice section the hardest. 'I've always found essay writing a bit easier so this wasn't too much of a problem. I know it gets sent to the college to be marked and I expected to be tested on it at interview, but it actually never came up – mostly we talked about my personal statement and my work experience at a barristers' chambers.'

When it comes to the multiple choice section, the difference between getting the answer right or wrong, depends on your understanding of the question and your comprehension of the passage. Successful Law students we spoke to say it can be helpful to deploy the following tactic – skim read the passage once, then read each the question carefully, and return to the section of text to which it refers for a more detailed analysis. While there are many different ways of reaching an answer, many applicants find it helpful to work through the five possible responses and eliminate those which cannot be correct, rather than searching for the right one immediately.

Remember that when answering these types of multiple questions, you must place language under the microscope. Just as is the case with the Cambridge Law Test (and even if you are applying to read Law at Oxford, we recommend you dip into our section on the Cambridge test) the LNAT tests your ability to identify assumptions, analogies and objective conclusions and a successful answer will depend upon the extent to which your mind can pick apart individual sentences and phrases to get at the core of their meaning.

When it comes to the essay, clarity and precision are more important than wit or flair. It is all to easy to forget that Law is a Social Science, not a Humanity, and therefore your answer should be detached and your arguments balanced. Now is not the time for opinionated waffle. A good way to practise for this section is to take a list of ten controversial topics and find points for and against in each case. See how quickly you can do this. Pay particular attention to the points on the side of the argument with which you instinctively disagree, and also see if you can find any middle ground or alternative to the proposition you are considering. This will get you into the good habit of objective thinking and teaches you to analyse arguments – in other words, it gets you thinking like a lawyer. Finding your own approach to planning essays, and learning to plot arguments both for and against a particular case, will, we believe, be more useful than writing endless unfocused mock essays.

The MAT (Maths Aptitude Test)

Test format

The Maths Aptitude Test is a two and a half hour test in two sections.

Question 1 (40 marks)

There are 10 multiple choice questions, each with four possible answers. Marks are only given for correct answers, although you are encouraged to show your working.

Questions 2-7 (60 marks)

Depending on which course they are applying for, candidates will answer four longer questions out of a possible six. Each question is worth 15 marks and marks will be given for correct working as well as correct answers. You must answer questions relating to your subject.

You are not allowed a calculator.

Do I have to sit it?

You do if you are applying to Oxford to read Mathematics, Maths & Stats, Maths & Philosophy, Maths & Computer Science or Computer Science.

When do I have to register?

You are automatically registered for the MAT test when you apply to Oxford for Mathematics, Computer Sciences and Mathematics & Joint Schools.

When do I sit it?

You usually sit the MAT in early November. In 2010, on 3rd November at 9am.

The Maths Aptitude Test is designed to test you mathematical ability away from your normal school work. The maths that the paper tests is general – and there is no specific knowledge needed as such. Just because you have followed a certain examination syllabus, this will not mean you are at an advantage or disadvantage. The test is a fair means by which tutors, as with all the admissions tests, can see you think, not how much you know.

While many of the questions will not require mathematical ability beyond your A level or equivalent syllabus, the questions can be structured in such a way, that the concept you are having to grapple with, appears new. The test therefore requires to think innovatively and apply your A level knowledge to solve them. As one applicant from last year said, 'the abstract thinking required to answer the questions was perhaps the hardest aspect of the test as they were asked in a very different way to A level questions.' This is echoed by another applicant who felt the most difficult things was 'was having to think in a different way to how I was used to at

A level. Instead of knowing exactly how to work through the problems, I had to take different parts of my knowledge and apply them in ways I hadn't done before.'

Many applicants also struggle with timing, especially in the long questions. 'I had to be really self-disciplined to move on to the next question or I would have run out of time', said one applicant. Another commented on how important it is consider the time factor, 'I would often run out of time, but would go back to the questions later and complete them. While my preparation did get me thinking about questions in the right way, I did not do enough practice to bring it up to speed and therefore did not feel I did myself justice. I was not offered a place.'

A good way to prepare for this test is to do lots of recreational maths. 'The questions I was asked were quite similar to the questions you get in the Mathematical Olympiad and the ones you get in advanced leisure maths books', said one successful applicant. Books such as *Advanced Problems in Mathematics,* by STC Syklos and the *Mathematical Olympiad Handbook,* by A Gardiner are a good place to start. It goes without saying of course, that you should ensure your knowledge of your A level work or equivalent is up to scratch, and if you wanted to take your preparation further, you could investigate topics such as groups, matrices or complex numbers in greater depth.

Applicants should aim for the highest score possible in the test. As one successful applicant recalled, 'I never saw my result, but at interview it was mentioned that I got 85%. My tutor told me that generally everyone who gets over 70% is invited to interview.' That said, unlike other admissions tests there is not a cut off point, and one applicant who achieved 60% was still invited up to interview and ended up being offered a place. This test is just part of the application process.

As with all exams, one of the most important things for the day of the test itself is to ensure you have a cool head. You'll come across questions that you do not recognise, but the test is not designed to catch you out. Admissions tutors want to see how you apply what you do know and so approach each question confidently and logically, and try not to let panic get the better of you.

'I think it isn't that difficult to do quite well on this test, but judging by my friends' results, which we found out afterwards, Oxford is only really interested in those who got pretty high scores.'

The PAT (Physics Aptitude Test)

Test format

The Physics Aptitude Test is a two hour test in two sections.

Section A: Mathematical Physics (50 Marks)
This section is made up of 11 mathematical problems.

Section B: Physics (50 Marks)
Section B is made up of three sections.

Part one (10 marks) is made up of 10 multiple choice questions, each with four possible answers.

Part two (20 marks) involves working through three problems.

Part three (20 marks) requires candidates to work through one longer question with three parts to it.

Do I have to sit it?
You do if you are applying to Oxford to read Physics or Physics & Philosophy.

When do I have to register?
You are automatically registered for the PAT test when you apply to Oxford for Physics or Physics & Philosophy.

When do I sit it?
You usually sit the PAT in early November. In 2010, on 3rd November at 9am. Test papers will be sent to your school automatically. If you are no longer at school you will have to fill in a test centre declaration form and sit the test at a test centre.

The Physics admissions test used to be quite informal and sat at the College when you came for interview. The more formal Physics Aptitude Test however is now an important part of the application process, and applicants should aim to do the best they can. 'I didn't actually see my final test result', said one applicant, 'I didn't think I did particularly well in it, but I did get an interview.' 'When I got there,' the applicant continued, 'we were told that everyone had got above 50% in the PAT.' The PAT tests whether you can apply the basic maths and physics that you already know to work out more complex problems. This is why it is so important to stay calm when you see a difficult problem and to work it through, and not panic that the style of the question is far removed from your school work. The questions have been designed to test your logic not your advanced physics.

In fact, as one applicant recalls, 'the only places where I got really stuck was on the relatively simple formulae I had actually learnt at GCSE but had not revised for a year and half. It is so frustrating if you forget simple calculus or trigonometry. I hadn't realised I had forgotten so much and so my advice is to brush up on those important basics!' Another aspect to be watchful of is the timing. A lot of applicants commented on how they ran out of time on the last question – and this is where you can pick up the most marks. 'I'm quite a strategic test-taker', said one successful applicant, 'so I had worked out how long I needed to spend on each question beforehand. In section B, part one, you only have just over a minute for each multiple choice question so you have to be really disciplined. This can be hard hard as some of the questions are quite long, but everyone is in the same boat.'

Oxford puts up a specimen paper on the Physics department page so prospective applicants can work through it. 'I found it quite difficult,' said one applicant 'although you don't need to know vast amount of Physics – you just had to be able to work through the questions in a logical and calm manner.' We appreciate this is obviously even more difficult when it comes to the real test, but remember, if you are applying to read Physics (either on its own or with Philosophy) at Oxford, you will have already proved you can excel academically and the PAT is an extension of your existing ability to grasp mathematical and physical concepts. Brush up on the basics – both GCSE and A level, and spend time working through specimen papers and mock-papers, so you know the format of the test. This will mean that when it comes to the exam in November you can confidently focus on the questions.

Cambridge TSA (Thinking Skills Assessment)

Test format

The Cambridge TSA is a 90 minute test made up of 50 multiple choice questions which assesses numeracy, spatial reasoning, problem solving, verbal reasoning and critical thinking.

Do I have to sit it?

It all depends on which course and college you are applying for. If you are applying for Computer Science, Economics, Engineering, Biological or Physical Natural Sciences, PPS or Land Economy you should check whether the college you are applying to will require you to take it when you come up at interview. Certain colleges, such as Queens', use it a lot, whilst colleges such as Magdalene and Trinity choose not to use it so much.

When do I have to register?

You are automatically registered to take the TSA when you apply to a college and course which requires it. The college will arrange for you to sit the test.

When do I sit it?

You sit the Cambridge TSA when you go up for interview.

When do I get my results?

You will never see your results. They are passed directly on to the college you are applying to, which can use the results at their own discretion.

Although Cambridge has been using the test for years, to many applicants the TSA can feel still feel like something of an unknown entity. In short, the TSA is a test of numeracy, literacy and quick thinking. It's not about what you have been taught to date, it's about how you analyse a problem or concept and use logical reasoning to pluck out what matters. It tests how you think under time pressure and how flexible you can be to unseen issues and problems.

Understanding the questions asked and identifying the small differences in the multiple choice answers is challenging and many students struggle with this. Many applicants found the best way to prepare for a test like this was to practise as many questions as possible – so you get used to the style of the questions and become more confident and skilled in knowing how to approach them. When it comes to the real TSA, timing is tough. As one successful applicant who sat the TSA last year said, one of the hardest parts about the test was the length of it, 'it feels like it goes on forever, yet you have such a limited time to answer all the questions.' So, if you feel under time pressure, don't worry, this is to be expected! Due to the speed with which you have to read passages and answer questions, applicants who do not have English as their first language might struggle with the amount of time you have for each question. 'I had problems even though English is my first language', says one applicant. 'I found that I was reading the questions but already moving on to the next question, which meant I wasn't really understanding the passages. That's why it is so important to keep a clear head.'

Applicants who are studying Maths and/or Physics at A level or equivalent naturally find the Maths-based questions a little easier to handle. However, pressure can still affect the best of candidates. One applicant recalled how she completely forgot one trigonometric identity, which meant 'I was unable to complete the question,' another student applying for Politics, Psychology & Sociology spoke of how he lost time trying to remember how to work out percentages. If you are a little shaky on some fundamental mathematical concepts, brushing up on your GCSE or equivalent syllabus will help to refresh your memory and lead to greater confidence and flexibility when approaching these questions in the fast-paced test environment. Other applicants we spoke to commented on their struggle with questions on spatial awareness.

The TSA is very different from your normal school work. The closest subject to it is arguably AQA's Critical Thinking A level which helps students to develop skills such as recognising sound arguments and how to use persuasive, influential language and present rational, convincing points. It is also designed to help students develop the analytical side of their brain, teaching them how to be critical, spot patterns and scrutinise statistics. Given the skills with which the A level equips you, it is easy to see why many schools encourage their students to take it, and why many recommend it as good preparation for such a test. Even if you are not sitting the examination for real, it is still possible to look over past papers, which many students find helpful.

Oxford TSA (Thinking Skills Assessment)

Test format
The Oxford TSA is a two hour test made up of two sections.

Paper one (90 minutes) consists of 50 multiple choice questions which assess numeracy, spatial reasoning, problem solving, verbal reasoning and critical thinking.

Paper two (30 minutes) is a writing task. Candidates must write one short essay out of a choice of three.

Do I have to sit it?
You do if you are applying to Oxford to read PPE (Politics, Philosophy & Economics), E&M (Economics & Management), PP (Psychology & Philosophy) or EP (Experimental Psychology).

When do I have to register?
Your school or test centre must register you. In 2010, you must register between 1st September and 15th October.

How do I register?
You are registered through the test centre where you sit the test, which is likely to be your school, although you should check with your examinations officer. If you are not at school you will need to register through another test centre and fill in a test centre declaration form.

When do I sit it?
You usually sit the Oxford TSA in early November. In 2010, on 3rd November at 9am.

When do I get my results?
For exams taken in 2010, results are released on 14th January 2011.

Just like the Cambridge TSA, the Oxford Thinking Skills Assessment tests an applicant's numerical, reasoning and logical thinking abilities. What makes the Oxford TSA different to the one required for Cambridge is that, in addition to the multiple choice section, applicants have to complete a short essay. Applicants are assessed on their ability to construct an argument in a logical and coherent manner and this section of the test is passed directly to the College applied to and is marked internally.

The Oxford TSA is an integral part of the admissions process and is used by Oxford to shortlist candidates for interview. On the university website, Oxford currently states that for PPE they expect 68.7% of applications to be shortlisted for interview (with an overall success rate of 18%) and for Experimental Psychology 75.9% (with a success rate of 24.2%). In contrast, for one of the most competitive courses at Oxford, Economics and Management, the university states that is expects to invite approximately only 30% of applicants for interview. Applicants should aim to do as well as they can in the TSA, to give them the best chance of being invited to interview.

An overwhelming majority of students said the hardest thing they found about the test was the timing. There are 50 multiple questions to get through in 90 minutes. There is a lot to read and you have to process the information provided in the passages, before you can understand them and thus answer the questions correctly. 'I found I kept getting stuck on questions where I thought there were two possible answers and had to go back and work the answers out logically', recalls one applicant.

The TSA is really designed to test your flexibility of thinking as well as how quickly you can solve problems. Some applicants find it hard to adapt to the style of the test, and the new information with which you faced. 'I found the test difficult' says one applicant, 'I had to do quite a lot of work to prepare for it. Lots of people thought that you couldn't work for it, but while it can be hard to prepare, there are definitely things you can do.' Just as with the Cambridge TSA, practising questions from the Critical Thinking A level can help to develop your analysing and reasoning skills. It can also help you practise how to structure a coherent and accurate argument, in a logical and concise way, which will be particularly useful for the essay section. 'I had forgotten quite a lot of the maths from my GCSEs says one applicant, and so to help me with the maths-based questions, I practised mental arithmetic and went over some of the basic principles.'

Applicants are encouraged to look at the TSA specimen paper as it shows you the types of questions you might expect and it gives you a good idea of how to structure your time – which is important given the time pressure when it comes to the real exam. 'I found practising as many TSA-type questions as possible very helpful, as it helped to build up my confidence and I found myself able to work through questions more efficiently and effectively the more I did. This stood me in good stead.'

Another top tip from successful applicants is to keep up-to-date with current affairs as you need to have lots of good examples at your fingertips for the essay question. And when it comes to the essay, it's essential that you take a little time to think before you start writing. You need to show that you can argue points consistently with good examples to support your case. Simply stating a view is not sufficient: you need to show you are thinking critically, and can write clearly. It does not matter what your conclusion is – there is no right or wrong answer, but you must ensure that you do come to one that seems appropriate.

'I did better than I thought I would on the multiple choice section, which I found more difficult', recalls one applicant. 'I achieved 68%, and I think you needed to get just above 50% to get invited for interview. We all thought that the essay wouldn't count for much,' she recalls 'and that it would just be a point of conversation at interview, however a friend of mine got the same mark in the questions as me but had a weaker essay and did not get invited for interview, and so it must count for something!'

And lastly, as much as you can, when it comes to the real thing, try to stay calm as much as possible. You have so much to do in such a short space of time, like all exams, you should avoid wasting time panicking. The questions require you to think logically – and if you let nerves get the better of you, it is likely you will find the test even more challenging. Every applicant is in the same boat. No one will have seen the questions before. The test is designed to see how you think, not how well you have been studying. If you can keep a cool head - that will really help you to show your logical thinking ability at its best.

The UKCAT (UK Clinical Aptitude Test)

Test format:
The UKCAT is an online test for Medicine and Dentistry made up of five equally-weighted sections

Verbal Reasoning (22 minutes)
Candidates must read 11 passages each with four statements, and then assess whether the statements are true, false, or if there is inadequate information to reach a conclusion. This tests critical and verbal reasoning.

Quantitative Reasoning (23 minutes)
Candidates must answer 36 questions based on tables, charts or graphs, each with a series of multiple choice questions. This assesses numerical, data extraction and graphical analysis skills.

Abstract Reasoning (16 minutes)
There are 13 questions each with five shapes which must be divided into two sets according to their characteristics. This assesses your ability to identify patterns.

Decision Analysis (32 minutes)
Candidates are presented with a single scenario and coded information and given 26 questions with four or five possible answers. This assesses ability to make decisions based on coded information.

Non-Cognitive Analysis (30 minutes)
Candidates have to answer questions in which they identify attributes that contribute towards being a successful doctor or dentist.

A basic functional calculator is available onscreen.

Do I have to sit it?
You will have to sit the UKCAT if you are applying for Medicine or Dentistry at the following universities: Aberdeen, Brighton and Sussex Medical School, Barts and The London School of Medicine and Dentistry, Cardiff, Dundee, Durham, UEA, Edinburgh, Glasgow, Hull York Medical School, Keele, KCL, Imperial (Graduate entry only), Leeds, Leicester, Manchester, Newcastle, Nottingham, Oxford (Graduate entry only), Peninsula College of Medicine and Dentistry, Queen's University Belfast, Sheffield, Southampton, St Andrews, St George's and Warwick (Graduate entry only). Neither Oxford nor Cambridge asks for the UKCAT.

When do I have to register?
You can register online via the UKCAT website from 1st May to 27th September.

When do I sit it?
You can usually sit the UKCAT from early June until 8th October. You sit the UKCAT at one of 150 test centres worldwide. It is advisable to book early to ensure you will be able to sit the test at a nearby test centre. You will need to bring photographic ID to the test centre.

When do I get my results?
Candidates are given their results on completion (marks are generated by the computer). The universities that use the UKCAT have access to these results online, so there is no need for candidates to send them. Subtests 1-4 are given a score between 300 and 900 and the four sub-test scores are averaged to give an overall score. The average score for each sub-test is 600 and most applicants score between 500 and 700.

In the past three years however, statistics have shown a tendency for candidates to perform better in the quantitative reasoning and less well in the verbal reasoning. Subtest 5 is not scored on a numerical scale, but you will be given a brief outline of your results, describing the personality traits tested. The results of subtest 5 do not indicate whether you would make a good doctor or not, and universities do not yet use the results in their selection processes.

The UKCAT tests your reasoning skills: how well you can think logically when confronted with questions drawn from outside the syllabus. It levels the playing field as it removes the influence of teaching and tests your inherent aptitude in five different areas.

It is difficult to know how to prepare because no part of it is related to the academic work you are used to. You require totally different skills to the ones you have been learning at school. 'I found the abstract reasoning (where you have to identify patterns in groups of pictures) the hardest', says one applicant. 'I therefore made sure I focused on this section in my preparation by doing as many past papers and practice questions as I could.'

Timing is also an issue as there is so much material to get through and you have to switch your mind from numeracy exercises to verbal reasoning instantaneously. The verbal reasoning passages also have long paragraphs, and applicants who are slow at reading tend to struggle more with the timing. As much as timing is tough, try to not to panic and just guess your response.

One of the best ways to prepare is to get to know the test format really well by doing practice sessions. A number of the students we spoke to found that once they knew what each section was testing they were better placed to be able to answer it. 'Talking to my friends,' recalls one student 'we all had trouble with a particular section,' although which section, varied from person to person.' If you are struggling with something and practice isn't helping, you could think about getting some special help with it. A number of applicants have said how helpful if can be to work through problems with someone who really understands this test and it can be well worth it in the long run as each section is equally weighted so low grades in one could dramatically affect your score overall.

How the results are used differs from university to university. However, common to all universities is the fact that the UKCAT will never be the only determining factor for interviews - it is used in combination with your AS grades, predicted A2 grades, personal statement and references to assist admissions tutors in deciding which applicants to interview. That means that keeping things in perspective is key. It is obviously good to try and do as well as you can in the UKCAT, but if you don't do as well as you would like, do not panic, as it is just one part of the application process.

6. The interview

Be prepared for anything

Stress free

What makes interviewers tick and how to keep your cool.

Oxford and Cambridge are world class, historic institutions and like most leading universities, they want to recruit the best and the brightest. Admissions tutors want to see students' academic potential, regardless of their educational background, so as to determine which applicants will flourish in the Oxbridge tutorial/supervision systems.

To excel in the Oxbridge teaching system, undergraduates must be able to listen, confidently converse, engage academically and absorb information about their subject. In essence, the interview acts as a mini-tutorial or supervision, to assess, along with all the other aspects of the application, whether you, the applicant, will enjoy learning in this environment and whether they in turn will like teaching you.

Interviews allow admissions tutors to explore exactly how the applicant thinks, how they adapt to new concepts and ideas and how they handle the pressure of reaching conclusions aloud. For example, if an admissions tutor gives you a physics formula to solve that you have not previously encountered – how do you react? Do you attempt to work through it, or do you freeze with terror? If it is the former, that's a good indication that you might be an interesting student to teach; you are showing you are responsive to new ideas and can apply your existing knowledge to problems you have not seen before, a skill you will have to exercise in a real tutorial/supervision.

If your opinion is questioned in an interview for Law, do you explore the cracks in your argument and seek to come to a strong conclusion, using hints and ideas that your supervisor throws at you, or are you inflexible and unwilling to consider another side to the argument? Do you enjoy exploring biological problems out loud, or would you rather keep the answer to yourself? How do you communicate your understanding of your chosen subject?

The interview is a platform whereby admissions tutors test whether a prospective applicant has the academic potential to shine. In successful applicants they are looking for genuine motivation and inspiration for the chosen subject, logical, critical, analytical and lateral thinking skills, an ability to think independently, listen carefully, and possess sound academic knowledge. Are you an interesting, agreeable and 'teachable' student? While we appreciate that might seem a daunting list, in truth, many bright applicants will already have these very qualities.

Like the personal statement, the interview gives applicants the chance to demonstrate whether their interest in their chosen subject is genuine or not. It is easy to say that you have understood a philosophical concept in your personal statement, but can you summarise the point in a sentence and then explore its application to a situation you have not previously considered? Have you been honest about reading the whole of the Bible and your engagement with it? Have you paid attention in class and can you show this when tested on your Chemistry syllabus? Genuinely passionate individuals will tend to be the ones who have really thought about why they want to read this course at university, and have a stock of solid examples to back up their points.

The interviews give admissions tutors the opportunity to test your ability in your chosen subject. Even if you have scored well on the university or college Maths or Physics test, they need to see whether you can answer a problem when it's put up on a whiteboard and you are under a significant amount of pressure. If you are a budding engineer, they want to hear you explain why your favourite bridge was constructed as it was, using basic concepts of engineering.

Admissions tutors may also use the interview to discuss how to approach material that has not been looked at in the application process, other than at interview. For example, in an Architecture interview, the tutor can talk through the portfolio that the applicant has brought and ask about why it has been arranged in that order and why the pieces have been chosen in the first place. In an interview for Music, the applicant can be given a score and asked to break it down to demonstrate their theoretical and critical appreciation of compositions. In a language interview, the applicant can be asked questions in the language they wish to study, to test oral ability. You may be able to talk confidently about topics you have covered at school or in your own time, but can you apply the logic you have to situations beyond your experience? Can you criticise a piece of rhetoric cut from a speech by Cicero, even if you have not studied this at A level? If you are given a new piece of information, can you work your way to a conclusion you have never considered previously? In short, can you think independently?

Many successful applicants are surprised to find the interview an enjoyable experience, and we promise you, that's not as crazy as it sounds! The interview is a chance to discuss your subject with someone who has dedicated their academic life to its study and you should try to relish the opportunity to talk about it, in the face to face environment. Think of the interview as a two-way conversation, not as an interrogation. Admissions tutors want to admit applicants who have real potential – and if you find yourself enjoying the experience, the chances are the tutor/s will be too.

In 2009, the overwhelming majority of those applying to Cambridge reached interview. Some applicants to Oxford were not invited, and in most cases this decision was based on scores in admissions tests. Interviews are the final piece of the application jigsaw, and it is from there that the university makes its ultimate decision.

What to expect from your interview

Both Oxford and Cambridge have fantastic websites with lots of information on interviews. They have mock-interview videos and podcasts you can download, peppered with explanations as to what to expect. We are aware that the type of interview you are likely to have varies depending on which subject you are applying for. This is why, in the later sections of this chapter, we explore how you might answer questions relevant to your chosen discipline. In this section we've put together some general advice on what to expect (based on over ten years of research) as well as practical steps on how to build up your confidence and skills so that you can demonstrate your potential.

The general rule is to be prepared for anything. You may be interviewed by one person or two, even three or four. In a room when there is more than one person, a good tip is to address your answers to the interviewer who asked the question, with regular glances to include the rest of the interview team. It may be the case that one party leads the interview, whilst another observes and takes notes. It can be off-putting to have a silent presence in the room, and the observer inevitably begins to scribble furiously halfway through your answer, prompting you to ponder what you have said, and lose your train of thought. If one tutor is clearly the driving force behind the interview, while another watches, concentrate on creating a rapport with the main interviewer.

You may have one general interview and one subject interview or two subject interviews. You may be interviewed at a college to which you have not applied (more likely at Oxford) or you might be interviewed at the college to which you applied, as well as one or two others. (Again, this is more likely at Oxford and nothing should be read into this decision.) You may be interviewed only by specialists in your subjects or you may have one general interview, by a tutor from another faculty (more likely at Cambridge). It is likely, if you are applying for a subject which is either Joint Honours or incorporates two disciplines that both departments will need to be impressed with your performance at interview. Indeed, last year, some applicants we spoke to were asked in their interview whether they would consider accepting an offer for Single Honours.

You may be interviewed by a man or a woman and they may be young or old. They may be friendly...or not. They may ask factual questions and they may ask for your opinion. They may be comfortable with silence...or not. They may ask you difficult questions...or not. Their questions may seem very relevant...or not. (If not, why not, have you really understood the question?) They may ask you about work experience or express interest in your personal statement. They may talk about your admissions test or submitted work and they may give you a problem to solve. They may give you a source before the interview. They may seem interested in you or barely look at you. They may want to shake your hand or simply tell you to take a seat.

Our advice is to control what you can control. You know you are there to try to show why you should be offered a place to study your chosen subject at undergraduate level. You know that competition is tough. What you cannot control however, is how the interviewer reacts to you. You may be faced with an aggressive or tough interviewer, who fires an intellectual assault at you, pushing you to reveal your strengths, and picking out weaknesses in your arguments or analysis. If you are faced with this, it is essential to keep your head. The interviewer does not want to witness you crumble but to see whether you can stand your ground in a heated academic debate. They want to see whether you can strike a balance between listening to your interviewer and taking their views into account, whilst also defending and maintaining your own viewpoint. 'I was surprised by the intensiveness of the first interview,' said one applicant we spoke to, 'she seemed to want to disagree with me the whole time.' This is echoed by another applicant who applied to read English. 'The interview was much more intense than I had expected. The interviewers were harsh and I did not get the opportunity to lead the conversation in any direction.'

If you find yourself in this situation, a key thing to remember is that you must remain respectful and rational. Be prepared for 'such as?' and 'for example' type questions, but don't let them put you off or force you into making a foolish point. Every time you make a case, ensure you have an example/s to hand to support and strengthen your point. Base concluding points on your examples – they are the facts the interviewers want to see you employ.

And lastly, do not be afraid to back down if you find yourself becoming tangled in a web of academic and oral confusion. The interview is not the place for stubbornness or pride. Remember that your interviewers have studied the topic under discussion for a lot longer than you and they might decide to play devil's advocate in the interview to see how you react under pressure. Try not to let a situation like this get the better of you. Ultimately, as successful undergraduates and graduates will tell you, interviewers want to see you at your best. They are looking to admit the best, not to exclude the worst, so try to hold that thought in your mind as you walk into that interview room, or find yourself caught up in a heated discussion.

Many applicants actually find the interview a much less intimidating experience. 'I was surprised by how nice they were,' said one successful applicant from 2009. Another remarked that 'the tutors were very encouraging, nudging me in the right direction whenever they felt it appropriate and I managed to arrive at the right answers and thoughts in the end for most questions.' 'I was slightly surprised at how much the tutors were prepared to help and explain things to me', said another, 'but, sadly, this led me into a slightly false sense of security. I was not offered a place.'

Friendly, arguably passive interviewers may appear laid back and open, however they are perhaps the toughest to read. With a passive interviewer, you do not have a ferociously aggressive combatant pushing you forward, challenging you and forcing you to perform to the best of your ability. Instead they fire a few direct questions, and the interview can feel like a monologue. The onus, in this situation, is on you to turn what feels like a casual conversation into an intellectual discussion, in which you demonstrate your academic potential. Passive interviewers may try to upset an applicant's thought process with interjections such as 'And?...' even though you, the interviewee, feel that you have come to a sensible conclusion. If you find your interviewer uttering one of these 'Ands?...', remember that you are being invited to explore your ideas in further detail or from a different angle.

There are two good tips when tackling this situation. You could either try to develop further your initial answer to its logical conclusion, or alternatively pause and reconsider the implications of the question. There may be a particular point the interviewer hopes you will grasp, which could be very close to points you have already made, or might require you to change track. If for example, your initial answer was 'Biology doesn't help Theology much, except to disprove through evolutionary theory certain creation myths,' you might expand your original answer into fleshing out the debate between creationists and evolutionists, or you might re-think the direction of your answer entirely and talk about the impossibility of trying to rationalise the existence of the conscious mind.

If you have tried both these responses and you are still met with 'And...?' it may mean that the interviewer has a specific response in mind that you cannot fathom. If you have explored your answers as far as you can take them, gracefully disengage yourself by asking them either to re-phrase the problem for you, or admit that you do not know the answer that they are looking for, and ask them to help you. A smile (not a grin) coupled with 'I'm afraid I don't know but I'd like to find out,' turns the problem into a virtue, as you seem (and we hope you are!) thirsty for juicy new knowledge.

Of course, most interviewers will not conform exclusively to any one typical style, but they are likely to demonstrate a mixture of traits. When it comes to the interview, what matters is that you can transfer what you can already do on paper into the oral context of the interview. Speak up - show your independence, your ability and your potential with every question. Don't be afraid to pause before you answer. It's ok to take a little time to structure your response in your own mind. The interviewers would rather listen to a coherent, well thought out answer, than a jumbled narrative ramble. Think about what you do in a written exam. It's about the quality of your ideas and how you communicate them.

Tips on preparing for Oxbridge interviews and beyond

Gwyn Day works as an Educational Coach advising individual students and top UK Independent and State Schools on how to improve sixth form success. He is a Master Practitioner of NLP (Neuro-Linguistic Programming). Since 2001 he has worked for Oxbridge Applications providing interview advice to aspiring Oxbridge applicants. Here he gives his top tips on preparing for Oxbridge interviews, with a view to controlling stress.

“It is never too early or too late to improve your interview skills. In my experience, practice gives applicants a greater sense of confidence, which tends to allow interviewees to express their ideas and thought process more eloquently, more logically and with less emotional cost. Practice really can help to conquer stress, with all its negative side-effects. The tips below do require effort and time. It is a good idea to play with these exercises months or weeks before interview, so that, by the time of the interview, you are not rigidly following the suggestions below and are comfortable with your own approach. This is not about turning you into a robot. Interviews truly are about being yourself. In my opinion, interview preparation should be about how you can be the most confident, honest and professional version of yourself, ready to tackle the unknown. Interview technique classes (and these tips) are not about giving applicants answers, but transferable skills which can boost confidence when tackling any interviewer and any question. The focus of the advice here is on knowing what to say and how to say it. Stress primarily comes from not knowing what to say or how to say it. This section looks at how you can conquer the fear of not knowing what to say so that potential shines through at interview.

Know how to use examples

One of the biggest mistakes interviewees make is giving fluffy, general answers without giving proof or examples to back up what they have said. As a general rule, steer clear of answers that someone with no detailed knowledge of the subject/concept could give. As an interviewee you need to demonstrate that you have understood the idea you are grappling with and your use of examples should demonstrate this.

Imagine interviewing a student yourself and being told that their favourite book is 'War and Peace'. Would you, like me, question whether they had actually read this (given its size), unless they proved through detailed explanation that they understood the subject matter and the techniques employed in the novel? How, through the use of examples, could you prove that you understood the book and had thought about it as a work of fiction? Using examples is perfectly possible in both the arts and the sciences.

Understand why you might need to use examples

An interviewee who uses examples helps interviewers to understand what they are interested in, and how they approach their chosen subject. If an applicant is forthcoming with examples (but not over the top), the interviewer does not have to work as hard. Further, if a student is generous with their ideas, it suggests they will be a keen contributor to academic discussions in the course of their studies, skills which might make them seem a favourable addition to a tutorial or class.

When asked 'What is your favourite book/building/structure/concept?' can you give a specific example? Can you understand that giving specific examples provides an important insight into the way that you think?

Remember that interviewers want evidence that you are engaged with a subject and that you have thought about why you want to study it at undergraduate level. They do not want your examples to seem contrived for the purpose of performing well at interview, but to be a reflection of genuine opinions and interests. If you are really engaged with a subject, you should want to think about it outside the classroom.

Build up a bank of examples, which you can confidently draw upon

This may seem obvious, but the majority of students still don't do this! You cannot predict what an interviewer will ask, but if you know what you think about certain topics, you will be much more confident when approaching the interview.

For example, prospective medical students may well have shadowed a doctor in Cardiology and volunteered in an old people's home. In both instances they should have knowledge of the causes, symptoms, treatment and recent developments in one or two of the cases they found most interesting. You should be particularly strong when discussing everything you have mentioned in your personal statement.

Compare and contrast

In an interview, a good applicant will show they can compare and contrast. It is likely that you have already started to do this as part of your normal school work. In English Literature, a range of examples linking themes in A level texts with wider reading across time periods, for example the use of landscape as an additional character, the importance of animal motifs or the role of science, can be extremely useful to demonstrate effort and genuine interest. You can read more about this in the next chapter.

Know how to roll with the punches

If the interviewer does not question you further on the topics you are interested in, this should not matter. The bank of examples you have made should serve to allow you to create a logically structured argument on the spot! Understand what type of question you may be asked – your answer will depend on which of the three main types of question is asked i.e. factual, opinion or linking:

A fact-based question

If it is a fact-based question, designed to test your memory, pause to allow your brain, which will already be moving quickly because of the adrenaline rush of the situation, to gather up the salient points. When you start speaking, slow down to give yourself more gravitas. The admissions tutors understand how important the interview is to you and know that students often rush. The more in control and demonstrably focused/interested you are in the ideas under discussion, the better you will do.

An opinion-based question

If it is an opinion-based question (including ethics) your 'answer' will not be simply to reel off facts but to answer: 'I think XYZ because REASON 1, REASON 2, REASON 3, although I appreciate ABC counterpoints.'

A linking question

The most searching question type is the 'linking,' for example 'Tell me about a banana.' OR 'What did you see on your way here today that tells you about the state of the British economy?'

Many students make the common mistake of immediately jumping into too much detail. For example, I saw rubbish bins were full, I saw buses and a lot of people. They fall into the trap of telling a story. Instead, the best way to approach these types of questions is to think about the big picture. For example, what do you know are the big issues in the UK economy (weak pound, immigration, public deficit/austerity measures) and then demonstrate how those issues are manifested by things you saw. Practice is the key to confidence. Interviewers have different styles and the more opportunities you take to practise your moves, the more confident you will become.

'Well I've always been told that I just need to be myself – so why do I need advice on that? I don't want to be a robot.'

I counter this with the challenge: think about your behaviour in different scenarios. Do you behave in the same way with your parents, a group of friends, your sports/music/drama peers, in a part time job or on work experience? For most people the answer is 'no'. You will have your own personal interview style and, as in any new situation, it takes time to learn the rules of engagement and how you as an individual can show yourself at your best. ”

Gwyn Day

So, we've done the theory of interviews - now we're going to look at how you might approach interviews in your chosen subject. Although there are general questions that might come up in any interview (such as: 'How can you justify studying your subject for three or four years to the taxpayer?'), interviews and an applicant's experience of them, tend to vary greatly from subject to subject. Over the years we have worked with schools and applicants, helping them to prepare for their Oxbridge interview. Just this summer we travelled the length and breadth of England's pleasant land, working with a number of students to help guide them on how they might approach their interview, working through past interview questions and strengthening skills at the core of their chosen subject. The sessions were designed to get students thinking laterally and logically, away from their school syllabus. The next section has been written to do just that – to get you thinking creatively, developing flexibility of thought and applying your existing knowledge to interview questions you have never seen before.

7. Approaching questions

Working with a team of Oxbridge graduates from different subject disciplines, in this section we look at how you might approach sample interview questions. Some of the questions discussed here are real and have been put to applicants at their interviews, others are based on past questions and have been carefully created by our team to ensure they give an insight into subject-specific interviews.

The key thing to remember is that there is seldom a right answer, unless it is a specific mathematical problem you are asked to solve or a fact-based question. Our graduates have made suggestions as to how you might approach a question, but their answers are by no means to be interpreted as a set 'model answer' or indeed suggest that there is a standardised approach to both generating or answering such questions. The points made are to serve as a guide as to how you might go about tackling them. You do not need an encyclopaedic memory to answer Oxbridge questions successfully. Nor do you have to be a genius in the making. Each year, interviewers come up with a host of new and appropriately challenging questions and problems to see how aspiring Oxbridge applicants go about tackling them. Therefore, please do not expect that just because we've concentrated on a question that you will be asked this in your interview – the chances of this are exceedingly slim and we do not recommend that you spend hours revising possible answers.

Archaeology & Anthropology

Questions to get you thinking...

How would you carry out the ethnography of a curry?

How would you describe the role of the media within American politics?

If you were shown the jawbone of an animal, how would you identify which animal it belongs to?

Some people say that in 100 or 200 years we will have one world culture. What do you think about this?

Describe your school in anthropological terms. (past question)

This question aims to encourage the consideration of the cultural make-up of your school and moves into wider discussion on issues such as multiculturalism, gender and class. It would be easy to meander and go off point. Be conscious of what you are saying and support your points with examples and evidence.

Anthropology is concerned with people and cultures, so the interviewer will be expecting you to be able to analyse your school as an anthropological field site. In anthropology, this kind of focused study (i.e. site-specific) is termed as an ethnographic investigation. The notion of an 'anthropological perspective' is very broad and encompassing, and this can be demonstrated even within the site of the school. For example, within a single site, an anthropologist could examine a number of topics, including cross-cultural, gendered, socio-economic status, and age interactions between people.

You could expand your argument to compare your own schooling system to another cross-culturally. A provocative current example is the expression of religious freedom, as exemplified in how lenient the schooling system should be in permitting religious symbols (such as the headscarf) to be on 'display' in so-called secular sites such as the school. You could link in issues of multiculturalism and secularism, and how this has been tackled in the educational system in different ways in different countries, comparing, for example, Britain's lenient approach to headscarves in schools in contrast to the French government's 2004 ban on headscarves in schools. Other possible issues you might consider: Is your school singlesex or mixed? How does gender impact on education? Is it a state school or private? Should education be free? Are school uniform regulations a breach of human rights?

You may also be asked how you would carry out this investigation. This relates to methodology, and you would be expected to demonstrate a range of approaches in your answer (conducting interviews, questionnaires, doing cross-cultural comparisons, utilising archival resources), including offering a realistic timeframe for such an investigation.

Would you agree that tourism, if it is led by indigenous people, will lead to a more positive result for the culture of the country? (past question)

In answering this question, avoid jumping straight in. Don't go for a wild stab and avoid a dogmatic 'yes/no' response. The interviewer will be looking for how you can engage intuitively and contemplatively with a complex current issue in anthropology.

A good place to start is to identify the key themes in the question. Here, for example, the question relates to cultural representation, identity, multiculturalism, and globalism. You could ask what defines the 'tourist'? Does the fieldwork ethnographer count as a tourist? What about the gap-year student? Note the problems in terminologies: 'tourist', 'indigenous', 'primitive', 'authentic' – such words are inherently ideologically fuelled and there is a risk that we are dividing them into two simplified cateogories, 'Us/Them'. Is there a need to distinguish between the categories of tourist and indigenous in this way? (especially in this time of so-called global cosmopolitanism).

You could argue that these categories – born specifically from a Western social setting – are ultimately deeply ingrained in a set of persistent and preconceived ideas – West/rest, primitive/modern, old/new. Yet with such cultural multiplicity, and in a time of increasing social change, such static constructions simply cannot hold force. By paying respect to the dynamics and differences of cultural situations, the task of anthropology is to re-contextualise the pervasive us/them polarities in favour of a more processual, scientific approach.

James Clifford argues in his book *The Predicament of Culture,* that one ought to hold all such dichotomising concepts in suspicion, attempting instead to replace their essentialising modes of thought by thinking of cultures 'not as organically unified or traditionally continuous but rather as negotiated, present processes'.

Top tips

If you are interested in studying Archaeology & Anthropology and want to find out more about the types of issues raised by these questions, you might want to dip into J. R. Bowen, *Why The French Don't Like Headscarves: Islam, The State, and Public Space*; Joy Hendry, *Reclaiming Culture: Indigenous People and Self-Representation.*

Architecture

Questions to get you thinking...

Does visiting a historical site give you a better appreciation of the architecture than you can grasp from a picture/photo?

What issues, important in building Ancient Greek temples, are still relevant today?

Why do we need architects?

Do you think architecture changes views of society?

What is your favourite building and why? (past question)

A handy hint with this sort of question is to try and think about specific details of why you like a building. Is it the building type, location, integration of sustainable/eco-friendly systems, material, shape, façade, interior, exterior that you appreciate? Remember that architecture is more than just 'buildings' as such. It is about design with certain proportional qualities, or design order with a conscious spatial awareness.

One Architecture graduate we spoke to said that her favourite building is the Dutch Embassy in Berlin by OMA. It is a good example of a modern building which uses interesting (and inexpensive) materials. The program is expressed on the façade through the building's materiality (cantilevered green glass) which gives it a subtly iconic look. When inside the building, the processional circulation allows one to experience the building from the outside in, which makes it an interesting building to visit. The details of the different working areas from an interior perspective make the place feel special and the employees take pride in working there. The building also responds well to its context on the Berlin urban block next to the river.

With a question like this, do try and choose a building you have visited. Remember that it is ok to pick a well known, iconic building but make sure you are very specific as to why it is you favourite. It may be more interesting to choose something that is perhaps more unusual and less likely to be chosen by another applicant. This is typical of the types of questions that have been asked in previous interviews and therefore it is good to have a few examples of different buildings that you like and that you are confident to talk about. You should also know which architect (if relevant) designed the building, and a bit about some of their other work which you might like to refer to.

Do architects need to consider light within buildings differently in different countries? (past question)

This question tests how much you have thought about the specifics of design with respect to context and location, as well as testing your environmental knowledge. It is asking you to identify that different countries have different climates and seasons which need to be examined with regards to construction and design in order to help maintain a comfortable microclimate within a building.

You could tackle the question by thinking of examples of why light may be considered differently. What is the building's function? Who are the end users? Where is the building located? Think about what other factors are dependent on light - heat (solar gain) and thus ventilation, and how these might be manipulated for different climates. Diagrams are always a good idea to help illustrate your answer. For example, you might want to show how light changes seasonally (low light in winter verses a higher sun in summer).

If 'yes' is your answer, you can support your point by stating that tropical countries around the equator have similar daylight hours all year round, compared with more northern and southern countries that have a large seasonal flux of sunlight. In order to prevent too much solar gain from direct sunlight, it would be preferable to use shading devices and materials with a high thermal mass to keep a building cool in hot weather. In countries where solar gain needs to be maximised to help heat a building, lots of glass might be used to let in large amounts of light (like a conservatory).

A poor attempt at the question would avoid the environmental issues related to light (i.e. for aesthetic purposes) and also one where the applicant simple stated a 'yes' or 'no' response, without elaborating further.

Top tips

Your portfolio is a key part of the application process. Do think really carefully about how to organise this. What is special about your portfolio and what are your individual strengths? Think about the order of your work, how you can explain why you have chosen the pieces that you have and the links between them. What skills can you show? Can you produce work in different media? Does your work illustrate what inspires you and your technique? It is a skill to be able to combine and present a multiple medium portfolio effectively and quickly. It is usually more convenient to have the pages free and not contained within plastic sheets so that interviewers can see the quality of the work better, and where possible original drawings (as opposed to scans/copies/prints) should be used. If models or art works are too big to carry then try and make sure they are well documented with photos.

Before the interview, do think about Architecture in respect of the profession. As one graduate stated, a great architect is, for me, 'a professional who understands the requirements and aspirations of a client (budget, aesthetics, functionality), with respect to designing a practical and buildable structure, and with the capability to respond sensitively to its context and potential environmental impact.' Take the time to think about what it really means to be an architect.

Biological Sciences / Natural Sciences (Biological)

Questions to get you thinking...

How does insulin function?

What is a mitochondrion? Why do you only inherit mitochondrion genes from your mother?

Why may a drug not have the same effect on a human as on a dog?

How do we know that species become extinct if we don't know that they exist?

What happens during PCR? (past question)

A good way to approach this question is to first state what PCR stands for - Polymerase Chain Reaction. Of course, if you do not know what PCR stands for, ask the interviewer to clarify. If you know what PCR is, a good next step would be to summarise it clearly: PCR is a technique used to amplify a single or few copies of a piece of DNA to generate thousands to millions of copies.

After summarising, a good approach would be to highlight the details of the technique: PCR is used to amplify a specific region of a DNA strand. PCR uses two primers which are complementary to the '3' (3 prime) ends of the sense and anti-sense DNA strands. A DNA polymerase (enzyme) is used to replicate the DNA between the two primers. The PCR mixture is first heated – this causes denaturation and separation of the sense and anti-sense strands so that the primers and polymerase can reach the nucleotides and allow replication. The mixture is then cooled slightly to allow the primers to anneal (bind) to the single strands of DNA. The mixture is then heated to the optimum temperature for the polymerase. The heating cycle is then repeated as many times as the user wants amplifications of the DNA, i.e. the first cycle turns one copy of DNA into two, the second cycle turns 2 into 4, and so on.

In your conclusion, you can discuss its practical uses: **Amplification** of small amounts of DNA to a volume that is large enough to be analysed. This is useful in forensic analysis when only trace amounts of DNA are available. **Isolation** of a particular DNA sequence by selective amplification. This is useful to quantitatively assess levels of gene expression for genetic fingerprinting and screening for cancer. **Identification** of a particular DNA sequence in a genome, i.e. PCR will only be successful if the chosen DNA sequence is present. This is useful in screening of bacteria following insertion of DNA sequences (recombinant DNA).

In the case that you have not studied PCR, the interviewer may instead provide you with information on the first two points above, and ask questions aimed to test your logical and lateral thinking skills, such as: 'How do you think PCR works?' In this case, you must use what you know about DNA replication and enzymes, applying it to explain how amplification of a DNA strand could be achieved.

What possible uses can you see for PCR?

In this case, you must use what they have told you about the process and think laterally. PCR is amplification of DNA volume – in what circumstances would you need more DNA? Only the specific piece of DNA is amplified – in what circumstances would you want to target specifically one piece of DNA?

Imagine a frequency graph of three different viruses over a 30 year period. One gradually increases and decreases, one peaks every other year and one peaks three times within a 30 year period. Why? (past question)

With a question like this, the information comes in graphical form but you are not actually supplied with a graph. A good approach would be to draw the graphs, as follows:

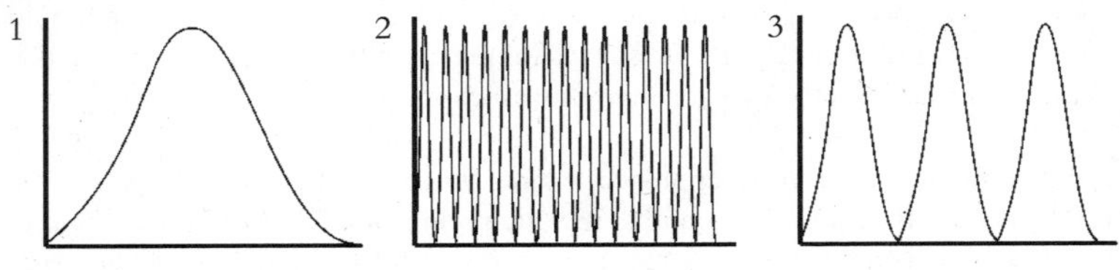

It would then be wise to check with the interviewer they agree that the graphs represent the information given. Do not be afraid to ask for clarification and if you need more information ask the interviewer.

Next, outline the factors that could affect frequency of viral infection in a population: **climate** – changes in temperature, humidity, seasons, etc, **mutation of the virus** – could improve transmission, give resistance, etc, **other viruses** – competition or symbiosis (e.g. infection with the influenza virus weakens the immune system and increases chance of other infections), **the discovery of a vaccine or other control methods.**

A good approach would then be to look at each graph in turn and apply the above factors to each situation, asking the question 'what could cause the change seen in each graph?' As far as possible I would use examples to illustrate my hypotheses:

1. Discovery of a vaccine could explain graph 1. An example of a virus dramatically affected by the invention and implementation of a vaccine is smallpox. Another possible explanation of graph 1 is environmental change affecting a virus. For example, if the UK climate warms to the extent that malarial mosquitoes can survive here, this would introduce an upsurge in the disease which might only be tackled by a strong response to the virus.
2. A virus that recurs biannually could be due to mutations that increase infection rates coupled to a constantly evolving treatment – for example, the influenza virus mutates every year and humans produce a new vaccine every year. A biannual recurrence might be caused by a slightly slower mutating virus.
3. It could be the same factor that occurs three times in 30 years, such as three particularly harsh winters or wet summers. It could also be three different factors causing three independent recurrences.

How would you go about setting up a blood bank in a developing country? (past question)

Please note: a question like this would not be out of place in an interview for Medicine or Biomedical Sciences. With a question like this, you are being asked to use your biological knowledge in conjunction with geographical, sociological and economical factors. As an interviewer you will be looking for a coherent plan-of-action that takes into account anything you know about blood donation systems in the UK or abroad.

To start, you might want to clarify the meaning of the term 'blood bank,' and once again, if you are unsure, ask your interviewer to clarify. A blood bank is a store of blood or blood components gathered from donations for later use in transfusions.

You can then move onto listing the factors you would need to consider in planning your approach: set-up and running costs; how to get donations; staff; safety of donating blood; location and logistics of storage; and transportation.

A good applicant would then move on to consider each factor in more detail:

Set-up and running costs: there will be a large initial cost associated with acquiring the necessary facilities needed; however, it would be equally important to consider how the project would be funded in the long-term. You might suggest approaching the government, WHO and charities for funding.

How to get donations: the National Blood Service in the UK relies on charitable donations, however other countries pay people for their donations. You could propose establishing a service in return for a donation. Due to the shortage of healthcare in many developing world countries, an effective strategy could be to offer a free health check-up to blood donors.

Location: the National Blood Service in the UK has multiple static and mobile facilities. The majority of developing countries have less well-developed infrastructures and fewer hospitals. Therefore, although mobile teams would make donating more accessible, you might consider multiple static teams working from existing hospital facilities across the country.

Staff: setting up the blood bank will provide new jobs for nurses, transport workers, administrators, etc.

Blood safety: there are two safety aspects to consider – donation safety and blood safety. Donation safety is vital so that nurses receive proper procedural and safety training. Any blood that may be used in a blood transfusion must be clean from transfusion-transmitted diseases. In the developing world, the main culprit is HIV/AIDS, although malaria, hepatitis B and C and many more are all also present. As many developing countries have tropical climates and poor living standards, the frequency of many of these diseases is higher. A blood donor would first need to be questioned and then tested for all of the diseases relevant to that area/country.

Transportation: a storage site would have to be acquired and fitted with refrigeration/climate control systems. It would have to be manned. The location should also be within easy access of the hospitals that will require blood for transfusions. The transportation of blood would require refrigerated trucks.

You might also go one step further and suggest that the blood bank is used to gather information about the population's health, as well as using blood for transfusions. A good way to end this question would be to give a brief conclusion, stating that safety is the most important factor to consider, although all factors would need research before a comprehensive plan could be formulated.

Top tips

It's very important that you know your A level syllabus as answers may require/ benefit from factual knowledge you have already acquired. Be prepared to discuss species that you have not encountered before and in these instances, apply knowledge that you have and lateral thought. Many successful applicants find watching nature documentaries and regularly visiting the *Scientific American* and *New Scientist* websites as helpful ways to keep abreast of your subject and its wider context. As one graduate said, 'there's nothing like a bit of David Attenborough to inspire you!'

Chemistry / Natural Sciences (Bio.& Phys.)

Questions to get you thinking...

What makes a material hard?

Explain how catalysts work.

How many atoms are there in a brussel sprout?

Name a reaction in which a bond is made.

Do you think O-H and O-D (deuterium) bonds differ in strength? (past question)

At any stage of the interview, do not be afraid to ask for help as you work through the questions. This is a purely theorising question. You are not really expected to know the answer but the interviewer will want to see how you approach it.

Start by thinking about what you know about deuterium ie. the fact that it has a significantly greater atomic weight than hydrogen. It is twice as heavy so you should be able to theorise that that the bonds will be very different.

Assuming the bonds do have different strengths, how will this affect the rate of exchange of hydrogen or deuterium ions in an aqueous solution? For example in a carboxylic acid? (past question)

Begin by thinking about what you already understand about dynamic equilibriums and how activation energy affects reaction rate. Based on this you can draw a reaction diagram of each dynamic equilibrium (one being the O-H equilibrium, the other being the O-D). Consider the reaction speed in both directions as well as how this affects the rate of exchange.

Don't be afraid to ask if you can draw diagrams as it will help you think clearly and follow through with your ideas. Drawing diagrams is also an essential part of the chemistry tutorials and supervisions you will be having in the future.

Given different rates of exchange, how will this affect the equilibrium point and therefore the acidity of the non-deuteriated and deuteriated forms? (past question)

You could start by explaining the formula for an equilibrium point based on reaction rates:

$K_p = k_1 / k_2$

where K_p is the equilibrium at constant pressure. Based on what you know about the different reaction rates for the hydrogen and deuterium exchange you can predict the different equilibrium points. This will then allow you to go on to explain the different concentrations of H^+ and D^+ and how this affects acidity.

If this interests you, you can go further by reading about the Kinetic Isotope Effect.

a. How does the radius of an ion affect the strength of its interaction with water? (past question)

You may already know that small ions are strongly polarising and will therefore have a strong interaction with water because their charge is more densely concentrated.

b. How do cation and anion radii affect the ionic bond strength in an ionic lattice? For example NaCl. (past question)

You may know from your school work that ionic lattice bond strength is affected by ionic radius and ionic charge. Greater ionic radii increase the distance between the ions in the lattice, and the strength of interaction is a function of 1/r.

c. What does the graph of $1/r^2$ (r squared) look like? (past question)

You are being asked this as a precursor to the next question. You will be able to use this graph to show that as the ionic radii increase there is a sharp drop off in the strength of the interactions.

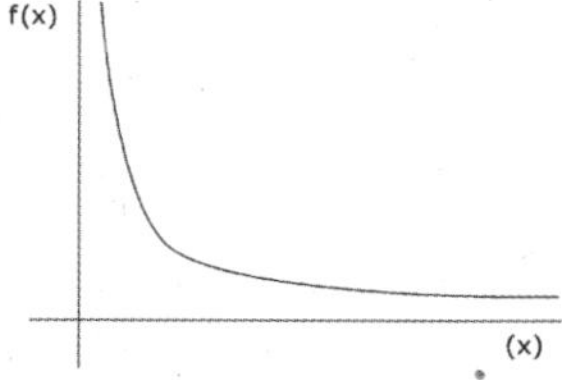

Given the answers to a, b, c how would you explain solubility trends in the series NaF -> NaCI and AgF -> AgCl?

This is the culmination of the answers you have given in the first three parts. You know the factors affecting the bond strength in the ionic lattice, and the strength of the cation and anion interactions with water. Using your knowledge that Na^+ is a relatively small anion and Ag^+ is a relatively large anion, you need to theorise about how the solubility trends down the halide group will differ. Drawing a Hess's Law diagram for this reaction would be a useful way of working through this analysis. You can use all of the knowledge and skills from your schoolwork and apply them to the question.

Hopefully you've seen from this that you can work through what seems like a complex problem by building on what you already know. If at any point you get stuck in your interview, you can ask for help. Even if you do end up with the wrong answer or make mistakes along the way, it doesn't matter too much as long as you've been thinking intelligently as you work through the problem.

Budding Chemists should also check out the questions in both the Maths and Physics section.

Classics

Questions to get you thinking...

What role did the chorus have in Greek plays and how well do they translate into a modern context?

What would happen if the Classics department burnt down?

Did the Romans or the Greeks leave a more notable impression on the culture of today? How?

What parallels can be drawn between the East-West culture today and the gap between classical civilisation and now?

Classics interviews often ask you to analyse a classical text. For the purposes of this exercise, we have chosen a particular poem.

Comment on this poem by Catullus.

odi et amo. quare id faciam, fortasse requiris?
nescio, sed fieri sentio et excrucior.

The interviewer will not expect you to offer a complete translation into English and you do not need to understand every word. An unseen commentary allows you to apply your existing knowledge of vocabulary, grammar and context intelligently and gives you the opportunity to offer insightful and analytical suggestions as to why Catullus chose that word, that image, that syntax etc. in his poem. Be instinctive and concentrate on your impressions of the poem - look, understand, evaluate, and respond.

You might start by commenting on the form of the poem – it is a couplet. You could point out that Catullus expresses paradoxical, conflicting feelings. 'Odi et amo' – 'I hate' and 'I love'. You could then highlight the fact that he exploits this couplet form well by asking a question in the first line and then answering it in the second line. What might strike you next as you look closer at the poem is the use of verbs – 'odi... amo... faciam... nescio... sentio... excrucrior' – six extreme verbs all in the first person, which focus the reader's attention on the author's intense feelings and actions, which are contradictory and successfully communicate the push-pull of emotions. He hates, he loves, he does, he does not know, he feels and he is in torment. Look at the first three words and the last three words, which mirror the same construction - verb - conjunction - verb. If you analyse the four verbs used – 'odi...amo...sentio...excrucior', you might notice that the two outer verbs indicate a negative feel and the two inner words are generally positive, producing an ABBA chiasmus in the poem. It can even be said that positioning the first word and the last word – 'I hate' and 'I am in torment' at the very beginning and at the very end of the poem suggests that the overriding feelings are negative, and renders the overall tone of the poem gloomy. You could suggest that his tight structuring is an attempt to organise and comprehend his conflicting emotions.

You might also know that Catullus was a member of the Neotericoi – the 'new poets', who were experimenting with a shorter form of poem, which they called an epigram and which aimed at brevity, succinct phrasing and intense emotion contained in few words. You might comment on how successful you feel he has been to this end. It is the structure of this poem, the syntax and the word choice which are the most notable features - the analysis of which can lead to the most thorough understanding of the state of mind of the author. Commenting on how and where certain words are used allows you, the reader, to understand the author's intentions and to impress the interviewer with your analytical ability.

Would ancient history be different if it was written by slaves? (past question)

A question like this calls on your on-the-spot intuition and it allows you to draw on your knowledge of any texts you have studied. The interviewer is looking for you to demonstrate an ability and a willingness to think for yourself and to develop an argument that cannot have been simply digested and regurgitated from another source. As an interviewer, you are looking for someone who has read enough ancient history to have sufficient knowledge of the subject matter to express an informed opinion, coupled with an ability to analyse the subject matter interestingly and originally enough to come up with a stimulating and persuasive argument.

Firstly, you might like to stress that there were many different types of slave, and many different possible experiences of history in the Ancient World. A Greek private tutor, a paedogogus, might have had very different ideas to a gladiator. Some household slaves, particularly those with an ability to educate Roman youth or with knowledge of medicine, would have had very different ideas to a German slave, prized for his physical strength, used in an auxilia army role. Secondly, you could mention how slavery in Greece varied from city state to city state: a helot would view things very differently to a slave in Athens (where striking a slave was forbidden and masters apparently tolerated back-chat from slaves). Here you could refer to the comedies of Menander, Plautus and Terence, where the slaves have a relatively jolly time of it. Thirdly, it might be a good idea to comment on how treatment of slaves changed over time and how the law evolved. A slave in the Roman Republic would have had fewer rights than a slave of the Imperial period (when the right to kill a slave at a whim was removed).

You could mention that it helps, when you are writing history, to have taken part in it. The majority of ancient historians were wealthy men with leisure and contacts. Herodotus travelled through many lands at a time when this was unusual. This required a private income (a big one) and free time (lots of it). Livy was a provincial of plebeian origin, but he was educated in oratory and Greek, indicating rank. The educational level required to write history, the leisure time, the breadth of experience, would have been so far removed from the experience of most slaves that an answer to this question is, at best, highly speculative.

That said, one of Claudius' freedmen (ex-slaves) would have had the ear of the emperor and would have had much to say about foreign policy-and would have been in favour of the Imperial system, as opposed to the romantic Republican (and historian) Claudius, or Livy, who wanted to abolish the system of Emperors (where slaves favoured by the emperor could wield real influence) and bring back the old Republic (where slaves could be maimed by their masters on a whim). We can speculate that an Athenian slave would have written favourably of the legislator Draco, who made the murder of a slave punishable by death, despite his prevailing reputation for severity. He might have had less rosy an opinion of Aristotle, for whom slaves were 'living tools' fit only for physical labour, or Homer, who wrote that 'Jove takes half the goodness out of a man when he makes a slave of him'.

Top Tips

In Classics interviews, you might be asked about overarching topics of Classical literature and your interviewer might touch on any of philosophy, history, archaeology, art, philology and linguistics. It is highly beneficial to develop in-depth knowledge of at least one of these topics, in order to enter into a discussion with your interviewer.

Developing a special interest can help. Soak up a particular author (e.g. one of the great Greek Tragedians Aeschylus, Sophocles or Euripides or study Ovid's use of myth), a genre (e.g. Latin love elegy, Ancient Greek political comedy etc.), an historical period (e.g. Peloponnesian War or the final days of the Roman

Republic) architectural style or period of art. Do not be afraid to have strong or even controversial opinions and reactions to ancient authors or historical events. The interviewer is looking for someone who has passionate reactions to the Ancient World, just ensure you use examples to support your argument. Show initiative and be proactive in your search for new knowledge. Visiting museums (for example, the Parthenon friezes at the British Museum), Ancient Roman and Greek archaeological sites, going to the theatre to watch an Ancient Greek play, or simply watching a suitable documentary on the BBC or History Channel, can show you are a motivated student, capable of going one step further to research your subject away from the classroom.

It's always good to brush up on grammar and your vocabularly to prepare for unseen passages you might be presented with in the interview, but do not spend hours revising. You may be asked about the essays or commentaries you have submitted as well as what you are studying at A level, what you enjoy about the Classics and what you look forward to studying on the course. Re-read any submitted essays/commentaries and develop new arguments and points in case you are questioned on them in the interview.

It's good to develop your critical thinking skills. Train your analytical responses to the literature you have already studied by reading scholars' critical responses (secondary literature) and deciding whether you agree with their views. You are entitled to have an opinion, you just need to have evidence to support your case.

Top tips for studying Classics ab initio

The interviewer may want to test your ability to react critically and analytically to a literary text, as this exercise makes up a large part of the course. Delve into a literary genre or start reading a particular author in any language and assess your reactions to the text in terms of style, language, context, themes, imagery, tone, register etc. Why did you like/not like it? Read a selection of plays/prose/poetry in translation to help you develop an understanding of the genres and periods and to get you excited about them! One possibility is to choose an author, for example Ovid or Aristophanes, who has left us a large legacy of work and track their literary development to gain a better understanding of the historical context.

It can be helpful to familiarise yourself with terminology used in literary criticism such as anaphora, pathetic fallacy, soliloquy, oxymoron and onomatopoeia, but do not get too caught up revising every single critical word and its meaning. Start familiarising yourself with the epic poets Homer and Virgil. Begin to learn the Greek alphabet and try translating some passages of Greek and Latin into English with the help of a dictionary and grammar guide to get to grips with basic language structures.

Computer Science

Questions to get you thinking...

What are the possible ways of making a secure transfer?

How would you ensure security between two people, A and B?

Why is the number 2.7182818... used in mathematics?

Explain briefly the difference between science and technology.

We spoke to a number of Oxbridge Computer Scientists, who experienced a range of interview questions, some mathematical or logic-based, while others tended to focus on the science of computers. We take a look at these types of questions.

If you have a sorted array of numbers, how would you find number n? (past question)

In other words, if you have a random array of 100 numbers, in ascending order, how would you find the number 38? The challenge is to answer this question out loud using logic. You might initially think to look at each number sequentially, but that would be inefficient. The tutor might suggest other starting points. What about the middle number? What if the middle number is bigger than n? What if the middle number is smaller? In these cases, which portions of the array might be sensible to focus on? What the tutor is looking for is for you to work with them. So really take on board their advice, articulate what you are thinking and why. They are there to help you get to the right answer (as they might do in the future with a successful candidate during their university lives).

What is the one fundamental difference between a spreadsheet and a database as surely both hold information? Perhaps there is no fundamental difference? (past question)

A good place to start here would be to acknowledge that both a spreadsheet and database hold information, but the way in which they hold information differs. A spreadsheet is a flat file document that stores each line of information in serial. There is a list of attributes, or columns that each record has a piece of information in. The spreadsheet can be searched for values and calculations can be made using information in certain columns, or fields, but without the use of macros and higher order coding, not much else can be done. In contrast, a database is more intelligent in the way it stores information. Moreover, the user must be more aware of the relationships between the data they are to store. Rather than just simply listing records, in a database there are different entities which each contain their own kind of record. There are relationships defined between these entities that ensure that data stored is correct - referential integrity ensures that related data is consistent e.g. 'John Smith' is always referred to as 'John Smith' and there is never the opportunity for 'John Smiht' to be confused with 'John Smith'.

In addition, you might add here that within the infrastructure of the database, inferences (otherwise known as queries) can be generated. These are smart, modifiable views of the data created by the user. In this way, a database can address a more complex requirement than can a spreadsheet.

A good conclusion will then come back to the initial question, stating that therefore, as illustrated, there is a fundamental difference between a spreadsheet and a database.

What is the structure of URLs? (past question)

Firstly, when answering a question such as this, it is always good to demonstrate that you understand the concepts to which the question is referring. In this instance, you should define a URL. URLs of the form http://my.example.com/page.html are pointers to a particular page on a website. They are unique, case insensitive and should make more sense to the user than the corresponding IP address.

You can then explain in detail, the major parts of the URL structure. URL's have five major parts as follows:

- The first http:// is the protocol being used to access the page. This may be https:// or even ftp:// if a file transfer is being done.
- Next is the subdomain. This is an optional part and is defined by the owner of the domain. It may signify a different section of the same site or simply forward to another URL.
- Then it is is the top level domain including the country code and/or organisation code. The suffix signifies the location of the organisation and its type. Options include .com, .co.uk, .org or even .edu.
- Next is the directory under the main domain. A homepage URL would not normally feature anything from this point onwards.
- Finally, consider the format of the file. Previously, this always featured html or .htm. Nowadays, it is optional.

Top tips

All aspiring Computer Scientists should brush up on their Mathematics and Physics as they often ask technical questions. Practise answering and articulating answers to maths and logic questions out loud. The interviewer needs to be able to understand and follow your train of thought and you need to be able to justify your problem solving logic verbally. Don't fret about not getting an answer right in the interview - this will probably happen and it does not matter. Be aware that the interviewer is there to support you and help guide you to your answer – be responsive to their suggestions and interact with them.

Economics/Economics & Management/PPE

Questions to get you thinking...

Who do you think is the greatest economist?

What do we mean when we say someone deserves a reward?

Would you support the privatisation of the NHS?

What is the biggest economic problem facing Britain today?

Economics interviews often test your understanding of economic theory and current affairs. For the purposes of this exercise we have created four example questions, based on similar ones that have been asked in the past. The first is an example of a microeconomics question, the second a macroeconomics question, the third an example of a logical thinking question and finally a mathematics question.

What factors could be expected to affect the price of houses in a free market?

At the core of this question is the interaction of supply and demand for houses. Given this, a logical way to answer the question, could be to work out the factors affecting supply and demand and then go on to explain how their interaction results in a final equilibrium price. To make your answer even stronger, it would also be good to consider what might affect the price of an individual house as opposed to what affects the price of houses in general in a free market.

Major factors affecting demand for housing include: the **incomes of households** in the economy, which affects the amount they are able to spend on housing in general, **mortgage interest rates** are key, as lower rates make houses in general more affordable and vice versa, likewise **expectations of future house prices** and future mortgage interest rates affect what householders might be willing to pay for housing.

The demand for a house rather than houses in general could be affected by: the **preferences of householders** in the economy, for example, are Georgian houses in fashion or is there a fad for the clean lines of modern architecture? This factor might also apply to houses generally, for example, if owning your own home is a sign of status in a society this may increase willingness to pay across the economy, the **size and nature of the house**, e.g. is it a cottage, flat, bungalow, mansion, and so on, the **location of the house**, for example is it located in a densely populated urban centre where there are many jobs or in a rural area; is it near good schools and local amenities?

Meanwhile, housing supply is determined by the existing stock of houses, and the building of new houses.

The next step in answering this question is to draw a graph of supply and demand and illustrate the equilibrium price. One thing to note is that because a new building contributes only about 1.1 per cent to the existing stock each year, the supply of houses is relatively inelastic even over long periods. This means that the supply curve will be steep. In contrast, demand is relatively elastic because consumers are highly sensitive to house prices. This means the demand curve will be relatively shallow.

You could also demonstrate how changing demand or supply conditions would affect the equilibrium. For example, during the mid to late 1980s incomes grew rapidly, while financial deregulation in 1987 made mortgages cheaper and easier to obtain. This led to a rise in demand, shifting the demand curve up and right and causing a housing market boom.

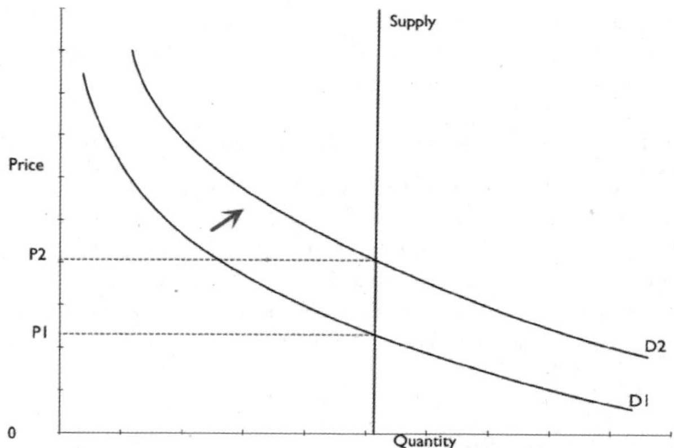

What effect would a tightening of monetary policy have on the value of government bonds in the bond markets?

The first step in answering this question is to define the various terms: 'monetary tightening' is a constriction of the supply of money by the central bank. 'Government bonds' are assets sold by the government to investors as a way of borrowing money. Investors hand over cash for the bonds to the government, in exchange for a promise by the government to repay this money at a specified future date. In the meantime, the investors receive interest payments too from the government to compensate them for the amount of money they could have made by investing this cash elsewhere, and also for the risk that the government will go bankrupt and not repay the debt.

Next, a good answer would then go on to explain how a central bank tightens monetary policy. It does this through 'open market operations' which work as follows: the central bank sells government bonds to investors from its own portfolio in exchange for cash. This reduces the supply of money the public holds. As we know from the law of supply and demand (see above question), an increase in the supply of bonds in the market for a given demand will cause the price of the bonds to fall. One thing to note here is that this is equivalent to a rise in the interest rate because less money is needed today for a given value in the future. Bond prices, therefore, are inversely related to interest rates.

At this stage, a strong applicant would look to expand further on the results of this action on aggregate demand in the economy. The rate of interest on savings in the economy has increased so consumers may be encouraged to save rather than spend. If foreigners want to buy debt then they must first buy domestic currency: an increase in the interest rate will increase their demand for domestic currency which, as we know from the question above, will make domestic currency relatively more expensive. Exports become more expensive and imports cheaper. You will add another layer of dynamism to your answer if you show knowledge of the current interest rate set by the central bank, the Bank of England, and recent changes in interest rates.

What is the angle between the hands on a clock at quarter past three?

This is a simple case of mental arithmetic. The best way to answer this question is to create a mental picture of a clock. Do NOT fall into the trap of thinking the angle is zero! There are 360 degrees in a circle and 12 hours on a clock face, so the angle between each hour is 360/12 = 30 degrees. The minute hand is directly over the '3' marking. However, the hour hand will be a quarter of the way between the '3' and '4' markings. Therefore, the angle between the hands is 30/4 = 7.5 degrees.

Draw a graph of y = sin(x^2)

As you will know from A level maths, the graph of y = sin(x) looks like this:

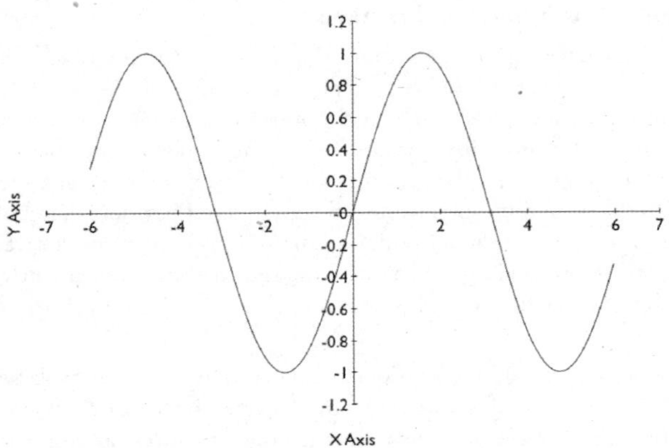

When working out how to draw $\sin(x^2)$, think about the fundamentals of the graph, rather than trying to plot specific points: first, evaluate what the maximum and minimum values for y will be. Since the maximum value of y for $\sin(x)$ is 1, no matter how large x, the maximum value of $\sin(x^2)$ will also be 1. Likewise the minimum value will also be -1, as this is the minimum for any value of x and thus x^2. Next, think about the frequency of oscillations. As x increases, x^2 increases exponentially, the rate at which y oscillates between 1 and -1 will increase. This will mean the gap between maxima and minima will decrease as x gets larger than zero or less than zero.

Finally, note that the graph of $y = x^2$ is symmetrical about the y axis, and thus so will the graph of $y = \sin(x^2)$. Hence the graph will look as follows:

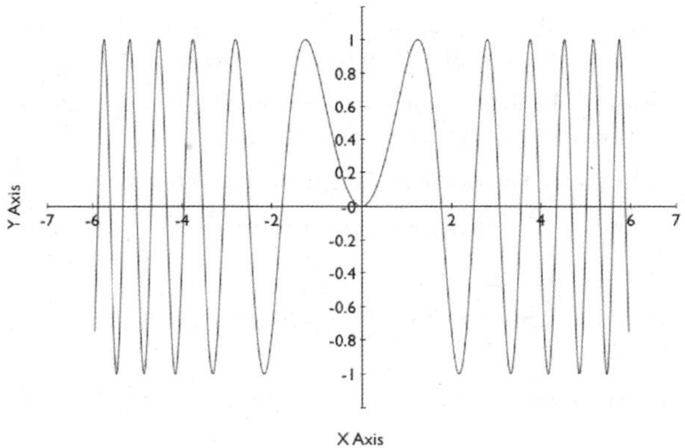

Top tips

Have a glance through our glossary. Economics is full of jargon. This can seem tricky at first, but as your understanding of the subject develops if will become clear how useful it is to have words for very specific concepts. Here are some examples of vocabulary that an Oxbridge interviewer may use:

Budget deficit/surplus - the excess/shortfall of government spending over government receipts from taxation.

Business cycle - the short-term fluctuations in the economy's output around its trend path.

Central bank - the institution responsible for implementing monetary policy (e.g. the Bank of England in the UK and the Federal Reserve in the USA).

Consumption - goods and services purchased by consumers.

Econometrics - the use of statistical techniques to quantify relationships in economic data.

Economics - the study of how individuals and societies allocate scarce resources.

Endogenous variable - one explained by the model.

Equilibrium - a state of balance between opposing forces, such as supply and demand in the market.

Exogenous variable - one taken as given; assumed rather than explained in the model.

Fiscal policy - policy on government spending and taxation.

GDP (Gross Domestic Product) - the total income/production of the economy earned/produced domestically.

Inflation - the rate of increase in the level of overall prices.

Investment - goods purchased by firms to increase their stock of capital.

Macroeconomics - the study of the economy as a whole; typical variables of interest include inflation, interest rates and exchange rates.

Microeconomics - the study of individual behaviour with respect to consumers' and firms' decisions about the allocation of resources.

Monetary policy - policy on the money supply and interest rates.

Monopoly - a market in which there is only one producer.

Profit - revenue minus costs.

Real variable - a variable which has been adjusted for inflation (as opposed to a nominal variable).

Unemployment rate - the percentage of the labour force without jobs.

You may be asked questions to test your comprehension of an article relevant to an economic topic. You may also be asked to talk about a couple of areas of the subject that especially interest you (such as economic growth in the third world), or an economist you admire (for instance John Maynard Keynes) and therefore it is helpful to think about how you might approach such questions. It is a good idea if you can, to talk about one or two books or articles you have read in your interview, particularly if they are mentioned on your personal statement. If you bring up a book, though, make sure you are able to talk in some detail about its ideas!

An understanding of mathematics is fundamental to economics and that is why Oxbridge Economic tutors deem mathematics an important subject to have studied at A Level or equivalent. If you are new to the subject, your interviewers will naturally not expect you to know as much as your peers who have done economics before and in this instance your interviewer will likely ask you more logic or maths-based questions. However, you should be able to show an initial understanding of key principles, to show you are committed and motivated to study the subject.

English

Questions to get you thinking...

Do you think that the director of a play should have absolute power, or should he/she be flexible?

Why study English at university rather than read in your spare time?

Can a play just be read, or must it be seen on stage to be understood?

What is tragedy?

The big picture

The biggest difference between studying literature at Oxbridge and studying it at school is that tutors are looking for students who can be independent thinkers. At Oxbridge, you are much more likely to have your accepted notions challenged with questions like, 'Why do you think that?' You must therefore be prepared to justify all your opinions. You'll be expected to be familiar with what critics, past and present, have had to say about particular works and to position your own responses in relation to theirs. Because the Oxbridge courses are structured chronologically, going from Old and Middle English texts all the way to contemporary works, you'll be expected to start making links between works from different periods and genres and show your understanding of how English literature has developed over the centuries.

Be prepared

You cannot predict what your interview will be like, but you should be prepared to have tutors really challenge your ideas; it might seem like they're 'putting you on the spot' but really they're trying to see how you respond when asked to justify what you think. Don't be scared, but rather view the experience as a stimulating conversation about literature. It may give you a sneak peak at what tutorials will be like if you eventually get accepted.

Come into your interview knowing which works of literature you can discuss most thoroughly and passionately. Tutors will be looking for students who have not just dutifully read the set texts for their A levels, but who are excited about literature and have gone on to do outside reading. That doesn't mean you should try to read everything under the sun: you can't do that, but the works you do know should be diverse. Think about which texts and authors you know best. Are they all from the same period? Are they all novels? Perhaps explore some older works or read some poetry. If you enjoyed the books by a particular author, read some of his other works, or read what the critics have to say. In short, if in the months leading up to the interview you are always reading some challenging, literary work and you are thinking about it critically, making connections with other works you've read, then you'll be in good shape. Look at the reading lists for the Oxbridge courses online to see what kinds of works you'd be reading there. This should give you some ideas for new things to dip into.

The interview

Be prepared to speak about any work that you've mentioned on your personal statement. The tutor may spend most of the interview talking about that, or they may not mention it. Make sure you spend time carefully choosing what to say in your personal statement. Tutors will pick up on statements that read like laundry lists, i.e. 'I read this book, this book, and this book.' Frankly, it doesn't matter that you have read the book – what's important is that you have something significant to say about it! Avoid generalities and do not drop in catchphrases you've heard about the books which aren't really your own. These are things tutors may challenge you on. One applicant was asked whether they thought David Tennant made a good Hamlet, having mentioned they had seen the production in their personal statement.

Writing the personal statement is good preparation for the interview. If you devote time to asking yourself questions like, 'Which works do I most respond to and why? What do I think literature's purpose in the world is?' and refine your answers so that they are strong and specific, then you will not only have a good personal statement, you will also have done a necessary self-evaluation which will make you more confident in discussing your opinions.

Your tutor may be interested to get into some of the biggest debates from the history of literature, such as 'Does literature have a moral purpose?', 'Should a work be judged based on an author's intentions or by some other criterion?' If you find a useful introductory anthology to literary criticism and browse through it, you can familiarise yourself with these questions and start to develop your own opinions. Remember, the big questions don't necessarily have a right answer: the key is to make a claim and be able to justify it, especially when the tutor challenges you by offering a conflicting opinion.

Don't forget to think about more personal questions, such as 'Why do you want to study literature?' or 'Why do you want to study at Oxbridge?' These are often the sorts of questions that students forget to ask themselves, but it is crucially important that you have good answers to them. This will demonstrate that you're excited about this field of study and that you've put some thought into the application process.

Tackling the unknown

Even if you have read beyond your school syllabus, it's highly likely that a tutor may mention an author or a work or concept that you're unfamiliar with. He may even present you with a text in the interview. Don't panic! The interview is not a trivia quiz: you don't get in just because you know the poem the tutor's chosen. What's more important is that you can look at it with the tutor and come up with some interesting things to say about it.

Do not be afraid to acknowledge when you don't know something. This is much better than blithely pretending that you do know and going down the wrong path. If you're given a poem by W. H. Auden and you're not sure if W. H. is a man or a woman, don't be afraid to ask. It's better than referring to Auden as 'she' throughout your interview. Remember that when faced with an unfamiliar text, you are working through it during the interview so there's nothing wrong with saying things like, 'Well, I'm unfamiliar with this, but having read it just now it seems to me that…' Be sure to have good reasons why the poem seems that way to you. Be able to point to the elements in the text that have led you to draw the conclusions that you've drawn.

Reading a text that's just been handed to you and coming up with interesting things to say requires a certain amount of skill and practice. It's all in how you approach it, really. A few simple pointers will help you: read the text all the way through (out loud if appropriate), then go back and read again, looking for key elements. Ask basic questions such as: Who is speaking? What is going on in this piece? Does it have a story? Move on to questions like: What is the tone of voice? What are the key themes, ideas, opinions being explored?

Get the technique right

Young literature students often focus too much on content and theme in a literary work and forget to make links with form and technique – a common pitfall too when it comes to Oxford's English admissions test – the ELAT (English Literature Admissions Test). Remember that poems and novels are different to essays: writers may have an intention or a theme that they have set out to explore but they're doing it through literary techniques. That's what makes literature different from, say, a philosophical essay or an opinion piece in *The Guardian*. Always try to identify the techniques that are at play in the text. Try to link form to content: often the way that a writer has chosen to express himself has a strong connection to the ideas that he is trying to convey.

There are certain basic literary techniques (especially in poetry) that you should look for every time you read a piece. As you do your first and second reading, you should register these things and ask yourself how they operate in this particular work: What are the divisions in the piece? Is it divided into stanzas, for instance? Why do you think the poet chose to place the breaks where they are? What is the meter (i.e. the rhythm)? Is it regular or does it change throughout the work? Does it follow a traditional meter like iambic pentameter and, if so, are there any points where that meter breaks or changes? Does the poem conform to any set form, such as a sonnet? Or is it freer in its form? Why is the overall structure appropriate for the nature of the theme or idea being explored? Is there any rhyme? Which words rhyme with which and is there any significance to that? What is the rhyme structure of the piece as a whole? Has the writer employed any other techniques, such as enjambement, where the thoughts being expressed spill over or 'run on' from one line into the next? Why has he or she chosen to make the line breaks that way? Are there any striking metaphors or imagery? If you notice a system of related images, such as images of nature or money or something else, why do you think the poet has selected these to present his or her theme?

Top tips

Try to ground your impressions about what the poem means by pointing to the places in the text where you can find evidence for your assertions. If you see evidence of poetic techniques such as those mentioned above, use the technical terms, but make sure you're using them correctly. Perhaps study the definitions of frequently used literary terms like irony or satire before the interview. If you do use them, be prepared to say what they mean. And, finally, it's almost never valuable to say that a literary work is interesting. The natural response to that is, 'Why? What's so interesting about it?' Skip that step and get into the meat of what the poem or text is doing. The more specific you are, the more substantive things you'll have to say and the more you'll impress the tutor.

Experimental Psychology / Psychology & Philosophy

Questions to get you thinking...

Who is the most intelligent: the straight-A Oxbridge candidate or the young mechanic living in Africa who left school at 14?

How do we test memory in animals, and can we apply the findings to humans?

Can you teach creativity?

What use is psychological study for society?

Why do we have handedness? (past question)

Questions like this, that contain unknown material, invite you to speculate, so make sure you are clear that you are indeed speculating rather than stating your opinions as fact. The interviewer may prompt you to aid debate, don't think that this is a negative action or that you are not saying enough, they just want to understand better how you think or the method behind your reasoning. Strong answers to questions like these would clearly take one or two approaches to psychology, attempting to explain how handedness can be explained by them, and then weigh up the two approaches against one another.

The biological or physiological approach to psychology may suggest that handedness occurs to conserve energy. If only one side of the body has to develop higher levels of dexterity to perform tasks efficiently then there seems to be little benefit in both sides of the body developing to the same and complex degree. It may also be that because language is located in one side of the brain – the left hemisphere – this part of the brain already has in place more complex neural connections, and therefore has a better capacity to form the dominant hemisphere. This is supported by the fact that the majority of people are right handed (which corresponds to having a dominant left hemisphere).

On the other hand, the question of handedness can also be explained from a behavioural perspective. There are two ways of explaining this. Firstly, modelling behaviour could occur when an infant sees their caregiver using one particular hand to do certain tasks they copy this. Secondly, conditioning may play a part. Perhaps, an infant uses a certain hand to pick up a cup of juice because it is on one side of their highchair. They then drink the juice and are rewarded by the good taste. The action of using this hand and being rewarded are linked in a form of classical conditioning.

You then might conclude that although both of these approaches have valid points, the biological approach punches more weight. It has been proven that handedness is linked to a particular cerebral hemisphere, and therefore seems logical that only one side of the brain should hold the capacity for handedness.

How would a psychologist measure normality? (past question)

'Very strong answers would include ways of measuring more than one type of normality,' says one Oxford Experimental Psychology graduate. They would also then give an opinion of which approach they feel is superior and why.

As we learn in mathematics, deviation from statistical norms is measured using the bell shaped curve of normal distribution (see image). The x axis shows the frequency/level of a behaviour/characteristic, and the y axis the proportion of people in the population displaying that frequency/level. Arbitrary norms are set for the lower and upper limits, and a person outside of these norms is considered to be abnormal. An example would be levels of anxiety. Very high levels of anxiety are abnormal, and may lead to a diagnosis of an anxiety disorder. Very low levels of anxiety may also be indicative of a mental health problem.

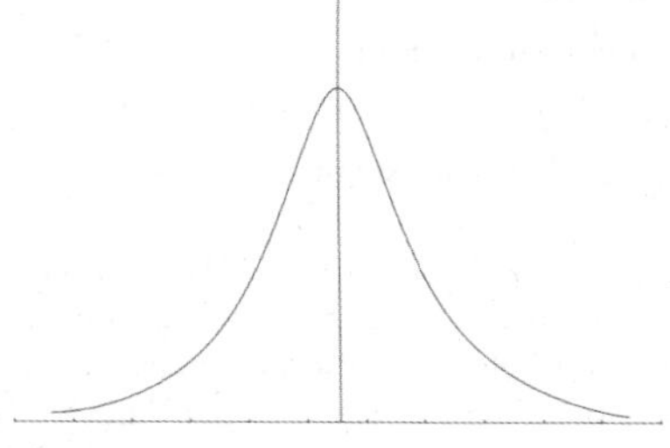

Another method of measuring normality is to define abnormal as causing distress to self/others. Whereas two people might engage in the same level of behaviour, for example checking their watch frequently, one may do this as part of their routine because they like to know the time, and are not overly distressed if they cannot access the time. The other may find it crucial to check their watch, infringing on their day to day happiness, and experience great distress/panic if for some reason they cannot check the time. This would be measured by a self-report diary, where the individual charted their feelings alongside their day to day experiences. It could also be measured through observations.

You might argue that monitoring the distress caused to self or others is a better way of measuring normality. This could be because it takes into account personal experiences of the sufferer, and therefore forms more of a basis for identifying and treating the condition. However, the statistical approach allows larger numbers of people to be more quickly identified, which could be advantageous.

Top tips

Ask questions: some interviewers will want you to assume certain things to formulate your answers, whereas for others part of the exercise will be for you to ask the correct questions to find out more about the situation. By asking a preliminary question you will be able to determine which of these situations you are in, and not deprive yourself of useful information. In answering questions, try to show logical development throughout your answer. Use terms commonly used in Psychology if they help you. For example, if looking at the question 'why would a 5 year old refuse to speak with you?', you could frame your answer by looking at factors which are internal (due to the child), external (due to the environment), stable (a problem that is always there), or unstable (a problem that is only due to this situation). Try to include a variety of factors in your answer. Perhaps also try to include a biological, physiological, social or behavioural factors. Do try to show your breadth of knowledge at all times.

Fine Art

Questions to get you thinking...

Can you use a variety of media to communicate your ideas?

Would you like to be treated like an artist from the word go?

Do you think artistically and does your work exist in its own right?

Having spoken to many successful Fine Art applicants, interviews for Fine Art tend to be a mix of testing artistic awareness, perception and skill. Our Fine Artists have offered the advice below, based on their own interview experiences, which they believe would be helpful to any aspiring Fine Art applicant to think about in advance of their interview, with its focus on both the theoretical and the practical. Fine Art at Oxford is an extremely competitive course (with only 20 students each year). The Ruskin school is world renowned, and applicants have usually completed an art foundation course before applying. Our Fine Art graduate explains elements of the application process.

Art tutors tend to be quite different animals to other academics. They tend to be very inviting and hospitable, incredibly patient, and somewhat laid back. It is true to say that they are like practising artists (as most of them are) and that they are intensively interested in what you make or more importantly what are you are going to make in the future, and they are there to help you achieve it. The more personal your artwork, and the greater relevance it has to you and your view of the world, the more likely it is that the tutors will believe your passion and sincerity.

Portfolio (go for quality not quantity):

Your portfolio should weigh no more than 10 kg, and should be submitted to the Ruskin School. In 2010, the deadline is noon on 13th November. You should demonstrate development and diversity in your ongoing approach to art by including:

Types of art:

Drawing should be central to your portfolio
Preliminary studies with final work
(Good quality) photographs of 2D and 3D work
BIG work is beautiful (it tends to hit home!)
Black and white drawings, not only colour
Art in a mixture of media
Work that isn't 'perfect' or 'finished'

Features of art work:

Make it recent and exciting!
Produce a spread of ideas and subject matter
Demonstrate your ability and potential
An evident commitment to art and design
Inventiveness and originality
Experimentation with materials and sources
Logical presentation

Sketchbooks:

Sketchbooks and personal notebooks are paramount to your application. They are of great value in recording images and exploring ideas, and should not be too contrived. They should also show your artistic thought processes and on-going development. Limit the number of sketchbooks you submit by providing those that show the greatest variety.

The Interview

'In my interview, a panel of five artists (four tutors and a current student) fired questions at me about my art work in a true climate of interrogation! Do not be afraid to argue and create a heated debate. I enjoyed bearing witness to the tutors' passionate and emotional debate about art, and to suddenly realise that I was contributing to it! In interviews, tutors tend to look through and pick out pieces of your art work, complimenting and questioning your work, in an attempt to locate your driving force and reason for creation. They may help you to see the relevance of your work to the greater art world and also suggest peripheral artists who are dealing with similar problems or issues. Taking new work to the interview is crucial. The tutors need to see that you are artistically inquisitive and continually researching and expanding on ideas. This will provide further fuel for the interview, and you must demonstrate a deeply informed awareness of contemporary art.'

Practical Test

One full day is spent on a practical test. The aim is to take you out of your comfort zone, but also allows you to be in your element (hopefully) while at interview! You should remember that they will probably compare your portfolio work with what you produce on the test, so try to approach the topic they give you with fresh ideas, while maintaining your usual thought processes or means of engaging with a topic. The work you produce in the practical test should not seem incongruous. Use the materials provided creatively and you may wish to bring your favourite charcoal or paint!

Geography

Questions to get you thinking...

What is the role of the media in Geography?

Describe a problem in your area which a geographer could solve.

What can we do to stop global warming?

How would you persuade an 11-year old to pursue Geography through GCSEs and beyond?

Geography is a multidisciplinary subject and the breadth of questions that applicants have been asked in past interviews, reflects this. For the purposes of this exercise, our geographers have created some sample questions, based on similar ones that have been asked in previous years, to help you think about the subject a little bit differently.

Should Physical and Human Geography be taught together and why?

This question tests the student's grasp of the purpose and scope of geography in an academic context. A good answer to this question may begin by breaking the question down, in other words, explaining what is meant by the terms Physical and Human geography. You might say Physical Geography investigates how the environment and natural habitats of earth operate. In contrast, Human Geography explores the spatial and temporal differences between human societies. The key point is that our physical and human worlds are mutually dependant and both Physical and Human Geography focus on exploring the links. You could then choose examples either from school work or wider reading e.g. volcanic eruptions to explain why such phenomena benefit from analysis of the human and physical impact.

This would naturally lead to a conclusion (and it is important that you do reach one) that Physical and Human Geography must be taught together. You might then wish to elaborate, suggesting that one of Geography's greatest strength is its ability to bridge the arts, social and natural sciences. Geography enables us to consider and analyse complex problems using a broad lens.

At school, modules on Physical and Human Geography tend to be taught separately. At university the boundaries are more blurred, with topics such as climate change discussed from a human and a physical perspective. In fact, at Oxford and Cambridge, undergraduate courses contain compulsory modules of Human and Physical Geography, while at other universities there is often a very real division between the two. If you choose to argue in favour of an integrated approach then it is useful to mention that this element of the Oxbridge course particularly appealed to you. This shows you have done your research and are up to date with contemporary teaching debates. Interviews may focus on Human or Physical Geography, or you may be tested on both.

What is more important, the economy or the environment?

This question tests a student's skills of evaluation and how well they can structure a logical argument. A definitive answer would require subjectivity, however, before you reach your conclusion, the interviewer is testing your ability to think objectively and to use examples and your existing knowledge to support your points.

Firstly, break down the two terms – the economy and the environment. The first refers to relations of production, exchange and consumption of goods and services. It is regulated by human structures. Issues of scale are important. National economies now operate globally and are increasingly interconnected. The environment refers broadly to the natural habitats of earth; the landforms and processes that operate to renew our eco-systems and provide the tools necessary for human existence.

Once you have defined these terms, you then need to consider the value of each concept. But how can you measure this? The environment and the economy are integral to our lives, and are extremely complex concepts. In evaluating the importance of each we are ultimately asking which do humans rely on more? Could we exist without one? Ultimately both are fundamental to our existence. With a question such as this, is it possible to reach an unbiased conclusion? Admissions tutors want to see evidence of your ability to interact with such a complex, macro idea and to have the confidence and intellect to ask these sorts of questions. This shows you have that ability to be flexible with your existing knowledge and are open to thinking and talking independently – exactly the qualities admissions tutors look for in successful applicants.

Top tips

At the core of geography are questions about place and space. Keep interested in these concepts and think about how they relate to you in terms of your reading, your studies and your daily life. One applicant last year was asked to talk about what they found interesting about their local area, another about what they thought made for an interesting geographic article in a magazine. You need to be interested and engaged with your subject, and in turn that will make you interesting!

In an interview you may be asked to analyse the key skills you have developed through fieldwork. The basis of your fieldwork investigation may be Human or Physical. Make sure, with this sort of question, you evaluate activities that you undertook during fieldwork i.e. why something was particularly useful or why something was not. You may be asked factual questions. This is more likely to occur if you have mentioned a particular topic on your personal statement or been given source material for the interview. Interviewers do not expect you to possess detailed knowledge on every geographic topic. Ensure you stay calm and use all the reading you have done before the interview to apply your knowledge to the question before you. Remain logical, think laterally and support your arguments.

History

Questions to get you thinking...

What is a historical source?

If you are closer to an event, will you record it more accurately?

How do historians obtain evidence?

What is the position of the individual in history?

Should history aim to please the public? (past question)

In this question you are being asked to comment on the subject as a concept. Your judgement is also being assessed. What is history? Who does it serve? And what is it for? These are all crucial questions that form the subtext. Your ability to define, conceptualise, and think deeply about your subject is what lies at the heart of this question. You have the opportunity to show here that you have thought long and hard about history – what it means to you and what it means to others. Remember that your interviewer will have, in all probability, some very fixed views on what his/her subject is about. You must, therefore, be prepared to defend anything you say. (There is nothing wrong with disagreeing, arguing, or debating with your interviewer – in fact it can be a good thing – but you must have a well constructed argument to do so).

There are three elements to tackling this question. Firstly, your definitions, both of history and what it means to 'please the public'. Second, your argument based on these definitions. Thirdly, your conclusion, following on from your chosen approach.

A good way to answer this question is to state your conclusion to the question – 'yes' or 'no' – and then go on to explain your answer. If it is 'no,' you might argue 'I do not think that history should aim to please the public. For me, history is about – or is at least aiming to be about – objective truth, and 'pleasing the public' should never be a factor in a historian's judgement.' History that is guided by what the public or certain people want to hear is nothing less than propaganda. It is subjective and therefore, in all likelihood, ignores counter arguments and facts that would lead towards a more accurate understanding. Most historians accept that it is impossible to be entirely objective in their work, but equally most – unless they are postmodernists – recognise objective history as the goal of their research.

As one Oxford History graduate commented, 'If I were an interviewer, I would expect candidates with views differing from my own to be able to engage in debate and to take the conversation somewhere interesting and new for me.'

Can you give me an example of where historians may be looking into the past for patterns that are not there? (past question)

In this question your knowledge of historiography, independent reading, and understanding of historical methodology are being assessed. You could perhaps give an example of a historian and then explain the nature of his/her work and the conclusions that he/she has drawn. You could then apply your analytical judgement to assess whether or not the historian was justified in looking for patterns. The obvious answer/example in my mind is Marxist historians such as Christopher Hill, E. P. Thompson and Eric Hobsbawm.

Another Oxford historian we spoke to said, 'as I understand it, Marxist historians – at least in their pure form (there are very few left) approach history from a unique perspective fostered by the political and economic ideology – Marxism. They believe, following on from Marx, that the "history of all hitherto existing societies" has been the history of "class struggle" [The Communist Manifesto]. In its simplest and crudest form, Marxists believe that the social hierarchy is divided into three – the aristocracy, the bourgeoisie, and the proletariat – and that there is a permanent antagonism between them. Based on their rather more complicated theory of the laws of production Marxists believe that the history of modern Europe (indeed of all societies) sees, or will see, the overthrow of the aristocracy by the bourgeoisie and then the overthrow of the bourgeoisie by the proletariat. This is not an objective conclusion, (although the Marxists try to prove their theory by facts), but an ideological conviction that has as much significance for contemporary politics as it did for history'. Therefore, Marxists historians have searched, within their individual areas of research, for social and economic patterns that point towards the proof of this theory.

Such is a bare-bones answer to the question, but a strong candidate would develop his/her answer further to involve a commentary on the pros and cons of Marxist history.

Top tips

Try and tackle questions head on. Pick a position and argue your case, showing an awareness of the complexities of the question. Definitely try and take a position rather than faffing in the middle, although 'not necessarily' is always a valid answer.

Do keep up your source work as this is likely to be tested at interview as well as through the HAT (History Aptitude Test) at Oxford University. You may be presented with a source at interview and asked to talk around it or to answer a specific question. Ensure that you work with what you are given. Do not underestimate the amount of information you can draw from the text. Try to leave your ethical and moral positions aside and look at the piece in the context of its style, its purpose and its meaning.

You should always be prepared to bow to the superior knowledge of your interviewer, if indeed he or she is right. (The likelihood is that they are!) There is no point in maintaining stubbornly that the battle of Trafalgar was fought in 1804 when it clearly wasn't. When you do give ground, however, (accepting a point of view is obviously a key part of education) you should do so in a way that shows your willingness to learn and grasp new ideas. Therefore try and take what you have just learned and run with it.

You may be asked factual questions, although this is not particularly common. Make sure you are hot on the work you have done at school, the arguments you have picked up from your reading outside school and be aware of what is going on in the press, particularly with regard to politics and economics. Try and demonstrate interest in societies and the way in which they interact.

Try and ensure that you show chronological breadth in terms of your reading and understanding of history. Many students come into the interview room with lots of information on modern history: Stalin, Hitler, Weimar Germany and Russia in the 19th century. Can you compare different periods and/or show understanding of ancient, medieval, early modern and modern history?

Although it is important to have facts at your fingertips in historical research, how you organise and draw conclusions from information is the toughest skill. When you are confronted with difficult questions, on paper or in an interview, remember that focusing on human motivation behind actions can be a good place to start and that, pulling apart a question or logically breaking down your approach to it, can take you somewhere exciting.

History of Art

Questions to get you thinking...

What is art?

Have you ever thought about why a building was constructed?

Are you interested in art created in a particular medium?

Do you enjoy art galleries and exhibitions?

These are some questions you should think about if you are considering History of Art. With so few places on the courses at both Oxford and Cambridge, our History of Art graduate suggests some ways in which you can successfully prepare for the interview...

What is the value of art?

What monetary value can art have? You should demonstrate an awareness of the modern art industry and how it works, such as who owns the art, who decides the price (for example, auction houses like Sotheby's), and the process by which it is commissioned, distributed and sold. Be aware, too, that the motivations behind selling art are sometimes different to those behind making art.

Who decided the canon of art and what is it? The responsibility lies with critics and art historians (such as E.H. Gombrich). Be aware of prejudices in their selection of artists (for example, Giorgio Vasari's Life of the Artists, published in 1556, selected the 'best' artists). They were all Italian, and the emphasis was on his great friend, Michelangelo. Why do Western universities still focus on the

Western canon when teaching their students? Does this propagate a one-sided approach to art? Have art historians attempted to look elsewhere?

What is the emotional value of art? An individual can connect with a visual stimulus in a unique way. Additionally, in the middle ages, the majority of people were illiterate and visual images on biblical stories allowed them to connect with their faith. Today, we can still connect with figures in art through powerful facial expressions.

What cultural significance can art have? How does art reflect culture and what role does it play? What can we find out about past cultures through art? To an art historian, art is a valuable source with which to research costumes, relationships, the role of women, and the role of foreigners.

Your response to a piece of art
Oxford requires you to submit a 750 word response to a piece of art or design before you come for interview. Both universities may use images you have never seen before at interview. Here are some points to consider:

General

Your initial response

Purpose and provenance

Material

Texture

Colour

Size and scale

Location

Style and period

Subject matter

Sculpture

Production method (carving or lost wax?)

Form (open or closed?)

Presentation (is it mounted?)

Painting

Type of paint

Colour of paint

Composition

Base (canvas or paper etc.)

Figures (if depicted): where are they looking?

Architecture

Line (angular or flowing?)

Structural elements

Decorative elements

How does form follow function?

Top tips

With your submitted written work, demonstrate that you can describe and analyse an image in words. Avoid simply dropping names of artists in your personal statement. Try to engage with some of their art too!

Human Sciences

Questions to get you thinking...

Are human beings still evolving?

Are there too many people in the world?

What is the purpose of religion?

Should gorillas have human rights?

Human Sciences blends creative and scientific thought. For the purposes of this exercise, we asked Human Sciences graduates to create different types of interview questions, based on their experiences of the interview.

What makes HIV/AIDS an interesting disease from the perspective of a Human Scientist?

A good answer to this question would be one that, in the first instance, addresses the biology of the disease. You could start by mentioning the fact that HIV/AIDS affects the immune system and renders the person more vulnerable to infection from other diseases. You could also mention that it is difficult to treat because of the ability of the virus to rapidly develop resistance to drugs. Don't be afraid to ask about the biological aspect of the disease if you don't know the science of the disease because the tutors will appreciate a demonstration of your interest.

To address the question from another angle, you could discuss where geographically HIV/AIDS is a significant problem (giving your definition of significant in your answer). Sub-Saharan Africa currently has a high number of HIV/AIDS cases as do parts of Asia. In these countries, the disease is often transmitted via sexual networks which include prostitutes and drug users. Transmission of the disease has been linked to poverty in the countries which have high prevalence rates. As an example, women driven to prostitution may be unable to refuse sex because it may be their main source of income. If condoms are unavailable or considered undesirable, these women may be at great risk because of cultural or religious factors.

HIV/AIDS creates problems within societies because it leaves orphans in its wake when parents die of the disease. Further, the disease may be transmitted to babies during pregnancy creating HIV positive children at birth. This means that governments need to find ways of caring for orphaned HIV positive children, who require general everyday care and treatment for the disease.

There are interesting instances of misinformation about transmission of HIV/AIDS. For example, some men believe that their disease can be cured by sexual intercourse with virgins, an act which may infect the women that they have sex with. Also, the use of condoms is avoided by certain people because they are associated with the infection itself. HIV/AIDS is stigmatised in many communities, therefore infection is often traumatic both for the patient and their family.

With your answer it is a good idea to show that you understand that HIV/AIDS is more than a biological disease; it has much wider social, cultural and economic implications which play an important role in the transmission, treatment and prevention of the disease.

What is the difference between marriage and mating?

This question tests your ability to identify ways in which human behaviour might differ from that of animals because of the existence of culture within human society.

You could answer this question by explaining that mating is natural, and likely to be driven by physiological desires which you could say are genetic or 'innate'. These desires are likely to be influenced by natural selection, and consequently behaviour which improves the reproductive fitness of an individual (the number of offspring they produce) is likely to spread within the population.

You could then go on to say that marriage in humans is determined by culture. Although men and women might have natural or innate preferences, the people they actually mate with are largely determined by who they marry. Rules about what makes a good marriage partner are often subject to cultural preferences, so for example in the West a woman may choose a marriage partner who has good levels of education, whereas in a more 'traditional' society a good marriage partner might be a man who is good at hunting. Another good point to add would be to raise the question of whether or not humans are still subject to natural selection because of the fact that our culture determines our behaviour?

It is important to demonstrate in your answer that humans are different to other animals, and that human behaviour is difficult to study because our culture influences our behaviour.

Top tips

You may be presented with graphical information in your interviews. If the graphs demonstrate a correlation between two variables, it is important to remember not to jump to a conclusion which assumes a causative relationship. Two factors can be associated without any real connection between them. For example, ice cream sales are high in July. However, July does not cause high ice cream sales; it is the hot weather in July which drives the purchase of ice cream.

Keep reading the news so that you are aware of developments such as the sequencing of the Neanderthal genome which has revealed that humans interbred with this extinct hominin species. The BBC news website has a great, trustworthy science section, so you can get some excellent talking points from here.

You may be asked to explain the purpose or function of an object shown to you in the interview. Remember that the interviewers may be assessing your ability to analyse objectively without assuming that objects have the same meaning for you as for people in other cultures. Objectivity is a skill which is essential in anthropology. Tutors aren't expecting you to have any specific knowledge about the object in question.

Law

Questions to get you thinking...

How important are jury trials?

When it comes to IVF treatment, should a male have rights equal to those of a female?

Do you think that anyone should be able to serve on a jury?

If A gave B £100 thinking it was a loan and B accepted the money thinking it was a gift, should he give it back?

At interview and throughout their degree, Law students are challenged to think analytically and this is reflected in the questions posed in interviews. For the purpose of this exercise, our legal minds got together and came up with this meaty law question, based on real past interview questions. The second question in this section is a real past question.

Are judges really necessary since they don't always make the law certain?

This question does require you to understand the basics behind judge-made law. While Oxbridge interviews do not strictly require prior knowledge of the law, you should have a grip on the basics here, from your awareness of legal cases in the news.

In summary, law in England and Wales comes primarily from two sources – statutes that are passed by Parliament and from judges (common law). Unlike other regimes (notably, civil law systems), common law allows that judges not only interpret and apply the law but that they contribute to the evolution of the law by laying down precedent. Essentially, a ruling by a higher court on a point of law, as long as it does not run in the face of a statute, is binding on lower courts and they must follow that ruling. For example, if the Supreme Court rules that a 'mobile phone' includes a hands-free kit in the above example, then a lower court cannot overrule this and rule that a mobile phone does not include a hands-free kit.

An initial reaction to this question could, and should, be questioning that perhaps judges are necessary for other reasons anyway so that even if they don't make the law certain, they are still necessary. You may argue that judges are necessary in order to apply the law, to be neutral arbiters in disputes and to sanction appropriately those who act contrary to the law. Question what the state of a regime would be if judges didn't exist – who would decide who was right or wrong if there was a dispute?

Next, you should go on to assess the claim that judges don't always make the law certain. First, try to understand why the claim would be made. It could perhaps be because judges are allowed this law-making power and so they are able to make rulings that change the law. Secondly, assess the claim. You may agree that judges don't always make the law certain – for example – taking the law stated earlier, if a judge ruled that 'driving' did include sitting at traffic lights, questions would still emerge such as 'does it matter if the engine is on or off?' or 'does it matter how long you expected to be stationary?'.

So the judge would not have made the law certain here, but perhaps you should question the state of the certainty of the law without this intervention. The law would be a lot less certain without a judge clarifying, to some extent, what 'driving' meant. So even though the judge did not make the law certain, s/he certainly went some way towards helping clarify the law and this may support the argument that judges are still necessary.

Smith sees Jones walking towards the edge of a cliff. Smith knows Jones is blind but does not like him, so allows him to walk off the edge of the cliff. Is this murder? (past question)

Obviously, murder has a legal definition. However, this question is not designed to test your understanding of the application of the law of murder to this situation (unless you have been given the law of murder and are expected to do this!) What it is really asking is whether Smith should be treated by the law in the same way as someone who commits a paradigmatic instance of murder, for example, a pre-meditated killing. Again, it is a normative evaluation testing your arguments justifying (or not) Smith's punishment. So your arguments should be on the issue of the moral blameworthiness of Smith and whether this blameworthiness is equal to that of a murderer.

In moral terms, it could quite simply be argued that if you know that somebody is going to die for certain, then you should stop them and prevent their death. However, this is obviously subject to various caveats which you should mention (or allow the interviewer to mention and respond to accordingly).

Is it certain that the person is going to die? In this case it seems from the facts that Jones is going to die for certain (especially bearing in mind that he is blind).

This probably adds to the moral culpability of Smith since surely there is not much of a burden on Smith to warn Jones bearing in mind the certainty of his death. Perhaps if the risk of death is not high, then there should not be this corresponding culpability e.g. if Jones was not walking towards the edge and only near the edge but aware of the drop.

How much do you need to do to prevent this death? In this case, if Smith is close enough to Jones that he could simply shout out to Jones to warn him then this is hugely morally blameworthy. Contrast this with the position whereby somebody is drowning in dangerous water – you should probably not be as morally culpable for failing to jump in to save that person as in Smith's case here. The fact that Smith knows that Jones is blind perhaps makes this even worse since he knows that Jones is less able to look after himself walking near a cliff. Although you could say that perhaps Jones is also not free of blame since should a blind person be walking near the edge of a cliff? Should anyone be walking that close to a cliff edge?!

So you could conclude that Smith is extremely morally culpable if he could easily have prevented this death without much burden on himself. In addition, the fact that Smith does not like Jones perhaps makes this worse since it may imply that Smith consciously did not take any steps to warn Jones and so Smith somehow wanted his death to arise as opposed to just realising that it would be a consequence.

However, you should go the full stretch with this question and compare this moral culpability to that of a 'murderer'. Take the example of a pre-meditated shooting in the head. Is somebody who omits to warn someone of their death, no matter how certain it is, as morally culpable as someone who takes the active step of getting a gun, pointing at somebody's head and pulling the trigger? You could argue that they are just as morally culpable or you could say that they are not – this is subjective. However, you could allude to distinctions such as omitting to do something versus taking practical steps or pre-meditation versus a sudden situation.

Top tips

Even if you do believe that you have some knowledge of the law in a certain area, ensure that you apply it with hesitance. Remember who you are conveying this knowledge to! Much of what is being asked is inherently subjective and there is no correct answer. Therefore, don't think that you may be 'wrong'. If you have a thought that sounds sensible then state it. The interviewers are looking to see your thought process so don't be afraid to think aloud and go through your thoughts step by step. Be receptive to contributions from the interviewers – they will help you formulate your views and your arguments but may also challenge any propositions. Take these on board and deal with them and remember that this doesn't necessarily mean accepting them. You are encouraged to think about what is said to you and challenge it if you feel that you can sensibly do so.

Mathematics

Questions to get you thinking...

Can you prove that any natural number consists of prime factors or is a prime number?

You are given an infinite square grid where each square contains a natural number and is at least the mean of the four neighbouring squares. Prove that each square contains the same number.

If I place a cube in water, what shape does it make on the surface?

Prove that any number consists of prime factors or is a prime number?

A body with mass m is falling towards earth with speed v. It has a drag force equal to kv. Set up a differential equation and solve it for v. (past question)

To answer this question, you need to be comfortable with the integration and differentiation you have studied at A level.

Try to work out which forces are involved, and draw a simple diagram to aid your understanding.

By Newton's Second Law of Motion we know that $F = m\frac{dv}{dt}$. This must be equal to the balance between the weight pulling downwards and the drag force against the motion.

Make sure you get the correct signs in the equation. The weight acts in the negative direction, and the drag force against it. Therefore, remembering that velocity is negative, mdv/dt = - mg – kv, where g is the acceleration due to gravity.

Dividing through by m we get $\frac{dv}{dt} = -g - \left(\frac{k}{m}\right)v$. For clarity let z=k/m.

By separating the variables we find that $\int \frac{\delta v}{g+zv} = -\int \delta t$

At this point it is helpful to make the substitution u = g + zv, and so du = zdv.

Therefore $\left(\frac{1}{z}\right)\int \frac{\delta u}{u} = -\int \delta t$ which gives us $\ln\frac{|u|}{z} = -t + C$, and so

$\ln|u| = -zt + C$

Remembering log rules gives us $|u| = e^{-zt} + C = Ke^{-zt}$.

Substituting back in we get $|g + zv| = Ke^{-zt}$, and so $v = -g/z + Ke^{-zt}$

Don't worry if you make a calculation error, it is your general approach to the problem that is more important. A tutor will want to see if you can think carefully about the maths involved.

If you pick 51 of the numbers 1-100, will you have: An even number? A multiple of 3? A square number? A square number plus a cube number? Two numbers, one of which is a multiple of the other? Co-primes? (past question)

This question builds upon easier problems to reach more complicated ones, to help you settle into the interview. Don't be surprised if you get something quite simple earlier on, the harder parts will come later!

There are 50 even numbers in the integers from 1-100, and therefore if you pick 51 numbers you will definitely have an even number.

Comparatively there are only 33 multiples of 3, and so a multiple of 3 is not guaranteed.

Simply list the square numbers – 1, 4, 9, 16, 25, 36, 49, 64, 81, 100. It is possible to choose 51 numbers not containing these numbers.

There are 5 cube numbers to consider, namely 0, 1, 8, 27, 64. Since there are 11 square numbers in consideration (including 0), there are at most 55 numbers equal to a square number plus a cube number from 1-100. However more than 6 of these numbers are over 100, and so it is possible to pick 51 numbers from 1-100 without picking a square number plus a cube number.

The question now becomes considerably tougher, and it might be tempting to look to the earlier parts for a solution. However instead partition the numbers from 1-100 into different sets generated by the formula $k \times 2^n$ where k is an odd number (for instance {1,2,4,8,16,...}). There are 50 such sets, and all numbers from 1-100 are in one of these sets. Therefore if we choose 51 numbers between 1-100, one must be the multiple of another.

Co-primes must not share common factors. If no two numbers amongst our 51 are to be coprime, it is clear they cannot simply all be multiples of a single number. Instead the most efficient way to make such a set would be for all members to have precisely two prime factors from {2, 3, 5}. However this set is smaller than necessary, and so we must have co-prime numbers.

There are a variety of ways to tackle this problem. Even if you cannot give a well formulated solution, explain your intuitions to the tutor.

Sketch the graph of: $y = \sin x$, $y = \sin(x^{-1})$, $y = x^2 \times \sin(x^{-1})$ (past question)

This is an interesting question and one that builds on school work. The interviewer will want to see you being as thorough as possible, thinking about the notable points on a graph.

It is possible to tackle the question in a systematic way – work out what happens as x approaches 0 or x approaches infinity.

- Draw the graph of y = sin x that you have studied at A level, marking where some of the turning points are.

- The graph $y = \sin(x^{-1})$ oscillates rapidly between 1 and -1 as x approaches 0, and is undefined when x = 0. y is greater than 0 when $x > \frac{1}{\Pi}$, and reaches 1 when $x = \frac{2}{\Pi}$. From this point x converges to 0 as it approaches infinity. The graph can be rotated around the origin.

- Again the graph of $y = x^2 \times \sin(x^{-1})$ oscillates rapidly as x approaches 0. However it does not oscillate between 1 and -1, but instead is bounded above by the graph $y = x^2$ and below by $y = x^{-2}$. As x approaches infinity, $y = x^2 \times \sin(x^{-1})$ diverges to infinity. This can be seen by the fact that sin x is approximately equal to x when x is small. Hence $\sin(x^{-1})$ is roughly equal to 1/x when x is large, and so $y = x^2 \times \sin(x^{-1})$ is large. Bonus points for a good explanation of why $\sin(x^{-1})$ is roughly equal to x^{-1}, using the expansion of sin x.

Top tips for Mathematics interviews

Make sure you are completely on top of all AS and A level work. It may be an idea to move ahead of the syllabus, if you have the inclination as this may give you more confidence.

Make sure you are comfortable with applying proofs and formulae to questions you haven't met before and be prepared to stand and write on a white board from the beginning of the interview. You may be asked to do this!

If you have forgotten a proof or a formula, do ask. Tutors are there to help you in tutorials and tend to be more excited by a mind that can apply information than a mathematician who can repeat rules they have learnt. That being said, do still revise so that you feel prepared and confident.

Remember not to neglect mathematics studied early in your AS level course and be prepared to answer logic questions using estimation and logic. In these cases, keep thinking about how numbers work. How can you show you think logically and how can you use numbers to illustrate your point? To be successful as a mathematician, you have to prove you can think with numbers.

Medicine

Questions to get you thinking...

What is the purpose of DNA?

How would you design a brain?

What are ulcers?

Why do we see things in the colours we do?

Having spoken to many successful Medical applicants, interviews for Medicine tend to be a mix of scientific and ethical questions. Our medical minds have therefore created some sample questions below, based on their own interview experiences, which they believe would be helpful to any aspiring Medical applicant to think about in advance of their interview.

If there was only one bird flu vaccine left, who would you give it to between you and me?

A good way to start this sort of question is to briefly mention what the bird flu vaccine is and what you know about the potential consequences of not receiving it. For example 'the majority of healthy people are able to recover from having the flu having experienced only normal flu-like symptoms such as a mild fever etc'.

You could then start looking at who should get this vaccine. Consider whether the person asking you the question is, for instance:

- In a position of having a lowered immune system so would be less able to cope without the vaccine if he or she contracted the flu: pregnant, elderly, on any other medication, suffering from any other illnesses such as AIDS.
- A person who has already recovered from the flu before and would thus be in a much better position to recover from the flu again. You could perhaps slip in here your knowledge of the primary and secondary immune response.
- A person who has dependents who would be affected if the person was to suffer from flu: children or a disabled person for whom they are caring.
- A person who spends/has spent/will spend a lot of time in a high-risk environment for the flu or around people who have, perhaps in a country where there is an epidemic at the moment.
- Suffering from any condition that may affect his or her life expectancy.

Having considered these factors you can reach a conclusion. With a question like this however, it is very difficult to reach an informed decision and a number of our medical graduates do believe it would be acceptable to conclude that 'without further information about your health and general circumstances I could not make an informed decision'.

In contrast, however, if you are one who would rather not sit on the fence, you could equally say that 'assuming that we are both of the same health and have the same circumstances, then, I may give it to myself because I am younger than you'.

If you were the new Secretary of Health, how would you want to improve the NHS?

Questions like this are very common, and admissions tutors are looking for an awareness of the problems currently facing the NHS.

One issue that all students should be aware of is the problem of the superbug MRSA and C-difficile. This is the sort of thing you could talk about here.

A good way to start this question would be to briefly talk about the problem caused by MRSA being resistant to antibiotics due to resistant strains mutating via natural selection etc., as well as talking about the problem this poses - patients come into hospital with a broken leg and may leave it with a deadly disease! The main problem with this is the lack of good hygiene in hospitals with visitors and staff not using the alcohol gels enough or properly as well as improper sterilisation of equipment used. As the Secretary of Health you may wish to improve training for the staff in hospitals to keep the environment clean and put more money into cleaning measures.

You might also say that you would like to put money into computerising a lot more of the work that doctors and their team do so that it is easily transferred and for safe-keeping. It is ALWAYS a good idea to mention something that you have picked up at work experience here. Be as specific as possible, drill down into detail!

One of the really big issues currently facing the NHS is the rise in obesity and its links to diabetes and coronary heart disease. Thus you might argue that more money should be spent on preventative measures to cost the NHS less in the long run. For example, increasing government campaigns to reduce childhood obesity by encouraging healthy eating and an active lifestyle - along the lines of what we are already seeing on TV at the moment. Again, you can strengthen your answer by referring to your work experience.

Work experience

Medical interviews tend to be different from other interviews because they are often carried out by practising doctors, rather than academics and therefore they expect you to be informed about the job of a doctor. Remember at the end of your course this is what you will be and your interviewer will partly be assessing your suitability for the role as well as for the course. Consequently, work experience is very important and it is highly likely that it will form part of any medical interview.

When it comes to questions about your work experience, questions tend to be along the lines of 'tell me about your work experience'. Many students can fall into the trap of simply listing all the different hospitals and surgeries they have visited, thinking that this sounds impressive. What's more interesting however is not the quantity of experience you have, but the quality. Tutors want to hear about an experience where you learned about what it means to be a doctor, and the relationship a doctor can build up with his/her patient.

Good students, might therefore approach this type of question by mentioning their observation of the importance of good communication – seeing a doctor smiling as he/she greeted the patient, the tone of the voice used (which helped to make the patient feel more relaxed). Indeed, one of the many difficult aspects of being a doctor is to make the patient feel relaxed enough in a consultation to give you all the information that you may need to know. Initially, doctors often do not know what they are looking for and must rely on the openness of the patient. You may have also noticed how a doctor spoke in simple, layman terms, refraining from using medical jargon to ensure the patient understands what is going on at every step of their treatment to ease worry and stress.

It may be that during your work experience you observed how important the wider team of other medical staff are to the role of a doctor, for example nurse and radiographers and doctors and how essential it is that a doctor has the confidence to work independently but also as part of a team. You might have seen certain negative aspects of being a doctor, including the amount of paper work involved or the strain of having to deliver bad news to a patient. You may have seen how important it is that a doctor be able to detach him/herself emotionally from the case.

Your answer will very much depend on your experiences. Really think about what you learned, and how it changed, strengthened or indeed weakened certain viewpoints or opinions of the role of a doctor that you previously held.

Top tips

'From my experience,' says one Cambridge Medicine graduate 'students are best off knowing the whole A level syllabus because admissions tutors may ask you about topics ahead of the level that your school may have got to. This was certainly the case for me but won't apply to all applicants. Of course, if it is something that you have not covered yet you should always say you do not know something, but they may expect you to attempt the question anyway using logic, common sense and an application of the knowledge you already possess.' Be willing to give each question a go – show you are open and willing to consider new ideas.

Modern & Medieval Languages

Questions to get you thinking...

Why do some languages have genders when others don't?

What is the difference between poetry and prose?

Could you say that an author is actually just another character in their novel or their play?

Do you notice any differences between English and European literature? If so, why might these be?

Literary analysis

Literary analysis is usually an important part of a languages interview at Oxford and Cambridge, as literature is a large part of the course. As such, you do not need to worry if you have not studied literature as part of your AS or A level course. You will, however, need to show an interest in literature and an ability to analyse and think critically about literary ideas, language and styles.

A good approach can be to read the work of a few authors or periods of literature which genuinely interest you. Find one or two authors you really like and read a selection of their works across their career with the aim of building up an understanding of the key ideas which preoccupied them.

Alternatively, you could pick a period or a theme (for instance, German literature about the Holocaust or 20th century East German literature) and read books by different authors (such as Christa Wolf, W. G. Sebald or Günter Grass) and appreciate concepts relevant at the time and their expression in the literature. Adopting one of these strategies should give you enough material to use in the interview as well as help you to explore your chosen subject in greater depth. You don't need to be an encyclopaedia of literature, but you do need to feel confident discussing literature intelligently with your interviewer. Remember too, that you could be asked to comment on any text you have mentioned in your personal statement. Be sure to prepare these texts thoroughly before the interview!

Speaking in your chosen language/s

You may be asked to speak in your chosen language in the interview. The first rule is, don't panic! This is a chance to demonstrate your ability. Arm yourself and prepare for this possibility by speaking the language as much as you can with friends, teachers or family members. It can be helpful to pick a topic to discuss and then practise defending an argument. You could put together a list of 'starter' phrases, or come up with and memorise a few useful phrases. While there are no guarantees that you will need to draw on them in the real interview, this exercise can give you confidence when answering an off-the-cuff question in the interview itself.

Analysing an unseen text

You may be given a text to read (normally but not exclusively a poem or a piece of prose), on which to comment and discuss. At first, this can seem a rather daunting task, especially if you are unfamiliar with some of the vocabulary, the style or the context. There are two key techniques you can apply to help you with such a task. Firstly, the 'analytical' approach: going through the text in a systematic and structured way may help you dissect and identify important points. Secondly, the 'building block' approach: start with something you definitely understand, however minor it seems. Building upon the word or sentence you know may allow you to deduce accurately meaning and context in the piece.

We've also put together some further guidelines that may also help you:

Getting started

Although there is no way of knowing which text you will be faced with, there are certainly things you can do to prepare. It is always a good idea to read as widely as possible to build up your vocabulary. You might consider making a vocabulary list which you carry with you on the train, on the bus or even into the bathroom!

While a broad vocabulary will help you, remember that literature goes beyond words and reflects historical, philosophical, scientific and emotional ideas. Therefore, you may want to consider the key literary developments in the country(ies) of the language(s) you want to read. This sounds grander than it is. In practice it simply means having an overview of the historical, political and social developments reflected in the literature of particular periods in history and how they interlink. For instance, if we were to isolate the French literature of the 18th century, we would see that some of the key ideas that influenced writers during this period were the (non-)existence of God, the dominance of reason over religion and the relationship between the state, the government and the people. Try and see the wider picture and ask yourself why authors wrote what they wrote. It may be helpful to make a timeline to illustrate the key developments and themes in history and literature and the authors associated with each period and theme.

You need to train yourself to think critically about language and ideas. Practise this by picking articles from newspapers, magazines or books, reading them carefully and thinking about how it makes you feel. Consider your instant reaction to the style, the content and the overall ideas expressed. In short, push yourself to have an opinion. The interview will test what you know and how you apply what you know to what you don't know. You need to show you can think on your feet and respond critically to unfamiliar ideas.

In the interview

When given the text, read it through several times and try to get a feeling for what it is about. Try and identify the key themes and the context. Perhaps try reading it aloud. This can be helpful if you are given a poem, as this tactic will help you identify some of the points mentioned below, such as the rhyme scheme. Take as many notes as will be helpful. Don't over-do it because if you write too much on the page you might end up confusing yourself and losing your key points. In short, jot down the most important points and highlight any sections you think are particularly useful.

If you come across words/a word you do not know, don't worry, this is perfectly normal and you will not be the only one! Really try and understand the overall sense of the text, concentrate on the words you do understand and take time to get to grips with the ideas expressed. Once you have understood the themes, you should be able to interpret the words you didn't understand. You may even find that they are not as important as you previously thought. If you do get really stuck, break the word down and try to decipher the meaning from the root. Call on all your powers of lateral thought here!

The basics

Start by assessing what kind of text you are dealing with. This usually boils down to one key question: is it a poem or a piece of prose? This should be clear from the form and structure of the text and once you have identified the form, there are a few basic technical points to consider.

If you are dealing with a poem, consider:

- The form and the structure: How has the poet arranged the lines and the stanzas of the poem? Certain forms and structures marry certain themes: the sonnet is often employed when love is the key theme, the ballad often lends itself to narrative poetry.
- The rhyme scheme: How does the pattern of rhyme contribute to the meaning of the poem? An inconsistent rhyme scheme can suggest conflict (possibly the poet's own, possibly external). How many syllables are there in each line? Which syllables are emphasised and why?
- The syntax: How are the lines broken up? Is it logical or disjointed? Does it serve to highlight a theme or an idea?
- The punctuation: Often used to emphasise an idea or a theme, how does it influence the reading of the poem? Be sensitive to the poet's use of punctuation and highlight particularly interesting constructions.
- The language: Examine carefully the poet's choice of words. Why has the poet chosen a particular word: to convey an idea or to create an aesthetic effect?
- Imagery: Think about whether the imagery used is abstract, literal or figurative. How does the imagery affect you?

If you are dealing with a piece of prose, you should consider:

The location of the extract in the text: Is the text taken from the beginning, the middle or the end of the work? How do you think the story will/has develop(ed)?

The characters: Who are they? What is their relationship to each other? How will their relationship impact the rest of the story?

The tone: The tone may be bound up with the narrator (see below). How is the story narrated? Is the narrator involved, detached, ironic or satirical? What effect does the tone have on your reading of the passage? Did the writer intend this?

The above points in relation to language, punctuation and imagery also apply and should be considered.

Poets and authors employ a tool kit in terms of language, rhythm, syntax, etc, which always serve a purpose. Techniques might be used to emphasise a key theme, for aesthetic reasons, to conjure a certain image or idea or to affect the reader. Be sensitive to how you feel as you read and share your ideas in the interview. The best answers are often the most honest, so be aware of your own responses to the text.

If you are unfamiliar with certain poetic forms or patterns of rhyme scheme, try and familiarise yourself with the most common (e.g. the sonnet, the Petrarchan sonnet etc) but don't worry too much about this. You are not expected to be familiar with every form of poetry ever written! Dip into different styles in English and your chosen language and familiarise yourself with how poetry works and, in particular, how poetry in a foreign language works.

The context

The style in which the text is written, the language employed and the main ideas expressed often shed light on when the text was written. This may not be obvious on a first reading and you may, therefore, have to dig deep into the piece. Reading widely across different periods can help you to develop sensitivity to context, (and should be enjoyable!) but this is by no means essential.

The historical context of a piece can be an interesting talking point in the interview. If you are able to deduce that the text is a product of the Spanish Civil War, for example, maybe you could use your knowledge of this turbulent period to comment on the poignancy of the writer's words. Do try not to go off on a tangent to show how much you know about 20th century Spanish history. Relevance and answering the interviewer's questions is key!

Do remember not to confuse context with the content of the story or the poem. This is easily done. Context relates to the surrounding circumstances in which the text was written. For example, the 18th century French thinker Voltaire wrote many short stories (known as 'contes') which are set in ancient Babylonia, in outer space, or in the Old Testament. However, the context remains 18th century France and the social, political and philosophical ideas of the day (see above).

The key themes

Identifying the main themes of the extract is important and usually fascinating! If the language or vocabulary is difficult, why not try employing the 'building blocks' technique explained above?

Once you have identified a few themes, look for links across the text. These links might be found in relation to one individual theme (i.e. look for the different ways in which the same theme is expressed) or to several themes (i.e. the way in which different themes are linked across the piece).

Remember to try and consider the points mentioned above in relation to style, language, punctuation, rhyme scheme, and how they add to our understanding of the theme (positively or negatively). This allows you to come across as a student aware of languages as an academic discipline.

Identifying the key themes of the piece (and considering the language used) can help you with the context. For example, if the text is littered with different ideas and images and the language is rich and textured it could be a Surrealist work and thus date from 1920s.

The narrator

Do bear in mind that the author/poet of the piece is not the same as the narrator and that the author/poet may have created a specific persona to narrate the piece. Examining the tenses employed will help you identify whether there is a first person narrator or a third person narrator. If the author or poet has created a narrator, it is important to be sensitive to how this figure is involved in the piece and how his narration of the story or poem affects your interpretation of it. For example, you could consider whether the narrator is trustworthy. Does his tone suggest he is treating the subject-matter ironically and thus not necessarily fairly?

The development of the piece

It is a good idea to think about how the text develops. Consider whether it starts and ends with the same theme, idea or style or whether it begins with one theme and progresses to another, and ends in a completely different place. How does this development bear on the overall theme of the poem? Does it convey a positive or a negative image of the over-riding theme?

Useful phrases

While it is important to be honest and genuine in answering the interviewer's questions, the delivery of your answer can be improved by beginning with 'smart starters'. Below is a short list of phrases that can be used to help you to introduce your arguments. Bear in mind that this list is neither exclusive nor exhaustive and is not a guaranteed recipe for success. It is merely there as a guide to delivering pertinent answers. More than anything else, having a phrase ready to use can increase your confidence and buy you a bit of extra 'thinking' time as you consider your response.

My first reaction was ... /A first reading of the text suggested to me ...

A closer reading revealed that ... /Scrutinising the text in more detail shows that ...

If we were to isolate the theme of ...

If we narrow the text down to the following themes ...

Summary

The above points can help you tackle any unseen text. The most important thing is to work through what you are given in a structured way. You won't have that much time to prepare so the better prepared you are to deal with an unseen piece of text, the more you will get out of your preparation time.

Above all, try to remember that exercises like this are designed to see how you react to unfamiliar concepts and how well you express your own ideas. The task is not designed to catch you out, this is why it is important not to worry too much about vocabulary you don't know. Focus your time and energy on identifying the key themes, examining the language critically and showing sensitivity to style. It is far more important to demonstrate a few insightful reactions to the text than to know all the words!

Bear in mind that there isn't necessarily a 'right' answer to some of the questions you are asked (for instance, there can never be a 'right' answer to the question 'what do you think of the poem?', since this question asks for your opinion). Most of the time the tutor will want to see what you think about a particular point – so don't get yourself worked up in the interview by trying to work out the answer the tutor wants to hear. Be as honest as possible, although admitting you don't have a clue is never advisable! If you really are unsure, ask the tutor to clarify areas of uncertainty, but show a willingness to find out the answer yourself by asking intelligent and probing questions.

A note on Joint Schools

If you are applying to read Modern Languages and another subject, the above still applies to the Modern Languages side. However, it might be a good idea to think about the links between your other subject and your chosen language. For example, if you are applying to read English and Spanish, you could consider the influence writers such as James Joyce, William Faulkner and John Dos Passos have had on Latin American authors, especially Mario Vargas Llosa and Gabriel García Márquez. Similarly, for History and French, you could think about the impact of French colonisation on writers such as Aimé Césaire and Patrick Chamoiseau. You will be interviewed in both subjects, but one of your interviewers may be interested to hear about the connections you have made between your two subjects and how you think the social, political and cultural developments of a country influence its literature.

A note on studying a language ab initio

If you are applying to read a language ab initio you need to demonstrate a natural aptitude for languages and an ability to pick up languages and linguistic concepts quickly. To test your ability, you may be given something to read and comment upon in the language. You might prepare for this by engaging with the language as much as possible. Further reading can help, study the grammar and try to build up your vocabulary, perhaps by making a vocabulary list. It is a good idea to show that you have dipped into the literature and begun to develop an interest in a few authors or periods. You could apply the same strategy as described earlier: pick an author, a theme or a period, look at the literature and start forming your own opinion about your chosen area.

Top Tips

Prepare thoroughly for the literature aspect but don't go overboard, even if you can swim! Focus on a few authors, themes or periods. Be aware of the wider context in which the literature you have read operates. Brush up on the grammar of your chosen language before the interview and make sure you are comfortable conversing on a range of different subjects. Re-read your personal statement and be prepared to answer questions on anything mentioned. Train yourself to respond instantly to ideas and arguments by reading passages from newspapers, novels or collections of poetry.

Music

Questions to get you thinking...

Is music useful within society?

Why are musical events written about?

Is the study of an instrument a valuable pursuit?

How is music related to free will?

The following questions highlight some of the issues within the study of academic music today. Our musicians have shed some light on all the components of their interview process, and the differences between Cambridge and Oxford, to help a potential music applicant jumpstart their interview preparation.

Is some music more important than others?

With a question like this, take time to consider the parameters. Are there different ways in which music is important? Is music more important if it is performed and heard, talked and written about, or can we see its impact on our past, present or future? Has it started a revolution or served as an anthem for an army or a nation?

How do we measure importance? Why are certain composers perceived as geniuses? Why does our regard for Bach, Mozart and Beethoven cause debate today? Should we use the term 'musical canon'? Are certain composers or pieces of music important because of their effect on a genre? Perhaps you could think about Wagner and opera or Beethoven and the string quartet. Is society aware that we marginalise certain musical styles? The study of ethnomusicology (music of non-Western cultures) is a hot topic in the academic study of music.

Use musical examples you feel comfortable with in tackling this question. This approach will allow you to support your arguments and speak with assurance.

Musical Analysis and 'Preparatory Study'

You may be asked to look at a score shortly before your interview, or in the interview itself. Without hearing the piece of music, you should be able to identify some of the following features: The form: Is it in binary, ternary or sonata form? How do the instrumental or vocal lines interact? Are the cadences perfect, imperfect or interrupted? What do you notice about the phrase lengths, climaxes, keys and modulations.

You may be asked to analyse a piece of prose, such as an account of an opera performance. Once again, remember to think critically about what the writer is saying and why they are saying it.

Performance: Oxford asks you to perform, on your principle instrument, a piece of music no more than five minutes in length. Choose a piece that suits you and is perhaps by a composer you mentioned in your personal statement. Tutors may enjoy something they do not hear regularly.

Harmony: Cambridge may ask you to harmonise a soprano line and/or transcribe a phrase of a four-part Bach Chorale (which will test both your harmony and aural skills).

Top tips for written work

You need to be able to write clearly about music – demonstrate this! Go beyond your school reading and demonstrate mature research skills.

Philosophy

Questions to get you thinking

How would you define infinity?

What is a lie?

Is death rational?

What's the difference between intelligent, wise and clever?

Oxford and Cambridge Philosophy interviews test your logical and lateral thought and require a critical and rational response to challenging philosophical questions. Our team of Philosophy graduates have put together some example questions, based on real ones, to help you to explore philosophical ideas and concepts, and give you a taster as to how you might approach potential interview questions such as these.

If a person is teleported by being destroyed and re-created exactly, is this the same person?

This question tests your ability to recognise issues of personal identity within this thought experiment.

That the person is destroyed might suggest that they no longer exist, but in their being re-created exactly, we are tempted to say that the re-created being is the same person. The bundle theory claims that if there is psychological continuity, where the re-created being has the same memories and personality as the destroyed being, then the recreated person is the same person. But what if two copies are made of the destroyed being? Surely they cannot both be you?

At this stage you could draw the distinction between numerical and qualitative identity. You are numerically identical to the person you were 15 years ago in that you are still the same person, but you are not qualitatively identical as you do not have the same qualitative properties, for example, you may have a different set of teeth.

For this thought experiment, you therefore might conclude that the person who is re-created could be the same person as the person who was destroyed, in the sense that they are qualitatively identical. This would also be the case if there were two copies of the re-created person. They are not, however, numerically identical.

If I am young today then I will be young tomorrow; if I am young tomorrow I will be young the day after that...so I will be young in 80 years' time. Discuss.

This question tests your ability to see past the tricks of language to detect the logic underneath, and your ability to argue rationally in the form of: premise one, premise two, conclusion. We can show that premise one is invalid by comparing, 'if I am young today then I will be young tomorrow' with 'if I am wearing red today then I will be wearing red tomorrow'. The structure 'if x today, then x tomorrow' is not logically sound.

Premise one would be true if it followed that, if you were young on day A, you would be young on day B. If we accept premise one, then premise two, 'if I am young tomorrow I will be young the day after that' logically follows, because what is true on day A would be true on day B (it would be a transitive property). Thus the conclusion, 'so I will be young in 80 years' time', holds.

As we have pointed out, premise one is incorrect. The quality of youth is affected by the progress of time. A person becomes progressively older each day. Therefore age, or 'youngness', is not a static quality, it is incremental.

With these types of question, admissions tutors are looking for you to demonstrate logical thought and reasoned opinions. Above all, they want to see how you a build and structure a coherent argument. Think aloud and be sure to work steadily through the question so that you come to a sound conclusion. And if you get stuck at any stage, do not be afraid to ask the interviewer. They want to see how you think and if you need to ask a relevant, intelligent question, this shows you are capable of thinking independently and willing to explore the subject.

Top tips for Philosophy interviews

In Philosophy interviews, students can all too easily rely on their intuition. Avoid this as much as possible. Think through your answers and support your arguments with evidence of logical thinking. Read books to help you to develop a genuine interest and understanding of the subject (not just A level material) such as Wilfrid Hodges, *Logic* and Edward Craig, *The Shorter Routledge Encyclopaedia of Philosophy.*

Physics / Engineering / Natural Sciences (Phys.)

Questions to get you thinking...

Explain how an aircraft flies.

What is time?

Why do sausages split lengthways rather than around the circumference?

If you are on a boat with a hairdryer and a sail, and you blow the hairdryer into the sail what are the forces acting on the boat?

Our team of Engineers and Physicists have put together questions for this section, based on the types of questions they and other applicants had to answer at their interview. All the questions are suitable for the above subjects, and some will be also be suitable for Mathematics.

Sketch the graph of $y = \frac{A}{x^4} - \frac{B}{x^2}$, where A and B are constants.

This is a fairly straightforward question that tests a range of A level techniques. The only real subtleties lie firstly in identifying those techniques and how they are useful in graph sketching, and secondly in noticing that the nature of the constants A and B affects the shape of the graph.

Make sure you understand what you need to draw by calculating intersections, for example, before drawing your graph.

A suggested approach to the problem

– Think about symmetries first. Is the function odd or even?

As all the powers of x involved in this curve are even (–4 and –2), the curve must be symmetric about the y axis.

– Then consider the x-intercept

The x-intercept occurs when y = 0, and can be found by solving the equation $\frac{A}{x^4} - \frac{B}{x^2} = 0$ for x (in terms of A and B). This gives $x = \pm\sqrt{\frac{A}{B}}$ at y = 0. Notice that these intercepts conform to the symmetry deduced above.

– Now consider the y-intercept

Similarly, the y-intercept occurs when x = 0. We cannot substitute this into the given expression as that would involve dividing by zero, so we know that there must be an asymptote. Instead we can consider the behaviour as x → 0 (x tends to 0), for example by trying small values of x, by taking limits, or by considering an expansion.

Trying x = 0.1 and x = -0.1 both give a value of y = 10000A – 100B, which is clearly large and dominated by the sign of the first term. Thus if A is positive (negative), y will go to positive (negative) infinity as x → 0, from either direction. This is symmetric about the y axis, as required.

By limits, which may not be covered in the Mathematics A level course (although keen students, or ones taking Further Mathematics, may well be familiar with their use!), the derivation proceeds as:

$$\lim_{x\to 0} y = \lim_{x\to 0}\left(\frac{A}{x^4} - \frac{B}{x^2}\right) = \lim_{x\to 0}\left(\left(\frac{1}{x^4}\right)(A - Bx^2)\right)$$

$$= +\infty \; if \; A > 0, -\infty \; if \; A < 0$$

and we see that the same result is recovered. Notice that this limit depends on the sin of the constant A.

– Look at the behaviour at large x

The technique of taking limits is also useful here. However, we are now considering the different limit:

x → ±∞

Trying x=10 and x=-10 both give a value of y = 0.0001A – 0.01B, which is small and dominated by the sign of the second term. When B is positive, y will approach 0 from below, likewise when B is negative, y will approach 0 from above as x → ∞. Formally taking limits:

$$\lim_{x\to\pm\infty} y = \lim_{x\to\pm\infty}\left(\frac{A}{x^4}-\frac{B}{x^2}\right) = \lim_{x\to\pm\infty}\left(\left(\frac{1}{x^4}\right)(A-Bx^2)\right)$$

$$= -0 \; if \; B > 0, +0 \; if \; B < 0$$

where '+/– 0' means '0 approached from above/below', and we see that the same result is recovered.

We now know enough to sketch the form of the graph:

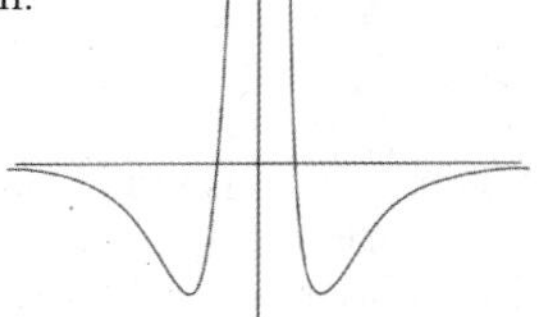

This is the form for positive A and B.

Note that we have not yet deduced that there are turning points. However, we know that this curve is symmetric, tends towards positive infinity as x tends to 0, and has only two x-intercepts, but the curve approaches 0 from below as x tends to either positive or negative infinity.

A complete sketch will have all the relevant points labelled, which we have not done here, so the final thing to do is to calculate the coordinates of these turning points. See if you can do this now.

– Turning points

We find the turning points by the usual A level method: setting the differential to 0 and solving for x, then substituting these x values into the original expression to find the values of y at these points, thus finding the coordinates of any and all turning points. A common, although minor, mistake here is to forget to find the y values.

Performing the differentiation gives $\frac{dy}{dx} = -4Ax^{-5} + 2Bx^{-3}$. Setting this equal to 0 and solving for x gives:

$$-4Ax^{-5} + 2Bx^{-3} = 0$$

$$\Rightarrow \left(-\frac{2}{x^5}\right)(2A - Bx^2) = 0$$

$$\Rightarrow 2A = Bx^2$$

$$\Rightarrow x = \pm\sqrt{\frac{2A}{B}}$$

and our two values for x. Note that these two values of x obey the symmetry we discovered previously.

– Conclusion

Now we find the value for y at these x values. By the symmetry, the value for y will be the same for both values of x, so we only need to perform one calculation. For simplicity, we will take the positive root:

$$y = \frac{A}{\sqrt{\frac{2A}{B}}^{4}} - \frac{B}{\sqrt{\frac{2A}{B}}^{2}} = \frac{A}{\frac{4A^2}{B^2}} - \frac{B}{\frac{2A}{B}} = \frac{B^2}{4A} - \frac{B^2}{2A} = -\frac{B^2}{4A}$$

Notice that the negative root would be either squared or raised to the power of 4, and thus give the same value as the positive root – this justifies our statement that we only need to calculate the positive root.

Thus we have found the symmetries of the curve, the coordinates of the x-intercepts and the turning points, and deduced its behaviour as $x \to 0$ and $x \to \pm\infty$ and thus sketched the graph.

Why do wind turbines have three blades?

A question that asks for why something is a certain size or shape, or as in this case has a certain number of something, is almost always the result of a compromise. If asked a question like this, a good strategy is to look for two (or more) competing factors in the design, driving to opposite extremes. The below model solution provides a good example.

This style of question is popular because it requires interviewees to consider a problem from a number of different viewpoints and identify the important factors. It also allows the interviewer to offer counter arguments to the 'correct' solutions, thus testing the student's scientific debating skills: whether they can defend a position and how they adapt to new ideas. Examples of this are given in the model answer below.

A suggested approach to the question

There are a number of elements that influence wind turbine design, such as theoretically-tricky aerodynamics and practical considerations, for example cost. We can immediately see that there cannot be one dominating factor. If there were, this would drive the optimum number of blades to either a minimum (one) or a maximum (a fan-like structure).

A common early idea is to consider practical limitations, such as cost, availability of materials and so on. Whilst these are relevant issues, and mentioning them displays an awareness of the reality of commercial engineering projects (thus demonstrating that the student has enough of an interest in the subject to know something about its practice), they do not display any scientific knowledge on the part of the applicant, and so should only be mentioned in passing. A student who focuses on these issues may, in the eyes of an interviewer, be doing so (either consciously or unconsciously) because they do not understand, or even recognise, the more fundamental physical issues.

For a wind turbine, the 'maximising' effect is a simple one – indeed, almost too simple, and could easily be overlooked; as the turbine wishes to extract as much energy from the wind as possible, it will be more effective if it can capture more wind. Thus, a high number of blades is preferable, to increase the surface area of the turbine.

A possible counter argument here would be to point out that adding more blades also adds more weight, and (assuming the blade design doesn't change) does not alter the surface area per mass. While more blades would capture more wind, the turbine would also now be heavier and require more force to move, negating the effect of the extra captured wind. While this sounds reasonable, a simple line of reasoning would deduce that each blade adds a given driving force to the turbine (in fact, the driving force will not be the same per blade, as discussed in the 'slipstream' argument below, but that is a different issue) otherwise the turbine would never move – each blade must capture enough energy from the wind to move, even with its weight taken into account, or the turbine would not work at all. Thus since each blade produces more than enough force to account for its own weight, adding blades adds to the total force produced.

This requirement is missed by a lot of students, and thus interviewers can use it to identify the applicants who are able to consider the 'big picture' and understand the question being asked, rather than diving straight into physics or maths without pausing to think carefully about the problem.

The 'minimising' effect is more subtle, and is a more straightforward test of the student's knowledge of physics. By the nature of a turbine, each blade follows the same path, and thus moves in the slipstream of preceding blades. At first this may appear to be a good thing – for example, in many racing sports (from speed skating to Formula 1) competitors prefer to race in the slipstream of their rivals, taking advantage of the reduced wind resistance, and thus move faster while using less energy. One may think that a blade moving in the slipstream of previous ones could move faster for less input energy, as with the racers, and thus turn the turbine more quickly and generate more energy. However, this approach shows some muddled thinking, and the analogy is not accurate. The turbine is not being powered from within with the aim of reaching a high speed, as with the racers. It is trying to extract energy from the air, so blades moving in slipstream (by definition, an area where there is little wind to affect the motion of the blade) will not be very effective at doing so. Each additional blade added to the turbine is less efficient at extracting energy than previous ones, so the most efficient option would be just one blade.

The above 'racing' analogy would be a good potential counter argument for an interviewer to use: it sounds plausible, and has a basis in physics that a student would recognise and is easy to explain and understand. However, it has flaws as explained above. A good student will examine the analogy carefully and spot not only that it is inappropriate for this situation, but also why, and use this to enhance their own understanding of the physics in the actual problem. Thus, we have two factors, one favouring a small number of blades, one a large. Balancing these two factors gives three as the optimum number of blades. However, deriving this quantitatively requires physical and engineering ideas and mathematics well beyond the scope of A level students and possibly even undergraduates, and would not be expected. The point of this question is to explore qualitative arguments, and to test applicants' ability to consider and balance opposing viewpoints without recourse to explicit mathematical formulae.

Integrate $\dfrac{1}{1+\left(\dfrac{\sin 2x}{(1+\cos 2x)}\right)^2}$ with respect to x.

This is a straightforward question that shouldn't pose much of a problem to a serious candidate. Nevertheless, there are a couple of subtleties to mention. A level students are taught a few methods of performing complicated-looking integrals, such as by parts or by substitution, and the interviewee will have to select the best option.

In fact, the best option here is not one of these integration techniques, but just to simplify the integrand before performing the integral. After the student has realised that this is the best method, the manipulation is simply a test of A level ability. Some interviewers may also insist upon the inclusion of the integration constant (usually denoted c). This manipulation uses trigonometric identities with which the student should be familiar from A level:

cos2x + sin2x = 1 the double angle formulae: sin2x = 2 sinx cosx and cos2x = cos2x – sin2x = 1 – 2 sin2x = 2 cos2x - 1.

The manipulation of the integrand, using these, is thus:

$$\frac{1}{1+\left(\frac{\sin 2x}{(1+\cos 2x)}\right)^2} \equiv \frac{1}{1+\left(\frac{2\sin x\cos x}{(\cos^2 x+\sin^2 x)+(\cos^2 x-\sin^2 x)}\right)^2}$$

$$\frac{1}{1+\left(\frac{2\sin x\cos x}{2\cos^2 x}\right)^2} \equiv \frac{1}{1+\tan^2 x} \equiv \frac{1}{\left(\frac{1}{\cos^2 x}\right)(\cos^2 x+\sin^2 x)} \equiv \cos^2 x$$

$$\equiv \frac{1}{2}(1+\cos 2x)$$

and the integral is now easy to perform:

$$\int \frac{1}{1+\left(\frac{\sin 2x}{(1+\cos 2x)}\right)^2}\,dx = \int\left(\frac{1}{2}+\frac{1}{2}\cos 2x\right)dx = \frac{1}{2}x+\frac{1}{4}\sin 2x + c$$

Top tips

Ensure that you make your assumptions explicit to the interviewer at all times. What is constant? What is changing? What simple concepts and formulae can be applied to the problem in front of you? (While the problem may look difficult, if you break it down into simple chunks, it should be possible for you to make sense of it if not reach a firm conclusion). Ask questions! Many interviewees are wary of asking questions of the interviewer and remember that Physics is a discourse, it is not just questions and answers. It is about ideas and communicating these ideas clearly. Make sure that you clarify terms of the question if they confuse you. And finally, think before you speak, especially with regard to mathematics problem and sketching graphs. Do not sketch prematurely!

Politics

Questions to get you thinking...

Is democracy the best system?

What would you say to someone who claims women have equal opportunities already?

Why do we need government?

Does the welfare state trap people into poverty?

Do you think political groups can have political legitimacy? (past question)

To answer this question, you need to ensure that you are clear about what a political group is, what political legitimacy is and then how (if at all) this political legitimacy can be obtained by these groups.

When we think of a political group, the most obvious type of group is a political party, but there are also other groups which could be classed as political groups. For example, there are groups which exert political pressure such as Trade Unions and lobby groups like Greenpeace.

Political legitimacy is the acceptance of a group as an authority, which has a right to rule. It is a basic condition for governing or exercising power as without it the exercise of power will struggle and collapse.

Political legitimacy can be created through the consent of those subjected to it, and the belief both by those exercising the power and by those subjected to it that the institutions and methods of ruling are the most appropriate ones for the society.

In your wider reading, you may have come across two political thinkers - John Locke and Max Weber. Locke (regarded as one of the most influential Enlightenment thinkers) believed that political legitimacy is derived from general explicit and implicit consent. Max Weber (German sociologist and political economist) identified three sources of political legitimacy: charismatic authority, traditional authority and rational–legal authority. It is suggested that people may have faith in a particular rule because they have faith in the individual rulers (charisma), because it has been there for a long time (tradition), or because they trust its legality, this is the rationality of the rule of law (rational–legal).

If we use Weber's three descriptive sources of legitimacy, you can see how a group may be able to obtain political legitimacy.

A group could have charismatic authority if people have faith in the individual leaders of a group. Traditional authority could stem from people simply accepting the authority of a group as it has always exercised power over them, for example a Trade Union. A group may gain legitimacy from rational–legal authority because people trust its legality, perhaps because it has been appointed by the rule of law they support.

People do not agree on how political groups can have authority. While someone may give authority to a group because it has been there for a long time this may not make it legitimate for others. This benchmark of legitimacy may vary from person to person, with some believing in democratic authority, where a group is legitimate if it is supported by the majority of people, while others might claim that authority could come from religion, such as a group appointed by God to rule, whereas others would suggest that even usual democratic authority is not enough for political legitimacy as the tyranny of the majority is not a legitimate way for a group to rule over all, for example, minority groups.

Are there always winners and losers in politics? (past question)

To answer this question we must look at what the different actors in politics are hoping to achieve, we can then see how they can win and lose.

For politicians in elections, it could be said that there is always a winner and a loser, lasting for the length of a political term. However counter arguments to this could be that the politicians are not actually winners or losers in an election but it is the will of the people which is expressed through the election which is always the winner. A politician who is placed second or third in an election, although not entering office, then has won if they believe in the democratic system. Furthermore, even from a selfish political point of view it may be beneficial to have not entered office in that election (due to political or economic turbulence) but to have participated in the democratic system with the possibility of entering in office after the turbulence.

In many political systems they also result in differing political parties having to work together, at both a local and national level. Whilst coalitions are common in more proportional electoral systems such as Germany and Italy they are not unknown (such as the current Conservative-Liberal coalition in the UK).

In such a coalition system it may be possible for the politics of compromise and consensus to overcome the partisan nature. It may be difficult however to avoid having winners and losers - it is unlikely that a coalition will include all parties and therefore there will still be losers, even if it could be argued that there are no winners due to the members of the coalition compromising.

Aside from the politicians, ordinary individuals in the distribution of public funds or taxation may be seen to be winners and losers, with some individuals paying higher taxes than others whilst receiving lower benefits and vice versa, it is difficult to see how there could be winners without losers.

With a question like this, draw on any extra reading you may have done and dip into your current affairs knowledge.

Top tips

Come prepared with opinions but remain respectful to established political theorists' views to avoid seeming dogmatic and arrogant.

Theology

Questions to get you thinking...

Are we in a position to judge God?

Is Britain a secular society?

Is it morally wrong to attempt to climb a mountain?

Would having a personal faith help or hinder the study of Theology?

Can you think of any circumstances in which murder would be justifiable?

A question like this tests your knowledge of applied ethics. It might work well to answer this with reference to Christian philosophers or theologians, for example Kant.

Kant was a deontologist (someone who considers the morality of an action to be intrinsically linked to its adherence to certain rules). It is likely that someone following Kant's ethical approach would take a firm view against murder.

A Kantian position would adopt the categorical imperative, which states that an act should only be pursued if you would want it to become a universal law. In the case of justifying murder, take a situation where we will gain a huge amount of money if the person is killed. In this instance, we could not reasonably wish this maxim to be universalised and therefore, following Kant's logic, we would judge the murder as unjustifiable.

Another example could be killing one person to save the lives of twenty others, for example, Bernard Williams' 'Jim and the Indians' thought experiment. Kant would respond, given that the other part of his categorical imperative demands that you treat people as ends rather than means, that killing one person as a means to save twenty is never acceptable.

You can conclude that murder, from a deontological Christian standpoint at least, would never be justifiable. From this point, the discussion would develop with your tutor, who may want to examine different sides of the problem.

Should the church compromise?

This type of question focuses on current and historical issues that face and have faced the church. A good way to approach this question is to start by breaking the question down and analysing the language used: 'Should the church' is a difficult start to the question. A good answer may make the point that there is no discrete entity called 'the church', so remember to make appropriate distinctions where possible between different churches. What does the question mean by 'compromise'? The word compromise suggests forsaking or adjusting one's own position in order to accommodate another view.

Here is one possible approach: there are many different churches, for the purposes, of this example, let's take the Church of England. The issue here is whether the C of E should stick resolutely to its position on a particular issue or whether it should be prepared to adapt and change with society. If the church is not open to compromise or change this would suggest the 'truth' resides solely within the church. However, from a Christian perspective, the Word has been created by God and the Holy Spirit can operate and inspire individuals, independent of the church. It is possible, then, for individuals or groups outside the church to discover truths that the church should accept. History provides numerous examples of this happening. The Church has compromised in the past and modified its views on a whole range of issues such as slavery, its relationship with other religions, and women priests.

You could then qualify this by saying that the Church should compromise on an issue for the right reasons – that is, because the compromise represents a more authentic witness to the life and vision of Christ than the previous position.

For example, you could suggest that the Church should allow certain sexual relationships outside marriage, provided they are a genuine expression of love between two consenting adults. An act of compromise, such as this, does not undermine fundamental Christian values, such as self-sacrificial love (agape). It is possible to justify a compromise theologically, with reference to scripture and other parts of the Christian tradition. Jesus, for example, privileges the commandment to love others, and was himself prepared to break the established laws on occasion e.g. Matthew 5:38.

Top tips

At your interview you may be asked a variety of questions. Generally speaking, our graduates said that it is unlikely you will be asked about any specific theologians unless you have mentioned them in your personal statement. Moreover, you are more likely to be asked questions either pertaining to ethical and philosophical issues within theology or a critical evaluation of modern theology.

Veterinary Medicine

Questions to get you thinking...

What do you think about kidney transplants in cats?

Why do animals have two ears (i.e. why not one or four)?

Is selective breeding tantamount to genetic modification?

Why do dogs behave badly?

What is the time difference from sound reaching one ear and the other? (past question)

The time difference between sound reaching the first and second ears is called the interaural time difference. The time difference varies depending on the location of the sound source. If the sound comes directly from in front of the face, say at eye height and equal distant from either ear, then there is no time difference in the sound arriving. We would describe this as sound arriving at a zero degree azimuth (the angle of the signal in relation to the head), interaural time difference being zero also.

If the sound comes directly from the right or left (i.e. a 90 degree azimuth), then clearly the sound will arrive at the nearest ear first, having further to travel to the second ear, and the interaural time difference will no longer be zero.

It can be calculated as follows:

$T = D/V$
where

D = distance between the ears (probably in the region of 20cm or 0.2m)
and
V = speed of sound (roughly 343m/s)

So in this case the interaural time (T) would be
0.2/343 = 0.00058s

If the sound is coming from a smaller angle than 90 degrees (or between 90 and 180), there will be a smaller difference between the distances sound has to travel to either ear (i.e. D is smaller) and the time difference will be reduced. The variation in the interaural time differences does not seem large, but it is detected by the brain when processing sound and is a key source of information in sound localisation.

How would you have solved the Foot and Mouth crisis? (past question)

A good way to approach this question, is to firstly show to the interviewer that you understand what Foot and Mouth Disease is – it is a highly infectious viral disease which affects cloven hoofed animals such as cows, sheep and pigs. Next, you could refer to past Foot and Mouth crises – explaining how in the past, the virus has spread rapidly and beyond control, decimating the UK farming industry. It is therefore important to take the threat seriously and act quickly and decisively.

You can then move into the 'meat' of the argument (no pun intended). Assuming it has only been reported on one farm, you could suggest that the affected farm and the surrounding area be immediately quarantined and that the animals that had been in direct contact with any sufferers culled. The virus can be destroyed by heat, sunlight and certain disinfectants, but it can survive for long periods of time in the right conditions. Thus the affected farm would have to be completely gutted and disinfected before the farmer could even consider going back to normal. The virus does not affect humans, but can be spread on vehicles and boots and so on, so movement from affected to non-affected areas should be strictly limited. Ideally any roads that neighbour the affected property should be shut until the virus has been controlled. Wild animals which could carry the disease between farms, for example deer, should be controlled (probably culled) if/when they are seen.

When the Foot and Mouth crisis hit in 2001, farmers were hesitant to use vaccinations due to difficulties that would later arise in selling the animals overseas. However the rules have since been changed to allow vaccination as an emergency measure in the event of an outbreak. There are several strains of Foot and Mouth Disease, so once the strain has been identified, you could propose recommending the vaccination of all cloven hoofed farm animals in an even wider area than the quarantined area - say county-wide. Airborne spread is known, so if conditions are right (i.e. windy, not too hot) then animals should be kept inside.

As an outbreak of Foot and Mouth Disease can be so devastating, you might point out that you do not think you can overreact to another outbreak. As much as possible should be done to prevent the virus spreading, and if it does the affected farms need to be identified immediately. Clear information should be given to the press and to farming bodies with what to look for in affected animals and who you should call if you suspect you have found a new case. The emphasis is on speed of reaction, and on ensuring that the movement bans/quarantines/culls (if necessary) are strictly adhered to.

Top tips

Make sure you know your personal statement inside out and that your knowledge is thorough and technical. If you don't know something, ask the interviewers – don't try and make an answer up. There is nothing worse than an interviewee desperately fumbling for an answer, after having claimed that they have understood something. Be honest about your ability and this will help the interviewer to assess your potential. You are not supposed to have all the answers now – that's why you are applying to university!

8. 'Beware of the man who knows the answer before he understands the question'

Anonymous

Past questions, for those with a thirst for more.

Here are a few of the past questions we have gathered over ten years of research from actual Oxford and Cambridge interviews. Of course, you may never encounter anything like these again, but someone who applied to Oxbridge (and made it through to the interview stage), did.

Having read the previous chapter, why not give the questions for your subject a go? Do remember though, this is not about revising and rehearsing answers; it's about thinking analytically and laterally and then communicating your answer, as clearly and concisely as possible, using your existing knowledge to support your points.

Anglo-Saxon, Norse and Celtic

What are some of the ways that [Latin] differs from [English] as a language?

How would you go about drawing a conclusion from differing written and archaeological evidence?

Archaeology & Anthropology

Are there boundaries that an anthropologist should not cross?

Why do you think Christmas is such a long-lasting and widely-celebrated holiday?

Architecture

How much do you think architecture changes views in society?

Do you think colour has a part to play in the way people feel about a place?

Biological Sciences

Why is carbon so important in living systems?

Design me an enzyme that could work in cold conditions and hot conditions.

Chemistry

What do you think is the most important issue in chemistry today?

How do you make aspirin from ethanoic anhydride and salicylic acid?

Classics

What were Plato and Aristotle's views of women?

Is it fair that Ted Hughes won a literary prize for a translation of an Ovid poem?

Computer Science

Sketch the block diagram of a TV receiver including the teletext, remote control and back panel connections to home theatre equipment.

If you were to transmit a signal into deep space for decoding by unknown aliens, what would you transmit and why? Do you think they are already listening to early radio broadcasts on long wave and do they understand them?

Earth Sciences

How does the age of ice change as you walk up a glacier?

Does a fridge in a sealed room get hotter or colder when the door is opened?

Economics

Explain how the Phillips curve arises.

Why is deflation a scare to the UK?

Education Studies

Is a faculty of education simply a 'teacher factory'?

What should be the government's involvement with education?

Engineering

Explain the following to someone with no knowledge of physics: force, momentum, power, work.

If you had a cylinder, sealed at both ends, with the pressure rising inside, would it blow at the end or split along the side first?

English

How is poetry linked to music and the other arts?

Can you have an authorial voice in a play?

Experimental Psychology and Psychology & Philosophy

What are the effects of recreational drugs on the brain?

How do we solve the nature vs. nurture debate?

Fine Art

(see History of Art)

Geography

Why should we conserve?

Can climate change be monitored?

History

Do you think that all of history is a history of thought?

What is the position of the individual in history?

History of Art

To what degree is it necessary to be an artist to study History of Art?

What is your opinion on the Turner Prize and Brit Art?

Human Sciences

What do you think is the single greatest difference between humans and animals?

Why are some societies religious and others not?

Land Economy

Why are wages higher in London?

How do towns grow?

Law

Do you think that anyone should be able to serve on a jury?

Should parents have the final say refusing a blood transfusion for their child in a life or death situation, or should the doctor have the authority to do what is necessary to keep the child alive?

Materials (Science)

I have a bar of chocolate, which has 12 pieces in it. I am allowed to pick it up and break it once then put it back down. How many times do I need to break the chocolate so that it is in 12 individual pieces?

If a human being was doubled in dimension would he jump higher or less high?

Mathematics

Imagine an octagon with unit edges, centred on the origin. What are the co-ordinates of its corners?

Estimate the fifth root of 1.2.

Medicine

What is your favourite organelle?

How could you justify the legalisation of cannabis?

Modern & Medieval Languages

How can the study of languages be justified when the majority of graduates don't go into jobs which need them?

Does every work of literature always have a moral? Is there such a thing as an immoral book?

Music

Is music a language?

Where does music begin for you?

Philosophy

How can you prove that anything exists outside your own mind?

Is happiness a basis for morality?

Physical Natural Sciences

(see Chemistry and Physics)

Physics

How is a rainbow formed?

Explain Newton's 3 laws of motion.

Political & Social Sciences

How would you deal with the problem of refugees?

Where does political power lie today?

Theology

How would you define faith?

What, if any are the ethical difficulties which arise in the classical theory of salvation?

Veterinary Medicine

Explain how the structure of a horse's hind leg helps it to run.

How would you tell if an animal was in pain?

And finally...

If you have made it this far - well done and thanks. We hope you aren't too exhausted!

We also hope that, having reached the end (unless you have sneakily jumped ahead to this last section) you feel you've been given some useful advice on how to prepare and how to ensure that your application reflects your true potential. We hope we've helped to oil those lateral and logical thinking skills, have fired your motivation to delve deeper into your subject and to apply that sound knowledge of yours (you had forgotten you had) to new questions and challenges.

Of course, there are no guarantees when it comes to applying to Oxford, Cambridge or any university. What matters is that you take responsibility for your own application and do this now. We can offer advice, research and experience, but only you can turn advice into success. Each year, thousands of bright, enthusiastic, talented, committed applicants - brimming with academic potential - receive offers at Oxford and Cambridge and one of those could be you.

This is the start of a very exciting journey and one that deserves your best shot. It's worth it we think (and we've spoken to thousands of students who will support us on this)!

So...you want to go to Oxbridge? We really do wish you the best of luck.

And if you would like to talk to us about anything we've discussed in this book or would like any more advice about applying, we'd love to hear from you... and we promise we won't ask you about a banana.*

Rachel Spedding, Jane Welsh
& the publishing team at Oxbridge Applications

+44 (0) 207 499 2394
info@oxbridgeapplications.com
www.oxbridgeapplications.com

* And in case you're wondering, the banana title stems from a real Oxbridge question asked in an interview for Medicine. The applicant believed that the interviewer wanted to know the nutritional benefits of a banana for the human body. So, now you know that... could you tell me about a banana?

With thanks to:

Peter Baldock, Jane Bennett-Rees, William Breame, Alex Caillol, Sarah Collier, Gwyn Day, Lucinda Fraser, Adam Hadley, Sophie Inglis, Tessa Jones, Charlotte Moss, Mark Shepherd, Sarah Slater, Jo Travers, Alexandra Tyson, Barry Webb, Sally Welsh, the Oxbridge graduates who work with us, the applicants we have supported and the teachers we have met and spoken to.